# WE CALLED
# THEM LIDS

# WE CALLED THEM LIDS

## Adventures of a Hippie Pot Dealer

Harold Stevens

A Memoir

Copyright © 2019 Lafayette Camp Felder, III
All rights reserved.
ISBN: 9781792711930

## Chapter One

There was a loud knock at the door and Jack barked. I had just fallen asleep and wasn't sure what it was that made Jack bark, but I thought it sounded like a knock. Then I heard it again and Jack ran to the front door. I looked over at the alarm clock. It was 5:00 a.m.

I got up out of bed, put on my bellbottom jeans and a T-shirt that were on the floor, and slowly stumbled out of my bedroom to answer the door. As usual, we had the wooden security bars across the door. I turned on the front light, pulled up the bars and opened the door. My eyes were a little blurry and a thick fog made it hard to see.

Standing in front of me were two tall sheriff deputies. They both were dressed in white starched shirts, khaki slacks, black cowboy boots and tan Stetson cowboy hats. One spoke up right away, "Are you Harold Dean Stevens, III?"

"Yes," I responded.

"The boys downtown would like to speak with you," one of the deputies stated.

"Now?" I sleepily asked.

"Yes, now!" both deputies said in unison.

That sounded like I didn't have a choice. One leaned around to see behind me. The living room was dark, but the porch light gave enough for them to see.

"Are there other people in the house?" one deputy asked.

"Yes," I said. "They are asleep though."

While looking at me straight in the eyes, a deputy said, "Well, we'll leave them that way, let's go."

"I've got socks on but I don't have any shoes," I said. "Can I get them?"

"Where are they?"

"In my bedroom," and I pointed to the door nearest to the front door. One of the deputies pushed me aside and walked into my bedroom. Just then I realized that the gunnysack of pot was leaning on the wall next to my bedside table. If he didn't see it, he would certainly smell it.

He came back out, handed me my boots, and didn't acknowledge the pot. I put my boots on and closed the door as they walked me out to the black and white Bexar County Sheriff's patrol car. We stopped at the back door of the car where they turned me around, pulled my arms behind me and placed the cold steel handcuffs on tight -- very tight. Then they shoved me into the back seat, got in, and off we drove. Evidently, no one in the house woke up or had any idea what had just happened except my dog Jack, who just stood there as I shut the door in front of her.

We drove towards downtown San Antonio on Highway 281. The streets had just come alive with people heading to work. The fog had lifted somewhat. My wrists were killing me and I tried to get them in a more comfortable position.

We pulled up to the west side of the Bexar County Courthouse, a historic red stone building in the center of downtown San Antonio. The deputy that was driving stopped the car at the curb and got out of the car. He ran up the concrete steps and into the side door of the courthouse. The other deputy stayed in the passenger seat. I asked him what we were doing and didn't get any response. The Bexar County Jail was only a couple of blocks away and I figured we were soon heading there.

The deputy came back out carrying a folded piece of paper and got back in the car. Nothing was said by either of them -- we just drove off -- south. It suddenly occurred to me that this was not the way to jail.

We then drove through the south side of town and I just couldn't figure out why. I thought that maybe that paper he came out with had something on it I could see. I leaned over as far as I could and read the title on the paper in the deputy's hands.

*WARRANT -- for the Commitment of Harold Dean Stevens, III to a Texas State Mental Hospital...*

Hell, I wasn't going to jail. I was headed to the *nuthouse*!

We proceeded to drive out South Presa Street and then made the turn through the big gates into the hospital grounds. The complex took up about thirty acres of land with many large, brick buildings clustered towards the center. We drove down the tree-lined entry road and around the back of the first group of buildings. They stopped the car, got out and opened the door for me. The metal handcuffs had been cutting into my wrists so I was hoping they would be removed soon. The deputies walked me up the concrete steps and into the back door of the building.

We went into a narrow hallway and up to a counter. The walls were painted institutional green and there was no furniture in the room. They turned me around -- still not saying a word -- and took off the handcuffs. Finally.

The clerk took the warrant from the deputy and proceeded to type the information on an electric typewriter. We all just stood there and watched. I could see more employees moving about in the background, laughing with each other while they were drinking their coffee. I noticed a time clock on the back wall and guessed they had just come to work and punched in. The clerk looked like he had been up all night and wasn't in the best of moods. I thought about my old roommate, Mike, who had worked at this hospital and told us plenty of stories about it. The clerk shoved an official-looking piece of paper across the counter to me and said, "Sign here."

"Why?" I said as I began reading the paper. It was a document that said I was voluntarily committing myself. I focused on the word *voluntarily*.

"So what happens if I don't sign this?" I asked sarcastically.

One of the deputies quickly spoke up, "Look Bud, you can either sign this here paper or we can put you back in the car and take you back to your pretty, little house in the country."

He lifted his arm, looked at his wristwatch and said, "Round about now the Narcotics Squad should be rounding up all your little pothead friends and all those drugs you had. You, too, can be included in all that fun. It's your choice. Wanna go back?" He had a big grin on his face as he spoke.

"No, I'll sign," I said. I grabbed the ballpoint pen off the counter and wrote my signature.

With that, the sheriff deputies' jobs were done. They turned around and left without saying anything more. The clerk stepped from behind the counter and opened a nearby door. He held it open, looked at me, and said, "Go in and take a seat." I entered the small room and sat in one of the plastic chairs along the wall. I was the only one sitting there. I couldn't believe this was happening to me.

I sat there for about an hour and then I asked permission to use the restroom. Then it was back to my chair. It was chilly in the room and I just had on my T-shirt. No one cared. I was angry. My world had just been turned upside down. I felt like I had been booked into jail. I hadn't. It was the *nuthouse*!

Finally, a man came in and said to the clerk, "Good morning!"

"Likewise," the clerk said and shoved some paperwork at the guy. He took the papers, read them quickly, and turned to me.

"This way," he said, and started to walk off. I got up and followed him out the door and down the steps. I followed as he climbed up into a small bus. He drove it across the grounds of the facility, passing building after building. They were all colonial-style with red brick and white trim, and two or three stories tall. The paved drive was lined with beautiful oak trees, manicured grass, and trimmed shrubs. We passed two gardeners who were busy raking leaves. One looked up and waved at the bus driver, who responded with little toot on his horn. The morning sun was casting a warm light through the trees and it lit up the inside of the bus in flashes. It looked peaceful, but I felt like I was being sucked into a whirlpool -- no escaping it -- and this was no dream.

The bus driver approached one of the buildings and slowly stopped the bus. Then he pulled a lever and opened the bus door.

"This way," he said, as he stepped down off the bus.

I followed him along the sidewalk to the building and up the steps. There was a large black number 10 attached to the front wall. When we got to the entrance, a male nurse dressed in a white uniform opened the heavy steel door and we walked in. The bus driver handed him my paperwork, then turned, and walked back out. Behind me, the nurse closed and locked the steel door.

I had been looking around the place, but the sound of the door being locked startled me back to reality. It was a large open room. In front of me was a nurses' station with a counter and heavy, thick, glass windows. The glass had a round hole in it to pass things back and forth. A hallway led off to the right, and to my left were big double doors made of metal bars, with windows on either side, also heavily barred. The whole room smelled of cigarette smoke.

There was a set of stairs to the left of the windows with barred doors blocking anyone from going up there without a key, and another hallway going off to the left. The floors were made of highly polished, beige terrazzo. The walls were the same institutional green as the first building I encountered. The wall to my left was just a series of closed doors and a TV set hung on the wall in the corner.

There were several rows of chairs with men sitting in them watching the TV and I noticed that the volume was turned up way too loud.

There was a table along the front wall where three men sat playing cards. The three of them looked up at me and quickly went back to their card game. It looked like Poker. Everyone wore identical blue and white striped pajamas and white slippers. I knew what was coming next -- pajamas and slippers for me.

A male nurse motioned with his hands, "This way." I followed him past the rows of chairs and I noticed that not all of the male occupants were adults -- there was also a boy who looked about eight. The group was mainly Anglos with a few Mexican-Americans keeping to themselves.

The men playing cards looked like regular businessmen. Others sitting around looked drugged. Some were asleep and slumped in their chairs. The kid was watching TV. It was certainly an odd assortment of people. I wondered what these people did to get put in there.

Two female nurses walked by looking very professional in their white uniforms. I could see other nurses busy behind the glass window. I followed the male nurse down the hall to the right and into a small room. He handed me a clear plastic bag. I was instructed to take off what I was wearing, place them in the bag, and put on the pajamas and slippers. I handed him the bag of clothes and he said, "You can have these back when you leave."

It was comforting to hear him say, "...when you leave."

*Okay, I'm not in here forever,* I thought.

"This way," he said.

I followed the male nurse back to the main room and continued down the left hallway. We stopped at a metal doorway on the right. It wasn't locked so we went on in. This was another large room -- only this room had rows of single beds around the perimeter walls and a few rows in the middle of the room. There were plenty of windows but all of them had metal bars. Housekeepers were in the process of making the beds. The *patients*, as I later learned we were called, were not allowed in the dorm while the beds were being made, so many of them were hanging out in the hallway.

The male nurse stopped at one of the beds on the right wall and said, "This is yours." I stood there looking at it. He proceeded to list off all sorts of information and rules, most of which I didn't pay attention to. I was still in shock. Breakfast is at blah blah; lunch at blah blah; dinner at blah blah; medication at blah blah -- on and on.

*Wait, did he say medication? Well, just what sort of medication do they have around here?* I wondered.

He finally finished listing off the rules and regulations. I thought to myself that his version of the list sounded a lot like Arlo Guthrie singing *Alice's Restaurant*, and I had to smile at that.

As he turned and left the room, he said, "Now you're on your own, Bud."

I wondered why everybody was calling me *Bud* as I sat down on my bed in my freshly laundered striped pajamas and slippers.

He poked his head back in the dormitory and said loudly, "You can't stay in here Bud; they're cleaning!"

I walked out into the hallway and made my way back to the area where the other patients were sitting, plopped myself into one of the chairs and closed my eyes. I was hoping all this would go away but I opened my eyes, and yes, there I was. It wasn't a bad dream. I was still in the *nuthouse*.

I closed my eyes again and tried to think about how I ended up there. What the Hell went wrong? If I had chosen a different path after high school maybe things would have been different. And maybe, had I not cracked my vertebra playing football, I would have been drafted into the Army and sent to Vietnam. That was a path many of my friends from high school in the sixties were forced to take. Not me, I've now found my way into a mental hospital.

---

I have to admit that I had a wonderful childhood. I was a good kid. So what happened? I came into this world at San Antonio's Baptist Memorial Hospital on September 30, 1948, and was one of the millions of post-war *baby boomers* born between 1945 and 1965. I had loving parents and was the only boy in a family of three sweet sisters, two older and one younger. To them, I could do no wrong. I got away with a lot.

As I sat there in one of the metal office chairs, I began to think about the small things I did wrong when I was young. I was sometimes bad, but didn't get caught. Maybe that's where I went wrong. I know I did some really nice things too. Heck, I was polite, respected my elders and was always nice to people. I never got in a fight, played my heart out in athletics, and excelled in my drafting and architecture classes. By the time I graduated from Woodrow Wilson High School in 1966, I had *lettered* in both football and track, but was most proud of my letter with a drafting T-square on it and three bars. I was in the popular group, dated a cute cheerleader, and was heading in the right direction. At least I thought I was.

My father worked hard to make a living for us. He had earned a six-year degree to become a chiropractor but arthritis had a different plan for him. Not being able to practice because his hands hurt so badly, he returned to work at the Buick dealership where his father worked as a salesman. He was there for 42 years, eventually becoming a vice president. For most of those years, however, he was an assistant vice president, working for a man who basically did nothing but play golf. Dad ended up hating that job but stayed anyway. Having lived through the Depression, a steady job was security that he wasn't about to give up. Dad just lived for the weekends and holidays. He loved to hunt and fish and was able to keep a little cabin at a Texas Hill Country lake where he taught all of us how to water ski. He also built a beach house on the Texas coast where we learned how to fish in the bays and enjoy the beach.

My mother was a saint, staying at home to raise the kids and participating in community activities such as the PTA, Girl Scouts, Daughters of the Republic of Texas, Daughters of the American Revolution, Daughters of the Confederacy and the San Antonio Conservation Society. As a little girl, Mom enjoyed the life of a millionaire's daughter, until her father lost all his money in the stock market crash of 1929 when she was ten. No longer having any money didn't keep my mother from making sure I took three years of ballroom dance lessons in case I wanted to be social -- which I didn't. I never talked about my dance lessons back in my middle-class neighborhood, most likely out of embarrassment. No one else I knew was taking dance lessons and learning proper etiquette. It was my secret.

---

I was a kid just trying to figure out my place in the world. My first shock of what was going on outside my personal space was the Cuban Missile Crisis. Revolutionary leader Fidel Castro overthrew the Batista regime in Cuba in 1959 and then the U.S. tried to overthrow Castro in what was called the *Bay of Pigs* invasion. It didn't work and then the Soviet Union began to support Castro's new communist government.

I didn't really want to know what was happening, but it wasn't my choice. The Soviet Union had placed guided nuclear missiles in nearby Cuba and pointed them at the United States. That was always on our minds -- and on the minds of our parents and teachers because they talked about it a lot. All of a sudden I understood that the whole world could be blown to smithereens in one day. One push of a button was all it would have taken. One misunderstanding between countries that didn't even speak the same language could mean the end of the world. The Communists were our enemy. Nikita Khrushchev, the leader of the Soviet Union, took off his shoe at the United Nation's Assembly and pounded it on the podium yelling, "We will bury you!" He meant us -- my family, my friends, and me! That got my attention!

To make all this even more real, my mother wanted to be a civil defense volunteer. She needed to take a course one night a week held at the Navy Armory in downtown San Antonio. My father wouldn't let her drive by herself at night and volunteered me to go with her. So basically I took the course alongside my mother.

We had plenty of mimeographed pamphlets to read, but the thing I remember most about those night classes were the films that showed the destruction caused by the testing of the Atomic Bomb and then the much more powerful Hydrogen Bomb. I learned that an H-Bomb dropped in the center of San Antonio would create a crater that would pretty much be the size of the area inside our Loop 410 and very deep. There would be no escape, no evacuation, no lives spared, and no use for the fallout shelters.

While Mom and I were learning these relatively unpublicized facts, we were being told in school to have blankets, extra water, and food in the trunks of our cars in case of attack. People were buying and installing fallout shelters in their backyards and arming themselves in case they had to fight off their neighbors who didn't have the resources or desire to build a shelter. Families were buying properties in the unpopulated Texas Hill Country where they could go to survive an attack -- if they could get there. Evacuation routes were being established in cities, showing people how best to get out of town. Large buildings around the city were chosen as good places to head when the missile defense sirens went off, warning us to take cover.

We learned in civil defense class that San Antonio had more military bases than any other city in the country. We were definitely high on the target list. Schools were showing films pushing the concept of *duck and cover* (duck under your desk and cover your head) -- as if there would even be a school left -- there wouldn't be. We were being lied to. At this point in world affairs, the only way to prevent the end of the human race was diplomacy, and that wasn't looking too good.

We had already seen the Sputnik satellite that the Soviet Union had launched. They beat us to Space! We watched it go by at a certain time of the night by walking out into the street in front of our house. We could see the light reflecting on the satellite as it went by in the sky. The Soviet Union was a real threat. We were in the *Cold War*. We had a democracy and they were the dreaded communists. That's how I grew up.

Then, on November 22, 1963, President John F. Kennedy was assassinated in Dallas. He had been speaking in front of our beloved Alamo just the day before. It was the tragedy to end all tragedies for us. We were devastated. It was my first year of high school and everyone in the country remembered exactly where we were on that day.

We heard the news announced over the public address system. Girls were screaming and crying while the boys were trying to keep their emotions in check. But regardless, our faces were red and tears were running down our cheeks. School was dismissed and we all went home to try to get some comfort from our parents who were equally devastated. Coaches tried to gather their athletes for a meeting so we could talk it out. But there wasn't much that could be said.

We didn't know who or what did it, but pretty much assumed it was a communistic plot. It left a deep scar in our minds for the rest of our lives. It must have felt like it did when our parents' generation experienced the news of the attack on Pearl Harbor or the more current tragedy of 9/11. JFK's assassination was just the first in a long line of U.S. leaders to fall. His brother, Bobby, and Martin Luther King would follow. Our world was being pulled apart and I was a teenager trying to figure out how to think and act. Like everyone else, I just kept moving forward.

---

I graduated from high school in 1966 and enrolled at San Antonio College (SAC). My father thought it was a good idea to start out my college education at a low-cost community college while living at home to save money. Dad said that he was willing to pay the tuition for one try at college. If I dropped out, or flunked out, returning to college was on my own dime. He helped with some basic gas and food costs but that was about it. I could eat breakfast and dinner at home but I needed some spending money.

When a football injury ended my athletic career, I started hanging out with a different crowd...the one that smoked pot. It didn't take long before I was swept up by the new movement of music, girls, and marijuana. In those days we bought pot in little matchboxes. I had one taped under my desk in my room until it came loose and my father found it. We had a pretty good argument about that and he said I should move out. He had read in *Life* Magazine that pot was just as bad as LSD. It really scared him and he didn't understand why I would do such a thing. I don't blame him. I would have felt the same way back then if I were he. He said his door would always be open if I wanted to change my ways.

I heard that a mega military insurance company, USAA, headquartered in San Antonio, had part-time job openings for guys who were going to college, so I drove over one day, applied, and was hired right away. I became part of the "Night Search Crew," trying to marry incoming mail with files scattered all over the seven-story building. This job was the beginning of a whole new direction in my life, with a new set of friends and a lot of ups and downs to come. Working there gave me some independence and would allow me to move out of my parents' house. Then, I could do what I wanted -- *Freedom!*

Meanwhile, the country was in turmoil and didn't seem to be getting any better. The Vietnam War was dragging on and some of my friends were going into battle never to return. I was determined to have a good time while I could.

## Chapter Two

    Reality set in. This was no dream. I was in the San Antonio State Mental Hospital. Will someone please save me from myself? I stood up and walked out the door of the dorm and down the hall back towards the big room. The other direction just looked like a row of locked doors. In fact, each of the long hallways that went down the center of the building ended in heavy-locked metal doors -- the kind with little glass windows centered at eye height -- just like the front door.

    I walked into the big room in time to see everyone getting up from their chairs and forming a single line at the nurses' station window. No one had told me to get in line so I sat down in one of the vacant chairs and watched each person turn and leave the window holding a little paper cup. Then I figured it out. They were getting their meds.

    Each one put a pill in his mouth, jerked his head back while tossing the water from the paper cup into his mouth, and swallowed the pill. Then each one wadded up his paper cup, threw it in the wastebasket, and went back to his seat. I figured that most of them had been doing this for some time. Before the last man got his pill, a nurse walked by me.

    I said, "Excuse me, am I supposed to get a pill?"

    She responded, "Well of course you are. Everyone in here gets one."

    "Well, what is it?" I said.

    She looked me in the eye as if to see what kind of patient she was dealing with, then stated, "It's Thorazine, sir. You have the right to know."

    "What does it do to you?" I asked.

    "It just takes the edge off -- and it might make you a little drowsy."

    "Do I have to take it?"

    She thought for a second.

    "No, not unless you cause problems here. Are you a troublemaker?"

"No."

"Well, then you don't have to take it," she said, "What is your name?"

"Harry Stevens -- well, Harold, that's my real first name."

"I'll let them know you won't be needing a pill," the nurse said.

"Thanks," I said, thinking for the first time that someone cared about me there. I watched as all these guys came back to their chairs and sat down. No one was talking. The TV was on but without any sound for some reason. Then one of the older men walked over to the big double doors opposite the entrance and looked through the glass. I had not taken the time to do that so I wasn't sure what was in there. He was followed by several other men, including the young boy.

"They say the boy killed his mother," the man sitting next to me said.

I turned my head to look at the man that spoke. He was a handsome Hispanic man with black hair and a mustache. He looked about thirty years old and had a nice smile and demeanor about him.

"My name is David," he said.

"I'm Harry," I replied, and we shook hands. He didn't act loony so I thought it was okay to shake. I gave it a good squeeze, just so I wouldn't be taken as being soft.

"Killed his mother, huh?" I said.

"Yes, the talk is that they don't know what to do with such a young boy, so they put him here. Why are you here?" he asked.

I answered him quickly, "I'm not sure but I think my parents were trying to get me away from drugs. What about you?"

"I'm here because my uncle in Mexico thinks I am too vocal about my politics and he had it arranged. I come from a wealthy Mexican family," David continued, "but that doesn't stop me from protesting all of the corruption in my country."

"They can do that -- just put you away like this for no reason?" I said.

"Money talks," he said. "My family has many connections in the United States." Then David stopped abruptly and pointed his finger.

"The breakfast line's getting long," David said, looking across the room where most of the men in the room had formed a line.

"Oh, is that what that is?" I said. "I hadn't even noticed."

Just then, a male nurse unlocked the big double doors from the other side and pushed them wide open. Everyone just stood there. Some were trying to look past the people in front of them to see into the cafeteria.

Then the male nurse said, "Okay, come on in -- don't run, walk slowly -- there is plenty for everyone."

The line started moving fast down the center aisle of the room. David and I waited for the line to get shorter, and then got up and went on in. I could hear the sound of all the slippers sliding across the floor as, one-by-one, each person inched closer to the breakfast line at the far end of the room. It looked like a typical school cafeteria with tables and benches down both sides, and the stainless steel cafeteria furnishings at the end. The cafeteria walls were painted a refreshing white. I guessed it made the room look cleaner.

The workers behind the food counters were dressed in white uniforms with little pointy white paper hats. The white uniforms were a stark contrast to their dark skin. As David and I inched forward at the end of the line, it occurred to me that it may have been what a prison cafeteria looked like.

Some unfortunate soul dropped a tray of food before reaching his table. It made quite a racket. The whole place started laughing. Several people clapped. The guy who dropped it was upset and a male nurse quickly came up and helped him back to the line for a new tray of food. One worker in white came out from behind the serving counter to clean up the mess. I got the idea that this happened a lot.

The room turned quiet again, aside from some mumbling here and there. Finally it was David's and my turn to get a food tray. It was typical cafeteria breakfast food -- scrambled eggs, toast with jelly, bacon, and coffee or juice. I filled my plate and followed David to an empty table. At least he was being nice to me. It seemed strange leaving the food counter and not paying for my meal.

David and I started eating. I was hungry -- I hadn't eaten since early the day before. Dropping acid spoils one's appetite. Maybe that is why I was losing weight during that period of my life. I had been pretty buff when I was playing football back in high school. When all that stopped, my muscles started shrinking back down to a more normal size. But my lifestyle wasn't putting any fat on my bones. One thing I did appreciate was that they didn't make me cut my hair when I checked myself in. I still felt like a human being –– just in blue and white striped pajamas and white slippers.

That made me remember how often I was hassled for having long hair. There was a popular restaurant in San Antonio called Earl Abel's on the corner of Hildebrand and Broadway. I had eaten in there many times before I grew my hair long, but when my friends and I sat down this time the waitress came to the table and said that she couldn't serve us. She said our long hair was a health hazard and we would have to wear a hair net to eat there. We promptly left, just like the management wanted us to.

Another time of trouble was at the Alamo Heights Swimming Pool, the same pool where we used to swim during summers when school was out. They wouldn't let us in with long hair because they said our hair would clog their drains. They said we could swim if we came back with swim caps. We left and never went back. I guess their plan worked.

So, yes, for just a short time in my life I, too, experienced discrimination. Here I was a middle-class, nice-looking white guy that was all of a sudden being treated like a minority based on my looks! It gave me a sense of empathy that has stuck with me my entire life. It also made me want to grow my hair even longer.

"How long are you here for, David?" I asked.

"I don't know," David said as he took another bite of the rubbery eggs. "I guess as long as my uncle wants."

"So tell me about all these people," I said as I pointed passed him.

"Hmmm. Okay, let's see," as he glanced around. "See that tall guy over there that looks like an Indian?"

"Yes," I answered.

"He goes by the name of Chief and is the president of our ward -- Ward Ten -- where they put a mixture of people who are supposed to be non-violent."

"What about the kid who killed his mother?" I asked.

"Like I said, I don't think they had any other place to put him," David explained.

"Why is Chief here?" I asked.

David sighed and said, "Cause he's an 'Alky' -- a lot of these guys are alcoholics. They check themselves in here to try to quit drinking and go through detox, then most go right back out there to do it all again."

"So that's why a majority of these guys don't look or act all that crazy," I said, as I took another mouthful of eggs.

"I guess so," David said.

Chief really did look like an Indian Chief. He was tall and thin with short graying hair. His face looked old with dark brown skin and deep wrinkles. It was hard to tell his age.

"So who is the vice president?" I asked.

David pointed across the room and said, "Ken is. He's the guy sitting next to Chief."

"What's his story?" I asked.

"I'm not sure. Maybe drugs," David responded.

"I can relate to that," I said.

We ate for a few minutes without saying anything. I looked around the room as I ate.

"They're looking for a secretary of the ward," David said, as he finished drinking down his juice.

"They can't find one?" I asked.

"They're picky," David said quietly.

"Who decides?"

"They do," he said, nodding his head toward two of the nurses standing nearby.

"You don't want to be the secretary?" I asked.

"Nope." David wrinkled his nose and frowned.

"What do they do as officers of the ward?" I asked.

"They are supposed to represent the patients, but I haven't seen them do anything yet. It's just a title for nothing. That's why I'm not interested," David said.

"Ah, I get it," I said, even though I actually didn't understand much of anything about that place.

Many of the patients had finished eating and were taking their trays up to the counter. Some just left their trays on the table. Others had made quite a mess. No one seemed to care. Slowly they left the room one at a time. David and I were among the last to leave. We walked out and into the main room where most everyone had taken a seat. The loud TV was back on with the morning news.

As we came out the cafeteria doors, I could hear sounds of female voices giggling and talking. David and I sat back down in the same seats we had been in before. I wondered if people had their favorite seats. I didn't want to piss anyone off. Some people had lit up a cigarette and the room started to fill with smoke.

I looked over towards the giggling and saw that the staircase to the left of the cafeteria doors was filled with girls and women. Some were sitting on the steps while others were hanging on the bars of the locked gate at the bottom of the stairs. A female nurse stood on our side of the doors with a key in hand. The workers were busy in the cafeteria cleaning up the mess that the men left. When that was done, one of the workers came out and gave a nod to the nurse at the bars. She unlocked the gate and opened the barred doors.

Then all the female patients wound down the stairs in single file and walked into the cafeteria. A number of them were looking over at the male patients smiling and giggling as they walked. Some of the younger men in the room made some remarks. I heard a whistle from one of the women.

Two of the younger women in the line were making obscene gestures at the guys. I thought the best gesture was made by the girl who was moving her finger in and out through a hole she made with her other hand. That made me laugh. The nurse herded them into the cafeteria and shut the doors behind. Two guys went up to the doors and stared through the glass after they were shut.

"The men get to eat before the women here. That's what I'm talking about -- women have no rights in our countries!" David exclaimed. "But saying things like that is what got me in here. I'm not going to stop. I don't care what they do to me."

I kept quiet -- just taking all this in. A male nurse went over and unlocked the front doors, letting in the same bus driver who brought me over. The bus driver, a black guy that looked to be about forty, went over to the nurses' station and gave them some papers.

One of the older nurses walked over to me and said, "Mr. Stevens, time for your hearing."

"Hearing?" I said.

"Yes, a hearing," she replied. "Let's go get you into some regular clothes."

I got up and followed her down the hall to where they stored our bags of clothes. She handed me my bag and I put on my jeans, T-shirt and boots. Then she walked me back out to the main room.

"Follow me," the bus driver said, as he gestured to me and walked to the door. I kept walking and followed him outside. No one seemed to pay any attention except for David who gave me a small nod. He was reading the morning paper, as were several of the other patients. The bus stopped at the Administration Building. We went in and the bus driver led me into a small room lined with chairs. There were several others sitting in chairs, two men and a woman -- now THEY did look crazy! Two male nurses sat with them. One at a time, we were all called to go in. I couldn't see where we were going but when my name was called, I got up and went through the doorway.

I entered the room by myself. It was a long room with a big conference table down the center. There was hardly room for the chairs to move back from the table without hitting a wall -- institutional green, of course. The table was full of professional-looking men and women in business attire. They all looked up at me when I walked in, several shuffling the papers in front of them.

A distinguished-looking man at the other end of the table looked up from his papers and said, "Please sit down."

I pulled out the empty chair at the end of the table and sat down without responding.

Then the same man began shooting questions at me, "Your name is Harold Stevens, III. Is that correct?"

"Yes sir, that's me," I said in an upbeat voice.

"Well, Mr. Stevens," he continued, "We understand that you have a problem with drugs."

"Uh, I don't have a problem with drugs," I said right back.

"Yet, you signed this paper to commit yourself here for 90 days," he said, never breaking the smile on his face. It was like talking to one of those ventriloquist dummies. The words were coming out of his mouth through a pasted-on smile.

"I had to sign," I explained, "but I don't really belong here."

"I see," he responded, drawing out the word for an extra second.

He looked around the table at the other participants. Most were still looking -- or should I say staring -- at me. One picked up his coffee cup and took a sip. Another shuffled some papers in front of her.

"Well, Mr. Stevens," the man continued," we are going to keep you here for the time period allotted for your treatment. Thank you. You can leave now."

"That's it? That's my hearing?" I could hardly believe my ears.

Leaving no room for argument, the man ended the meeting, "You can leave now, Mr. Stevens. Thank you."

The door opened and a male nurse came in. He escorted me out the door and handed me back over to the bus driver who drove me back to Ward Ten. I was then relieved of my clothes once again. Soon I was sitting back down next to David in my pajamas and slippers watching TV.

The same routine I described at breakfast took place at lunch, only with hamburgers and French fries this time. Again I sat with David, but his political ranting was getting a little old for me. I couldn't imagine listening to him spout complaints about the Mexican and United States government over and over again, day after day. He was starting to repeat himself. Maybe he was crazy after all.

The afternoon was uneventful and boring. Some of the older men were enjoying a card game over in the corner. Most were slumped in their chairs. Some were taking naps, probably due to their dose of Thorazine, which they were all given again after lunch.

*Now that's a way to keep the peace in a nuthouse*, I chuckled to myself.

After dinner and more TV watching, a male nurse walked from behind the glass window and announced that it was time for bed. It had barely turned dark from what I could tell from looking out the iron-mesh windows. Slowly the men started to get out of their chairs and shuffle towards the dormitories. There were several bunkrooms down the hallway. I stopped at mine and went in. People were going over to their beds, pulling down the covers, fluffing up their pillows, and so on. Everyone looked like they were moving in slow motion. It occurred to me that this whole experience was like some kind of dream. But it was real. Ninety days.

Chief's bed was in the corner at the end of my row. Mine was next to his. He looked over and introduced himself.

"They call me *Chief*."

"I know," I responded. "David told me."

"What are you in for?" he asked. His raspy voice sounded like a scratched record.

"Drugs," I said, not wanting to go into any more detail. "And you?"

"I drink too much," Chief volunteered. "The doctors think it's my Indian blood. I checked myself in because I was about to hurt someone."

"Oh," I whispered half to myself.

"You want to be an officer?" he asked while crawling into bed.

"What do I have to do?" I asked.

"Nothing," Chief grunted.

"Okay," I said.

"Fine then," Chief said, "You're the secretary of Ward Ten. I'll tell the staff in the morning. Welcome," and he turned the other way.

The whole time I was talking with Chief, this short stocky Hispanic guy on the other side of me was doing something with his hands as he sat on the side of his bed with his feet on the floor. I put my head on the pillow but turned my head towards him to see what he was up to. He had his pajama top off and just wore the bottoms. His upper body was filled with weird tattoos -- most looked like he did them himself. He had huge muscles and scars -- and he looked dangerous. Damn, and I have to have the bed right next to his? I wondered if they reserved this bed for newbies and it was a cruel joke.

Then I saw what this guy was doing. Patients who smoked are given a small bag of tobacco and rolling papers. It was the cheapest way to give them cigarettes. This guy had rolled some and now was in the process of tearing them all up next to his bed. He would tear at it and then jump up out of bed and stomp his feet. Then he'd fall back onto his bed.

Tobacco was everywhere. He kept mumbling something fast in Spanish with a grimace on his face -- angry -- crazy. When he looked up, he didn't look at me. Instead, he was looking right through me and on into the distance as if I wasn't there. I knew right then that there were some people in this hospital for good reason. He was one of them. But hey, I thought this was the ward where they put the people who weren't dangerous!

They turned the lights out. I could still see the room with the soft light from outside coming in the windows. The room took on shades of blue. The guy stayed sitting on his bed but I still felt extremely vulnerable. My crazy-acting new neighbor gave new meaning to the phrase –– *sleeping with one eye open*. I kept my head turned towards him and kept opening my eyes to make sure I was safe.

## Chapter Three

While trying to fall asleep in my new hospital surroundings, I thought about the choices I had made and how I ended up sleeping next to this maniac. I thought about my friend, Mike Wilson, who was also going to San Antonio College in 1968. He lived on the right side of a small wooden rent house on Lewis Street at the edge of the SAC campus. Mike knew some of my friends from high school and needed a roommate. I moved in and we soon became great friends.

I remembered that Mike had worked part-time at the San Antonio State Mental Hospital. That's when we first started calling it the *nuthouse*. Mike was one of the staff members at the hospital. He worked the night shift and would attend classes during the day. He would come home and tell us some hilarious stories about his job and the crazy people he took care of. Now I was about to experience that for myself.

Of course, Lewis Street became the meeting place for all sorts of people, a party-house for sure. We had plenty of pot and pills around, mostly LSD and a few uppers and downers. Music was always loud and sometimes live when friends would come over to jam. The kitchen was disgusting so our girlfriends would clean it for us. They thought it was worth it since they had to go through it on the way to the bathroom.

After a while Mike had taken all the classes he could at SAC, so he transferred to Texas A&M University in College Station. I spent my second year at SAC living with different roommates on Lewis Street. One was Gary Day, a friend from high school who played an electric guitar. Gary was medium height with long, blond, curly hair and a ruddy complexion.

Mike would drive in from Texas A&M on the weekends and join us for some fun Lewis Street jam sessions. Mike played bass and another close friend, Pete Thompson, played lead guitar. Pete was the first of our friends to have really long hair, mainly because he had gotten a head start. He was a little older than we were and was in Architecture School at the University of Texas at Austin. Pete's hair was dark brown and hung in a ponytail down his back. He had a small mustache along with a little goatee. Pete was thin and dressed the *hippie* part in tight, bell-bottom jeans, tank top and sandals.

Gary would play rhythm guitar. I would sometimes play drums, as would another friend, Allen Griswald. Gary moved into the Lewis Street house first for a short while, followed by Allen, who we all called a *girl magnet*. Allen was kind of short with very long, blond hair and a blonde mustache. His blue eyes and soft voice were irresistible to beautiful girls.

One girlfriend of his was a stripper at a local club who moved in with us for a short time. Nothing lasted very long in those days. I enjoyed her company, particularly when she wore her see-through blouse around the house, but everyone treated each other with respect, and her work was just a way for her to make money. I tried my best not to look at her boobs. The only thing that bothered me was when I was trying to sleep and she and Allen were making noisy love across from where I slept. Not fair. That should have been me over there!

Our group had other places to party also. My family's Texas coast house was made of cedar siding and was built on telephone poles so it didn't flood during heavy rains or hurricane surges. I had many memorable parties down there before being banned from the place by my father. After a wild high school graduation trip, I had a new set of friends but still hung on to some of the others. I asked permission to use the coast house again and my parents said I could. Not giving it much thought, I planned a coast trip to our house that included both sets of friends, my conservative football buddies from high school and my new liberal ones from college. That turned out to not be such a good idea. They all had a very hard time relating to each other.

That trip was the first time I took acid. Everyone was to meet up at my coast house and they all knew the way to get there. There were twelve of us total. I was in Gene Day's car with his brother, Gary, our friend, Dean Satel, and Allen, my roommate. I had gone to high school with Gene, Gary and Dean. Allen was from the other side of town but knew everyone in the car. Dean was always the first to try something new and obtained the acid for the trip. And what a trip it was! We had only driven about ten miles out of San Antonio on Highway 281 South when Dean said, "Pull into that bar up ahead."

The bar was in an old stone building right on the highway at the edge of Floresville. We pulled into the gravel parking lot and Dean went inside to use the bathroom. When he came out he got back into the car and passed out little yellow tabs to everyone in the car and said, "Here, take this."

We each had a can of beer in our hands, as was the custom on the drive to the coast back then, so we washed the acid down with beer. It would soon be a life-changing experience for all of us in the car.

So we took off again on our merry way down 281 to the coast. I'd say it was about at Karnes City that the LSD started to kick in. We all had big smiles on our faces as we cruised through the small towns obeying the speed limits and red lights to perfection. Colors became brighter and exaggerated. Gene was driving and enjoying the new sensation but was still able to function well. When we looked at each other, all of our faces looked red and splotchy, but we didn't really know if that was the acid that made our eyes see things differently, or if our faces really were red and splotchy. To this day, I've never been completely sure.

We crossed over the ferry to the island and arrived at my house in good spirits. After unloading all the stuff from the trunk of the car, we opened up the house to air out. The rest of our group showed up shortly thereafter. Everyone was ready for a party.

The first thing we did was head to the beach, only about a mile away, making the traditional drive along the water to check out the chicks. Once back to the house, the second group started getting some lunch ready. Those of us who had taken acid were not hungry and the *non-druggie* guys were puzzled, not knowing that the rest of us dropped acid. Their high would be from their usual large consumption of beer and liquor. There was a lot of laughter and loud talk in the room. The booze started flowing and the fun had begun.

The stoned group put The Beatles' new *Sgt. Pepper's* album on the record player we had brought and cranked up the volume. The guys who were drinking complained throughout the whole album and wanted to play some country-western music they had brought. This light-hearted conflict went on until we headed for home a few days later. We had come down from our acid trip after about twelve hours or so, caught some needed sleep and ate food again. It was an extremely enlightening experience, complete with vivid colorful and harmless hallucinations, and discussions about the world around us that would have only happened under the influence. I enjoyed it immensely and was ready to try it again once we got home and the situation was right.

What was also glaringly obvious was the fact that my two groups of friends just were not going to work out together. The athletic jocks that got drunk that trip just didn't understand the newly-ordained hippies. Never again would I try to mix the two. I loved all of them, but I was heading in the direction of only one group. I had made a choice and hoped I wouldn't lose my other friends in the process. So I just charged ahead not knowing what the actual consequences would be. But I knew my life would never be the same. It became a different kind of fun. Instead of getting drunk and acting stupid, we were getting high, having intellectual conversations, and being careful not to be busted.

---

Back in San Antonio, a group of us were sitting around the Lewis Street house watching TV late one afternoon without much to do, so we decided to get high and drop some acid. About an hour later the evening news said that the Goodyear Blimp was at the San Antonio International Airport and they were allowing visitors. We just had to go! So six of us piled into one of our cars and headed out to the airport. In those days you could pull up near the entrance to the terminal, park your car for free, and just walk in. Most people didn't even bother to lock their car doors and security guards were scarce.

The blimp could be seen from a distance as we drove into the parking lot. The sun had gone down and the famous Goodyear Blimp was out on the tarmac. It was well-lighted with portable lights on large stands surrounding the blimp. Several clean-cut men in blue jumpsuits were standing near the blimp talking. The front of the blimp was tethered to a large pole and long cables came down from the sides to hooks on the ground made for holding planes down on windy days.

Gary, Dean, Allen, and I got out of our car and just stood there for a moment. We were parked right in front of the four-foot chain link fence that divided the parking lot from the tarmac. Our group slowly walked towards the blimp after passing through a narrow gate. There were only a handful of other people looking at the blimp. It was the largest object we had ever seen floating in the sky and being stoned on acid made it look incredibly huge.

Soon our group of stoners were standing under it and looking up. The huge blimp moved slowly back and forth due to the light breeze that evening. It was like a house floating above us. Dean gave a nod over to the men in the jumpsuits and they nodded back with smiles. They had no clue that we were stoned and none of us really cared. We didn't have any drugs on us -- only in our bodies -- so there wasn't much to worry about. Besides, everyone was functioning fine. The four of us walked around and stood under the giant blimp for about an hour before feeling like it was time to leave. A few other people had come and gone.

It was an awesome experience. That's the kind of thing my friends and I loved to do while stoned. Search out unusual places to go tripping.

---

On another occasion, under the same influence, we drove out to Inspiration Hills on the Northwest side of San Antonio to get a view of the city lights. There was a hilltop where guys used to go park and make out with their girlfriends. I was driving and wandered around until I found the turn that took us up to the very top. There was a water tower up there, but no houses were built yet.

The view was spectacular. We could see all the way to downtown San Antonio, about ten miles away. I parked the car, set the emergency brake, and Gary, Allen, Mike, and I sat down in the middle of the paved street facing the view. No one said much as we gazed straight ahead. It was a quiet summer night, complete with the stars above and the lights of downtown in the distance. There was no moon and it was pitch black. The only thing that could be heard was the sound of the crickets. No one spoke.

I was the first to notice them. I had brought a small flashlight, checked first to make sure nothing weird was on the pavement before we sat down, then turned the flashlight off. There were no curbs and the grass overlapped the pavement to our sides. I was sitting closest to the grass and the sound of the crickets seemed unusually loud. I thought maybe it was the effect of the acid making my senses more intense. So I decided to turn on the flashlight to look over at the grass while everyone else kept staring at the view ahead.

"Look at this!" I said, and they all turned their heads. "The crickets," I yelled, shining the light into the grass. "They are everywhere!"

"No shit," said Gary. "Just look at them."

The grass was crawling with black crickets and they were moving down the hill towards the city. We knew about them from years before when the highway department had to close the freeways on the north side of town because so many crickets had been run over by cars that it created this gross, oily slick on the roadway. They cleaned it up only to have more slicks to deal with just hours later.

Watching insects while on acid is either the most interesting thing you can do or perhaps the most terrifying. After a few minutes, we just needed to get out of there. We hopped back in the car, carefully turned it around on the steep hill, and started for home. We had to laugh at our discovery of the crickets. As we entered Loop 410 off the Inspiration Hills access road, someone started yelling, "The Crickets are coming! The Crickets are coming!" We all chimed in. That part was the most fun.

---

We did our share of hippie decorating in the Lewis Street house, with lots of color on the walls, music posters, and stuff we either bought at Pier One Imports or at a head shop. The house had one large room with a fireplace and a sofa. We made two sleeping areas at the far end with tapestries from India. Most of the furniture was picked up off the streets. People used to just put used items on the curb to get rid of them and that stuff was perfect for our taste. Walking between the beds, you entered a small room with a refrigerator on the left and a double-hung window on the right. When the window was open, you looked right into the bathroom, which must have been an outside porch at one time before the house was converted into a duplex.

I loved the artwork of Peter Max in those days and painted one of his stylized female heads on the window with Day-Glo paint. But, I didn't stop there. The floor was covered with an awful, pink shag carpet. The white fridge in the room was one of those old, rounded kinds, probably from the 1940's. So to continue my decorating, and most likely under the influence of something or another, I painted the walls of the little room black and started painting a flow of colorful Day-Glo designs on the wall...

and across the carpet... and up the front of the fridge. The paint was water-based and would come off easily if I needed it to.

The room came alive when we purchased a fluorescent black light. The black light hung from the ceiling on chains. Black-light posters and painted rooms were pretty common then, especially in the dance clubs downtown. The one bad thing was that the house was infested with roaches and they were all over our black light room. We didn't have money for an exterminator and neither did the landlord. A poor Mexican-American family that didn't speak a lick of English lived on the other side of our apartment wall and even if we did something about the roaches, they surely wouldn't have.

So, what do you do to keep roaches from crawling on you when you are enjoying the psychedelic effects of a black-light room? How do you keep tabs on them? Well, you catch them and dab on some Day-Glo paint of course! Now you have something fun to watch -- a moving circus of activity that would last all night! With a little different paint scheme on each one, you could give them names and cheer them on -- which we did.

---

I signed up for the Military Draft in 1966, like all of us guys had to do when we turned eighteen. But while I was still a student at SAC, the local news announced that President Lyndon B. Johnson was considering doing away with the College Draft Deferment. That sent chills up my spine. I had friends fighting in Vietnam and really didn't want to join them on the front lines. I didn't think we should be over there anyway.

Joe Sinclair, a close friend from high school, was also worried about being drafted and he proposed that we both try to join the Navy Reserve in order to not get drafted into the Army. There was a recruitment program called the *Buddy System* that allowed friends to join the Navy at the same time and stay together through boot camp and possibly beyond. I thought that had to be better than being drafted.

So Joe and I went to the local Navy recruitment office in San Antonio. The guy in the office told us that it wasn't that easy to get in anymore, but would give us a written academic test to see where we stood. We each sat at a desk, completed the exam, and turned them in. The exam really wasn't that difficult. The recruiter scored our tests and said they would accept us both right away.

The next thing I knew, we were on a bus going across town to Fort Sam Houston for a medical exam. I wasn't sure I was ready to join the Navy on THAT day! But the wheels were in motion and I just went with it. During a series of medical questions by the Army doctor, I mentioned that I received an injury to my back playing football in high school a couple of years ago. He immediately sent me to radiology for an x-ray.

When all the testing was done, Joe and I were bused back to the recruiter's office with medical papers in hand. The Navy recruiter said that Joe had been accepted and I was rejected because of a hairline crack in one of my vertebrae -- they were never going to take me. Joe and I looked at each other.

"Sorry, Joe," I said.

"Yeah, right," Joe responded.

So Joe went in and I went on. I told everyone that football kept me out of the draft. It was a life-changer. I have always wondered what my life would have been like if I had not injured my back and had been accepted into the Navy. Joe served his two years on a ship in Vietnam and came home in one piece. He eventually forgave me for not going in with him and remains a close friend to this day.

Although I was excelling in my design classes at SAC, I was less than enthusiastic about a particular architecture class on how to write a specifications document. I hated the class and I wasn't sure I could stand a whole semester of it. I liked designing buildings, but all those specifications made my head swim -- too much math.

I decided that I had had enough of college at that point and dropped out. I had excelled in my other architecture classes, earning the only A in the class in one of them. My three years of drafting in middle school, and my four years of architectural drafting in high school, made the design classes easy for me. My professors were dumbfounded. I told them I wasn't ready to finish right then, but thought I might someday return to it.

Soon I started helping some of my friends score some pot from other friends I had recently met. I wasn't making a ton of money selling pot, but it was helping to pay my share of the rent on Lewis Street. I needed a job, but most jobs required me to keep my hair short. Even though I was living in a very conservative city by national standards, I was determined to be that hippie I had seen on TV and in magazines. I wanted to be part of something cool. Slowly, I was getting there.

I was driving a little Corvair Monza at the time, which was a pretty neat car, but I wasn't married to it. One day I noticed a really unusual car while driving past a used car lot on Fredericksburg Road. My dad was the used car manager at a Buick dealership at the time and he sold many trade-ins to his friends that owned car lots around San Antonio. Many of them became his fishing and hunting buddies. I thought my Dad might know this guy too.

I turned my car around and came back to take a look. I got out and walked over to this very cool car. It was dark green with a black convertible top and brown leather seats. The body was long and low with running boards along the sides and a long, louvered hood in front ending in a rounded nose. The dash was made of polished wood, the body was wood with a metal skin, and with the back seat the car would hold four people. It reminded me of a stretched version of an old MGA, or maybe one of the German WWII cars I had seen in the movies.

Earle McDaniel, the owner of Earle McDaniel's Used Cars, came out of the small metal sales building with a big smile on his face as he walked towards me.

"You interested in that car?" he said.

"What is it?" I asked.

"It's a Morgan plus four, 1963."

"I've never heard of one," I said.

"Guys used to race them. They have a TR-4 drive train and they haul ass!"

"Oh, say, you may know my Dad," I said.

"Well... I don't know. What's his name?"

"Harold Stevens," I replied.

"Harold! I know him well. So you're Harold's son!"

"Harry," I said, as I shook his hand.

"Well... I'll be. Nice to meet you," Mr. McDaniel said. "I can give Harold a good deal on this car. It's the only one in town that I know of."

"Does it run okay?"

"Runs great!" he said. "It'll do one-forty on a straightaway."

"I'll have to trade in this Monza," I said and right then we both heard the telephone ringing from the direction of his little office building on the back of the lot.

"Tell your dad to give me a call and I'll see what I can do," Mr. McDaniel yelled as he ran towards his office to answer the phone.

I drove away from his lot with a big grin on my face. This was my fantasy car and I would really look like a hippie in it, particularly since my brown hair was growing long. *Girls are gonna love this car!* I thought to myself. Later I spoke with my Dad and he made a deal with Earle over the phone. I picked up my Morgan the next day. Yep, definitely a hippie car!

---

As my group of pot-smoking friends expanded, I was introduced to Michael Bartok. Michael was a good-looking, hip kind of guy –– tall with short, black hair and a somewhat sinister looking, well-trimmed black beard. He dressed in expensive bell-bottoms jeans perfectly pressed, polished leather boots, and colorful silk shirts. His signature wardrobe always included a paisley-print silk scarf tied around his neck and in the winter he wore a wine-colored velour smoking jacket. Michael had a booming, deep voice that would have been the envy of any disc jockey.

Michael was working in a hip clothing store on St. Mary's Street that was also a head shop, so he had a lot of hippie friends. He had a fun personality and a great laugh that could both attract people and scare them off. His stepfather was a local attorney and Michael had an extraordinary command of the law -- particularly the laws about substance abuse, drug smuggling, and the legal system pertaining to them.

By the time I met Michael, he had already spent two years in a Texas prison for smuggling pot out of Mexico. He was a veteran of drug smuggling in the mid-sixties before the *War on Drugs*. We hit it off right away and when Allen decided to move in with his girlfriend, Michael and I moved in together in a small, single-story apartment that faced the alley of a larger house on Locust Street, not far from SAC's campus. That older part of town was prime for renting an apartment without the neighbors calling the police every five minutes to report suspicious activities -- everyone looked suspicious.

Michael introduced me to a whole new set of people and I saw less and less of my other friends from high school. Selling a little pot didn't give me enough money, so I applied at the local Pizza Hut on McCullough Ave near SAC. My high school friend, Lee Jackson, was a manager at the Pizza Hut out on San Pedro and told me about the opening at the other store. I was hired because I knew Lee and, for about four months, I did just about every job there was at Pizza Hut -- waiting tables, prepping, making pizzas, and cleaning up. It didn't pay that much, but it gave me enough money to get by.

Well, the owner of all the Pizza Huts in San Antonio found out that I was the same friend of Lee's that he had heard about. I used to go into Lee's Pizza Hut to visit and drink a beer. Lee may have talked about me to the other employees, but one way or another, the owner knew that I smoked pot. So he instructed the manager at my store to give me a drug test in order for me to stay employed. I said I wouldn't take it and the manager fired me. Thus ended my first and last fast-food job, and after spending so much time with pizza ingredients, I couldn't even look at a pizza for about five years.

I needed another way to make a living so I concentrated on what I knew best. Besides, I would never have to take a drug test. Michael and his friends provided a readily available source of pot and LSD so I became a dealer. I wasn't interested in selling any *hard drugs* and, thus, didn't think it was a big deal to sell the stuff that wasn't addictive. It seemed like such a natural thing to do at the time, and so adventurous! I had plenty of friends who wanted to buy from me, like my old friends who would smoke dope on the weekends and who just needed a safe, reliable, and steady source.

Michael and I had a great time partying and dealing out of the little apartment on Locust Street. One day he introduced me to an old pot smuggling friend of his named José who had gone to prison with Michael. José made it clear that his days of smuggling and dealing were over. He became a travel agent instead. Prison cured him of that little habit, but he still smoked plenty of pot and was fun to be with. José was Mexican-American with light brown skin, brown eyes, black hair, and a big smile. He would come and go from our apartment, staying out of trouble and not drawing any attention to himself. He was super-intelligent and I always enjoyed our conversations while passing a joint back and forth.

Michael continued to get our stuff wholesale. We were really just small-time dealers, making enough money to cover the rent and expenses without taking too many chances. But the added benefit was that we didn't have to pay for our own drugs. Of course, we dreamed of making more money with larger transactions but the fact was that dealing gave us a cheap supply of pot and pills –– and what an interesting group of people I was meeting! It was the beginning of an adventure that was hard to turn my back on. I was having a lot of fun and making money at it. I just went with the flow, not knowing exactly where that was taking me.

    Like other small-scale pot dealers, Michael and I would buy a few kilos of Mexican pot in a compressed brick wrapped in plastic, then break it all up and put it into sandwich bags called *Baggies*. When we rolled up the bags, we had what back then were called *lids*. A lid would weigh anywhere between an ounce and two ounces, but we didn't actually weigh it. We just grabbed a handful of pot and stuffed it into the Baggies, stems and all, until it looked big enough that people would like it. There was enough profit in it that weighing seems pointless. We just wanted people to be happy buying from us. Ziploc bags had not been invented yet, but the Baggies had a flap on one side so you could roll one up, put your thumbs into the pocket and flip it over to make a pretty good seal. We got extremely good at this. Our kitchen table would have piles of pot, Baggies, and brown lunch bags that we would place the finished lids in.

    We paid about $30 for a Mexican kilo and got about 40 or so lids out of it, selling each lid for $10. Kilos back then varied in weight. Some friends would buy two or three lids at a time, getting some extra for their friends. That's just how it worked. Now that was easy money! Who needed a real job? A lot of pot smokers around the country were doing a little dealing on the side to provide them with a free stash and make some extra cash. I thought I could do the same. It seemed like a harmless way of making a temporary living while I was young, unattached, and having fun. And I could grow my hair long and look like a *freak*! Now there was a goal -- looking like a *freak*! That was one of the names hippies called themselves back then. I was tired of being normal and looking normal. I saw all sorts of *long-hairs* in the media. I thought it would be cool to look like that -- to be part of something -- a worldwide movement of young people who looked like their ancestors did in days of old. Now how bad could that be?

There was an old two-story house that bikers rented on McCullough Ave. just down the alley from our apartment on Locust and right across the street from that Pizza Hut where I had been fired. Michael knew the bikers because they bought drugs from him. They were the *Clacker Chapter* of the local motorcycle club. Biker gangs in the U.S. were territorial so each area of the country had a club. On the West Coast, they were known as the notorious *Hell's Angels*. In the South, they called themselves *The Galloping Gooses*. In Texas, we had the *Bandidos*.

But the Clacker Chapter of the Bandidos wasn't exactly the best chapter in the club. In fact, it was the worst. There were about twenty members in that chapter. Some of them lived together in the McCullough house and a few just hung out there. Most of them had some sort of job and some made money stealing motorcycles and rebuilding them by mixing the parts. I went along with Michael to meet the Bandidos one afternoon. We walked down our alley then turned and walked up the steps onto the broken-down wooden porch. Michael knocked on the door. Michelle, one of the biker *mommas,* opened the door and gave Michael a big hug. He introduced me and she gave me a hug, too.

We walked into the front room and there were five bikers sitting around watching TV on old stuffed sofas and chairs placed over worn, oriental carpets. Motorcycle posters hung on the walls covering up some of the old wallpaper. There were a couple more guys talking and laughing down the hall. One was on the phone.

The head guy of this chapter was named Rabbit. Most club members had nicknames. He was tall, slender, and of course, extremely dirty. You had to look dirty if you were a biker in those days. Rabbit wore tight blue jeans that looked like they had been painted with grease and a dirty white T-shirt under his *colors*. That was the name they gave to the gold-colored club vest they all wore. They were the typical motorcycle club vests with their club's insignia across the back which, in this case, was the club name surrounding a caricature of a Mexican Bandido. It reminded me of the old *Frito Bandito* in commercials, although the spelling was different.

Of course, they had their nicknames written on their colors and a variety of patches and trinkets sewn on. I never did know what all those meant. Most of the bikers had long, unkempt hair. It was either the type of hair that went all over the place or slicked back in ducktails. Rabbit kept his hair like that using a handful of Brylcreem, the hair grease of choice back in the day. Rabbit was glad to see Michael, especially since Michael was bringing him a lid he had ordered.

I was introduced and welcomed by the group without hesitation. Rabbit paid Michael for the lid as he handed it to him. As customary with a new batch, Rabbit threw it to another guy who picked up a pack of Zig-Zag papers off the coffee table and proceeded to roll a joint. Soon we were passing around three joints and the mood of the group got a lot happier.

Bikers in general were a rough bunch of guys. The media called them the *misfits of society.* They were the ones who got in fights after school, didn't like authority, and spent a lot of time sitting in the vice principal's office. Many didn't graduate from high school or barely did. Only a few had jobs. There was only one thing that held them all together and gave them purpose –– their *choppers*. They loved going on rides with the rest of the club, but members of the *Clacker Chapter* were always on the verge of getting kicked out of the Bandidos for not behaving themselves. It was as if the club held a meeting, voted on who were the worst members, and put them all together in the *Clacker Chapter.*

We didn't stay long that day, but while we were there listening to some of the stories these guys loved to tell, I noticed out of the corner of my eye that Michelle was staring at me with an odd smile on her face. As far as I could tell she was the only girl living in the house to take care of the cooking and cleaning –– if you could call it cleaning. Everything looked filthy to me. But that didn't seem to bother them at all. It was how they liked it –– dirty like themselves. I did, however, hear Rabbit bitching at a big guy down the hall because he stunk so bad and needed to take a bath. Evidently, a bath was a rare event for those guys. Even changing clothes was a rare event.

The guys sitting in the living room with us kept yelling towards the hall in agreement that a bath was needed. Although they occasionally washed clothes, there was one thing that was never cleaned -- the *colors*. It was disrespectful to do so. In fact, during initiation when a member's colors were ordained, everyone in the club had to pee on the vest. I never knew if that was done while the honoree was still wearing it or not, but I was not about to participate.

As we sat there, Rabbit started telling one of his favorite stories about Michelle. Michelle kept interrupting to add something funny. It seemed she was at one of their drunken club events out in the Hill Country north of town. The event was for the initiation of a new member -- Michelle. Yes, she was about to become a true *biker momma*. They could hardly stop laughing as each of them chimed in to tell the tale. Michelle was laughing too.

The event was held at night around a big bonfire at someone's uncle's ranch. Evidently the ranch had chickens. Most people who grew up on a ranch or farm back then was used to having chickens around -- and used to how chickens went from scratching dirt in the barnyard to becoming dinner on the kitchen table that same day. They started the event by dropping acid and tapping the 16-gallon keg of Lone Star beer.

Then the drunken and stoned bikers went about trying to catch a chicken. And they did. They cut its head off and chased Michelle around the bonfire hitting her with it while the group laughed and cheered. I doubt that Michelle was doing much laughing. My guess is that she was doing some serious screaming! Blood was everywhere. It was the most fun the Clacker Chapter had had in a long time. So she passed the test because she was a good sport, became a biker momma and laughed about it later. You have to give her some credit for that!

I'm not sure exactly how it happened but somehow Michelle took a liking to me the day we met, and the next thing I knew, she had moved into my little room of our apartment down the alley from their house. Michelle wasn't the prettiest girl but she wasn't bad looking either. Rather plain with long, dark, brown hair, Michelle had a plump figure. Like most of the hippie girls, she wore a lot of T-shirts without a bra, tank tops, and cut-off jeans. She also wore a pair of soft brown leather moccasins, the fringed kind that come up high above the ankle.

Michelle went about her day keeping the apartment tidy and doing most of the cooking. She enjoyed making love regularly and I had no complaint. She and I would also spend some time over at the Bandidos' house -- sitting around listening to their stories and smoking pot. They had no problem with the fact that I wasn't a biker. I was a dealer and believe it or not, that came with a certain amount of respect from these guys. Not for one single moment did I ever think about being a biker and joining their group. I'm not sure what I was doing with Michelle but for the time being, I was having fun learning about this crazy and dangerous lifestyle they were living.

We heard some motorcycles outside the Bandidos' house one night and then there was a knock at the door. Michelle, in keeping with her biker momma status, jumped up and opened the door. In walked two bikers that I had not seen before. They just moved right past Michelle without a word.

These were not the typical Clacker Chapter bikers. These guys were older and much more serious looking. I had not seen anyone like them before. They reminded me of a modern day Davey Crocket or Daniel Boone with their old worn brown leather biker clothes -- the kind with fringe like a mountain man might wear. One was tall, thin and clean-shaven. The other was short, stocky with a *Lincoln* beard. They never cracked a smile and said they were only staying one night and planned to leave first thing in the morning. Rabbit didn't know them, but said they had called ahead for a place to stay while coming through town on their way to California from Louisiana. The biker *brotherhood* was like that.

Everyone in the room was quiet as the unknown bikers sat down. No introductions were made. The bikers said they were on their way to a huge biker funeral in San Francisco. Evidently one of the top Hell's Angel leaders had died and the whole biker nation saw it as their duty to try to make it to his funeral -- except the Clacker Chapter, who didn't even consider it. But they were doing their duty by putting up these two guys for the night.

I was a little bit scared being there but was curious enough to stay. One of them brought in a thin black, case that looked similar to a small briefcase and placed it next to him on the floor. Everyone got a beer and several joints were lit while Michelle went to the kitchen and brought out a bag of potato chips and a few more beers. I sat back and just listened to the conversation.

After a few minutes, the short biker picked up his black case and placed it on his lap. He unlocked the two locks and opened the lid. There in front of God and everyone, he proceeded to pull out gun parts and put together a serious weapon while we talked. Everyone watched as he wiped each part carefully with a soft cloth before its assembly. I didn't know much about guns at the time, but this big pistol thing looked like something an assassin might use -- all *blued* metal, short stock and a long barrel. Once assembled, he pulled out a black silencer and threaded it onto the barrel. He didn't say what he was getting it ready for and no one asked.

It turned out his actual biker name was *Assassin*. Well, I had had enough education in biker lifestyle for one night, so I nodded to Michelle and we said our goodbyes and walked back down the alley to our little apartment. The traveling bikers were gone early the next morning and that was the end of that.

The next week, we were back at the biker house and the guys were making fun of Michelle for not having a bike. After all, biker mommas are supposed to be riding bikes, aren't they? I certainly didn't have any money to buy a bike, not even a used one. Michelle was happy to be with me regardless. She liked the fact that I bathed on a daily basis and wouldn't give her any sexually transmitted diseases and the risk of me beating her up in a drunken rage was pretty darn low. But still, she loved riding on the back of choppers and I could tell that she was embarrassed that she and I didn't have one.

So what does a biker gang do when they need a bike? They steal one. Yep, they were going to get us a bike –– and soon. They asked me what I wanted. I said I didn't want a stolen bike. Sounded like a lot of trouble to me. They said I had to have one if I was going to stay with Michelle. I got the picture then –– she belonged to them, not me. Rabbit said that since I was a *newbie* to riding, they would get me a Harley Sportster and make some modifications to it, like filing off the serial number. Sounded like I didn't have a choice in the matter. For the time being, I was just going with the flow.

I suppose the good news was that they never found one they liked for me, at least in the short time Michelle and I were together. I don't remember exactly why we broke up, but as I recall she just left one day and didn't come back. All she brought with her in the first place was one of those large hand-made cloth purses that hippie girls used to carry, so that's all she left with. I was fine with it.

## Chapter Four

Back at the *nuthouse,* I was sitting in my usual chair one morning when a female nurse came up to me. I had watched her walk out of her station. She was an older nurse. Some nurses were kind of hot looking -- she was not.

"Mr. Stevens?" the nurse said while walking up to me.

"Yes?" I answered, looking up at her from my chair.

She stopped and asked, "We would like you to join us for an interview today. Would that be okay with you?"

"I don't know. Will it hurt?" I said, trying out my humor on her. She didn't even smile.

"The meeting starts in about thirty minutes," she said. "I'll come get you when they are ready, okay?"

*They? Interview?* I was curious as to what she meant but I just nodded.

The nurse came back about forty-five minutes later. I was ready. It was something different to break the monotony. I got up and walked side-by-side with her down the hall. The nurse opened one of the heavy, steel doors down the left side of the hallway and followed me inside. We walked to the middle of the room where there was one wooden chair. The nurse motioned for me to sit and I did. Then she walked over to a chair by the door and sat down.

I looked around the room. Right away I knew this was not what I would consider a normal interview. It was a large room -- maybe thirty feet by forty feet. The room was empty of furniture except for all the wooden chairs along the walls and, to my surprise, each chair had someone sitting in it.

I looked all around me at their faces. There must have been thirty people in the room. Most of them looked like doctors with their suits and white coats. There were a few in white nurses' uniforms, too. I had not seen any of them before.

*What was THIS all about?* I thought. *Why all this interest in me?*

One of the men in a suit introduced himself.

"I'm Doctor Blanchard, Harold."

"They call me Harry," I blurted out.

"Oh, excuse me, Harry," he said, and turned to a nurse sitting beside him. "Make a note of that please." Everyone had a pad and pen in their hands and made notes.

"Well, Harry, do you know why you are in here?" Dr. Blanchard politely asked.

"I think I do," I replied.

"Then please tell us," Dr. Blanchard added.

"You don't know?" I said, now feeling embarrassed that I was sounding cocky. I continued, "I'm sorry. Well, my guess is that it had something to do with my parents, probably my father."

"And why is that?" the doctor quietly asked.

"Because my parents are not very happy about the lifestyle I have chosen and are trying to do something about it."

"And what lifestyle is that, Harry?" Dr. Blanchard continued.

"I guess a hippie lifestyle," I said.

"And does that hippie lifestyle include using drugs?" he asked.

"Yes, it does," I said.

Since I was in a mental hospital already, I figured that I couldn't get in too much more trouble by admitting to using drugs.

"So, Harry, if you will, please tell us about the drugs you've taken," he said.

"Okay, let's see... you should know that I'm not a *hard-drug* user.

"*Hard-drugs*?" he said. "What are *hard-drugs*?"

"You know –– heroin, meth, cocaine. I only like the fun stuff. I know better than to use stuff that I could get hooked on. I'm just one of those people who likes to smoke a little dope and do a little tripping. See some color and laugh with friends. I don't see anything wrong with that."

"'Smoking a little dope' would be smoking marijuana, right?" the doctor asked.

"Right," I said. I was starting to think that this interview was just a little juvenile. He knew what *smoking dope* meant. I realized that I had rolled my eyes when I answered. I needed to not use rude body language or they might get the wrong idea about me.

"And 'tripping', what is that?" he asked.

"Dropping acid -- taking LSD," I told him and the group.

Dr. Blanchard paused for a moment. The lady next to him leaned over and whispered something to him. Everyone in the room was staring and listening carefully. I felt like a celebrity all of a sudden. All this attention to what I had to say. It felt strange.

"How many times have you dropped acid, Harry?" he finally asked.

"I've lost count," I said, "but probably over a hundred."

"Did you have any bad things happen on any of those occasions while you were under the influence of LSD?" he asked.

"No, I've always had a pretty good time," I honestly explained.

"I see," the doctor said. "Now Harry, would you mind explaining to our group what it was like to be under the influence of LSD?"

"That's pretty hard to explain," I said.

Everyone in the room leaned in closer as if to better hear what I had to say. My first thoughts were, *These people really want to know what acid is like. This isn't going to be easy, but I'll give it a shot.*

"Well, after you swallow a tab of acid, it doesn't have an immediate effect," I said, "It starts out with just a hint that something strange is happening. You begin to notice little things around you that are different, such as lights flickering, sounds you may not normally notice, and colors that seem exaggerated. It gets more intense as it progresses. I would say it takes about thirty minutes to really be tripping. You start getting this funny feeling, like maybe the feeling you get when you have taken an upper," I said.

"You didn't mention taking uppers," the doctor noted.

"I don't really like uppers, but I have taken some to stay awake so I could party longer," I told the captive audience.

"I'm sorry I interrupted," Dr. Blanchard said, "Please continue –– you were feeling funny at first?"

"Well, I don't exactly know how to describe it," I continued. "You just know that it is starting to *come on*. Then things start getting weird. It's like objects might move a little –– maybe out of the corners of your eyes at first –– then things right in front of you start looking different. Like they move on their own. And colors! Colors are all intensified –– and you notice a lot more detail about everything you look at. I guess that's why you might sit there and stare at something for a long time, just groov'n with it." I realized that I was doing all the talking now –– but I continued anyway.

"That goes on for maybe an hour or so before you peak. I'm not sure," I said. "Maybe it's different with different people, but I seem to be on the same track with the other people around me who have also dropped acid."

"So you do this as a group?" he asked.

"Usually, I guess. It's more fun that way," I said. "I've never taken any alone. There's always at least one person with me."

Dr. Blanchard smiled and asked me to continue.

"Okay, let's see if I can describe this. The whole experience seems to build up, and up, and up," I explained, as I gestured with my hand going up each time I repeated it. "Until you notice that the drug is wearing off. Everything seems to be slowly returning to normal, no one is laughing anymore and you start coming down from the high."

"Coming down?" Dr. Blanchard asked.

I leaned back and thought for a second before replying. "You know when you no longer feel anything."

"And how long before that happens?" he asked.

I was on a roll now. "Well, on a good trip, I'd say about eight to ten hours. I've never timed it. Time doesn't really matter while you are tripping." I started using gestures more as if I was on stage.

"Let's get back to how you feel while you are tripping," he said.

"Okay," I went on. "Well, before long, you are buzzing along, almost like humming along. You are wide-awake -- very wide-awake, but you don't feel like moving much. You can function if you need to most of the time. You are looking at everything around you for the first time. I mean *really* looking. You notice everything. Everything starts having meaning to it -- even the smallest things. Like you could focus on an ant in the kitchen and follow it around for an hour just thinking about what it would be like to be an ant. Like, what would you do if you were an ant? That sort of thing -- like everything matters -- everything!"

I paused, realizing that I was getting excited now -- able to say things to older people that I normally wouldn't have been able to say in a different setting. It felt a little bizarre and I looked down to the floor.

"I see," Dr. Blanchard said, "Please continue. We all would like to know how you were feeling."

"Okay," I said, as I snapped back into my oratory mode, "Not only are things important and your feelings about the things around you important, but people are important, too. It's like your feelings for people are also exaggerated. Like you care about them and their wellbeing more. People who have dropped with you are going through the same things you are, noticing the world around them in a new way. Maybe the things right next to them, or maybe the things going on across the ocean -- or even under the ocean! All of a sudden anything and everything is in your sights. They say it expands your mind, maybe opens up those places in your brain that have been dormant, or maybe places in your brain that you don't normally use."

I decided to get down to the nitty-gritty of how doing acid affects your mind. "I can give you an example of seeing something cool that you know is not there, if you want."

"You mean a hallucination?" he said. "Yes, we would like to hear about that."

"Yes, I guess hallucination would be the right term for it," I said. "But it's not like a dream. It's more like you know you are seeing something in a different way -- and enjoying it. You are aware of being alive and pretty sure things would be different if you weren't tripping on acid."

Then I told them of an experience I had while living on Ira Street. "I once lived in an apartment that had a tall wall of bricks on the inside. I was sitting at the dining table tripping out, and out of the corner of my eye, I noticed that something was happening to the red brick wall to my left. I turned and focused on the wall and, all of a sudden, all the bricks, and the mortar between the bricks, looked like they were moving. It looked so real! The bricks turned into little gears and the grey mortar turned into chains or belts moving along the gears. The whole wall turned into one giant machine -- everything turning in different directions, everything connected and all working off each other. I just sat there with my mouth open. I have always said it was my best hallucination and I doubt that anyone had ever seen the same thing looking at that wall. You see tripping is unique to each person -- each brain."

Dr. Blanchard pondered aloud. "Harry, do you know of any LSD research that proves that?"

"Yeah, my own research. No, I guess that's just what I think," I responded.

"I see," he said, "and then what happened?" Everyone was still paying close attention.

I continued, "I watched the wall for a few minutes until someone in the house interrupted me. When I turned back around, the wall was just regular bricks again. I tried to make it move again, but couldn't. It was a big disappointed to tell you the truth."

All eyes were on me. The doctor wanted more. "I see. Please go on," he said.

"So my friends and I try to make our acid trips as colorful as possible -- just to see how cool we can get things to be. Like having colored lights in the room -- maybe a black light hanging from the ceiling and day-glow posters on the wall. Oh, and the lava lamps are fun to watch stoned. Some acid is more colorful than others. My favorite is *Sunshine*."

"*Sunshine?*" Dr. Blanchard asked, "What is *Sunshine?*"

Everyone in the room was on the edge of their chairs so I went on. "Oh, it's just a name for some good quality LSD. It is made into a little, yellow tab... you know, like the color of sunshine. They say it comes directly from Timothy Leary's own lab, but I'm not so sure that is true. People say anything to sell you something."

"I see," he said, "Please continue, Harry."

"Well, uh... screwing! Oh, I'm sorry. Can I say that here?" I felt a little embarrassed with the women in the room, but I did notice that everyone sat up straight all of a sudden.

"Like... you know, making love," I said, "Like when you'd like to *ball* somebody." I stopped and didn't know if I'd said too much.

"You can say anything you want here, Harry. We would like it to be in YOUR words so we can understand you better." Dr. Blanchard's deep, calm voice started to bother me.

*Understand me better? I was telling them about drugs -- not ME. Maybe this was about me.* I didn't care one way or another. I was just telling them as much as I could think of. Besides, I was on a roll and I was enjoying talking about it.

"Okay, uh, making love is what I am talking about," I said. "It feels great stoned on acid. Well, when both people are stoned on acid that is."

"I see," the doctor said. Everyone continued to stare. I was about to blow their minds and wondered if my description might make some of them want to try acid.

"It's like both people are extremely sensitive -- both in mind and body," I said. "You can feel someone touch you like you have never felt before. And you feel something magical when you are touching someone, too. All your senses are enhanced. And it doesn't have to be such a serious thing either -- you are enjoying it so much that you are mostly just giggling and laughing together. It's like you are lost in each other -- nothing else beyond two people matters. It is an intense feeling. Really nice!"

I had been looking at the doctor and people sitting next to him as I described having sex while high. I stopped and looked at the other people around the room for a brief moment. They all seemed mesmerized.

I couldn't think of any more descriptions of sex on acid so I tried to think of something else to tell them about tripping.

"And music!" I blurted out, proud of myself for not missing that one. "Music is fantastic on acid -- particularly with headphones on. It's best when there are several sets of headphones and everyone is listening to the same music -- like sitting around together groovin' to something. Everyone is nodding their heads and keeping time together -- with big grins on their faces -- just enjoying it so much. We sometimes listen to music for hours. You know, volume up, keeping the beat together. It's just a lot of fun and feels wonderful. Hard to set the needle on the record though when you get really high."

There was a pause, then the doctor asked, "What about feeling paranoid? Do you ever feel paranoid when you are tripping?"

"Some people get more paranoid than others," I said. "I'm not that bad about it, even though sometimes you think you hear things and imagine the sounds are something they are not. You have to learn to stay in control and not let your mind go there. Some people have a hard time with that. I try to only trip with people whom I trust. I'm not too paranoid as a rule, so maybe those things don't get to me so much. I'm not sure. I've heard of people having bad acid trips, but so far, I've done fine with it."

"I see," Dr. Blanchard said. "And what else?"

I realized that people were still writing notes on their pads. They had been pretty busy all this time between staring at me and writing down things I had said. I felt like I was in control of the whole room. I didn't want to stop. This was about ME and I really liked that for some reason. I wasn't used to being the one out front. I preferred to be second in command, letting someone else take the lead. Now, I wasn't sure where I was going with all this.

"I'm not sure what else," I said, "When people read articles about taking acid, they don't seem to understand what it is all about. That article that came out in *Life Magazine* on LSD was all wrong. It's like the people who write that stuff never took it to know what it was like -- if they had, they wouldn't say the things they say about it. It's like the world is getting split up somehow between the people who get stoned and the people who don't. I think more people should try it. It might help stop these wars. How can people try to kill each other if they are smiling and giggling and passing a joint?"

"I see," he said. He paused for a moment, leaned over to the lady next to him and whispered something. She whispered back and he turned and asked me another question.

"So, Harry, why do you really think you are here today?"

"I guess I'm here because someone was going to bust the house I was living in because the sheriff deputy said if I didn't sign the paper he was taking me back to the house -- and I would join my friends in jail."

I wasn't about to start telling them about dealing -- I just wanted to sound like a user, not a dealer. People in the room started shifting around in their chairs. The lady next to the doctor looked at her watch and whispered to him. People started making noise with papers, folding up their notepads -- some reaching down for their briefcases. I figured that we were about to end the interview.

"Well, Harry," he said. "We want to thank you for sharing this with us today." I saw a few people smiling and nodding their heads in agreement.

"We all wish you the best of luck. You can go now," he said.

No one got up. They were probably waiting for me to leave. So I got up from my chair and turned around. The nurse who brought me in got up from her chair and motioned me over to the door. I walked down the hall with her and into the main room where I plopped back down on my favorite chair. I bent over and stared at the floor. I thought about what had just happened -- things I had said.

I felt glad that I talked about it and maybe a little sorry it was over. Heck, my first experience at public speaking. That was fun!

Many of the people from the interview passed by me on their way out of the ward. It was really boring just sitting in that room watching TV and just waiting for the next meal. So I got up and started walking down my dormitory hallway. About half way down, two young nurses in white uniforms that had been in my interview came up to me.

"Harry," one of them began, "We're really interested in knowing more about your acid trips."

I definitely got the feeling that these cute nurses weren't asking me because they were trying to study acid for their class -- they wanted to know for themselves. At least that's what I'd like to think. They weren't much older than I was and were whispering as if they didn't want anyone else to hear them. They were almost giggling as they asked me about the acid. I could tell they wanted to try some. I spent a few minutes telling them more about tripping. It was really funny to me. They acted like groupies. I felt like a rock star -- another chance to experience my youthful, overblown feeling of self-importance.

Right then and there, I started to realize how sexy nurses looked in those pressed white uniforms, white shoes, and little white hats. Was I crazy? Now I had nurses asking about acid? The nuthouse was stranger than I had ever imagined!

After about five minutes of talking, they said they had to go and walked on. One looked back at me. It was just like in the movies. I hung around the hall for a few minutes thinking about all that and then went back and sat down in the living room. I didn't feel like watching TV so I just did some people watching, thinking about each individual patient and why he ended up there. Now my rock star fantasy was over and I was just one of those guys sitting around in the ward of a mental hospital again. I thought I should be in jail, not in the nuthouse!

## Chapter Five

The next day, I went through the usual morning routine in Ward Ten. After lunch I returned to my favorite chair and tried to pass the time. I was sentenced to ninety days! Just sitting there with nothing to do was starting to get to me, so I again focused on my adventures while living with my friend Michael Bartok. I thought back to what had happened over the last year.

Michael and I were enjoying life in our apartment for a few uneventful weeks and driving around in my 1963 Morgan. Friends would drop by to score some pot on a daily basis and we sat around in the dark apartment listening to Eric Burden and *The Animals* play songs like, *San Francisco Nights* and *We Gotta Get Out of This Place*, sometimes dropping acid and just groovin' to the music.

Janice Joplin was one of our Locust Street favorites. Her songs, *Summertime* and *Piece of My Heart,* still reminds me now of that little apartment. It was always dark except for the mood lighting. We could sit there for hours passing a joint, listening to music, and waiting for the next buyer to call or just come knock on the door.

The drug scene took off with such intensity in 1968 that the San Antonio narcotics squad could hardly keep up. We weren't really worried that we would be caught. To us, everyone our age smoked dope and we would have an easy way to make money for years to come if we were careful. We were off their radar -- at least I thought we were at the time.

Our hippie pad was all decked out in the trappings of that lifestyle with lots of tapestries, mattresses on the floor, big pillows, soft light, lava lamps, and oriental carpets. The place smelled like a head shop since we always had incense and candles burning, and we smelled like old leather from patchouli oil, which the Urban Dictionary now refers to as *hippie perfume*. But nothing ever stays the same does it? In

1969 our lives were about to change when two real hippies came to town from San Francisco.

Tall Tom and Bambi showed up at the Bandidos' house one evening while I was there hanging out with the gang, smoking dope, and drinking beer. Tall Tom knew Michael from his earlier dealing days and they gave each other a big hug. Tall Tom grew up in San Antonio and was a few years older than all of us. He had been part of the early hippie scene in San Antonio, hanging out at the now-famous bar near his house called the *Blue-Note Lounge*. He had left San Antonio for San Francisco three years earlier when Michael went to prison, and now he was back.

Tall Tom stood about six-feet-three and was skinny as a rail. He wore the serious trappings of a San Francisco hippie –– tight bell-bottom jeans, a flowery silk shirt, and a brown leather jacket with long fringe. His light brown hair was very thin and fell past his shoulders. He was always running his hands through it as he talked. He also had a wispy, thin brown mustache that he liked to twirl. Tall Tom was a jolly person, always ready to laugh and giggle. Girls loved him, but I never saw him get serious with one. Everyone loved Tall Tom.

Bambi was different –– much younger than Tall Tom and maybe a little better looking. His real name was Dennis but no one called him that. This was Bambi's first trip to Texas and he wasn't impressed. He was only seventeen and was short with a medium build. He wore a heavy, wool, navy-blue pea coat –– originally worn by sailors but then adopted by hippies –– over a white T-shirt and old worn-out black bell-bottom jeans. Bambi's hair ran down his back and was very blonde and frizzy, and he had a big blonde mustache to match. He had grown up in San Francisco but moved out of his parents' house early to join the San Francisco Haight-Ashbury street scene. That's where he met Tall Tom.

We all sat down in our living room and began talking. Then Tall Tom asked Michael to step outside with him for a minute. They both got up and walked out to the front porch to talk. Tom had heard that Michael was dealing again and wanted to make him a proposal. It seemed that Tom and Bambi had come to town with a whole lot of drugs that they wanted to sell, but no longer had the local contacts. They were staying in a girl's apartment in Alta Vista, just off San Pedro, and needed to find a place to put their large stash. She told them they couldn't keep it at her place any longer.

Tall Tom told Michael that in exchange for holding it for him and Bambi, they would not only let us sell what we wanted but also let us consume what we wanted, and they would be coming by ever so often to do the same thing. Tom said that the drugs they had were all in the harmless pill category. No hard drugs, just the fun stuff. That seemed too good to be true. Michael said, "Sure!" He told me later on the walk back to our apartment. I was all for it.

The next day, Michael and I followed the guys over to the girl's apartment in Alta Vista. It was in a row of two-story, red brick buildings with four apartments in each. Tom's friend who lived there was at work when we entered the apartment. Tall Tom went into a bedroom and came out with a large black duffle bag.

Tall Tom turned to us and said, "Here it is, now please get this shit out of here." That made us all laugh.

Michael and I said goodbye and quickly left with the duffle bag. When we got back home, we set the bag in the middle of the floor and proceeded to assess the contents. The bag was full of an assortment of containers. One by one, we pulled out large bags of pills and eight big Folgers Coffee cans. We laughed each time we opened one up and saw what was inside. Most of the cans were full to the brim with hundreds of capsules and tablets. We could hardly believe our eyes. We had thousands of pills at our disposal.

Those were the days when you knew what most pills were just by looking at them. Most of what we saw in the bag were *Black Mollies*, which were a stimulant similar to what later became known as Ecstasy; yellow *Sunshine* acid tabs; white synthetic Mescaline capsules, normally obtained from the peyote cactus, but produced in the lab; and *Purple Barrel* acid tabs that were of the same quality and consistency as *Sunshine*. We didn't even bother to try to count them all. Tall Tom was right. There was plenty for everybody. We took the risk of holding them and, as the days went by, we were all making some good money selling them.

The newly-found drugs were a big hit among my old friends and new ones as well, particularly the synthetic Mescaline, since no one I knew in San Antonio had ever had any. They were like acid but without the weirdness and paranoia. I called them *acid light*. Synthetic Mescaline was like being high on pot combined with colorful hallucinations. As far as our own usage, we would consistently take a mixed dose of tabs each evening –– like two or three of one, one or two of another, then maybe one more of something. It was all pure, colorful and lots of fun. Ah, those were the days.

Well, that lasted for about four weeks. By then a lot of people knew what we had, including our friend, Bill Krumb. Bill was a preppy, frat-rat who was in his second year at San Antonio College. He loved drugs, but didn't look like a hippie at all. Instead, he looked like an insurance salesman, often wearing plaid pants, suspenders, two-toned leather shoes, and a bow tie. But his money was as good as anyone's, as long as you could put up with his constant, obnoxious chatter whenever he came by. Michael had known him before we were roommates, but he was new to me.

One day I got a call from Allen Griswald, who drove a nice Triumph TR-3. He wanted to go to Houston to hear *The Children* play at *Love Street* and had a couple of other friends with sports cars already lined up. Allen said it would be a sports car rally and we just had to go. Bill Krumb was over on a Thursday night and sat around with us as we discussed the trip. We didn't invite him along. He didn't drive a sports car anyway and besides, no one wanted him riding with them anyway.

A discussion began about what to do with the stash of pills. Too many people knew we had them. Michael and I were worried that maybe they could be stolen from the apartment. Krumb said he would be glad to hold onto them for us but we declined because Tall Tom and Bambi didn't know him. We decided that the best thing to do was to bury the stash somewhere in the yard before we left. The next day we gassed up my Morgan and were ready to head out. The others were going to meet us in the alley that morning. So we went out to the alley early, before anyone was walking around, dug a hole at the base of a telephone pole near our apartment and buried the treasure. That seemed like a reasonably safe thing to do. I scattered leaves and rocks around to cover up the spot.

The trip was a lot of fun. Michael and I stayed with some friends from San Antonio who had moved to Houston, ate some of their food, and smoked some pot. As night fell we headed for the *Love Street Light Circus and Feelgood Machine*. There was lots of dancing, light shows, pot smoking, and loud music until all hours of the night. We slept in the next morning and headed back to San Antonio later that day.

Arriving back to San Antonio, we drove up the alley and parked the Morgan. The first thing Michael and I did was to walk over to check out the stash but all we saw was a dirt hole. The stash was gone! We looked at each other and both thought the same thing –– Bill Krumb! He was our number one suspect.

Allen got us to go out of town, but there is no way he would have set this up. He just wasn't that kind of guy. The only thing we could think of now was finding Krumb. We headed over to the Bandidos' house to get their help. How better to find someone than to have a whole gang of bikers looking, too? They loved the challenge. They were on a mission to help find the bad guy. At least we thought it was Krumb. It could have just as well been some alley bum who just happened to notice that some dirt had been disturbed. We never saw the stash or Krumb again, but not because we stayed there to find out. Bad news followed bad news.

Father Jim was a hip Catholic priest in our part of town that got to know young people and tried to help them stay out of trouble. Michael knew him and heard that Father Jim needed to talk to him. He was a trusted person you could tell anything to, so Michael went to his church to see what the father wanted. Michael came back to the apartment very upset. It wasn't like Michael to not be in control at all times. He seemed to have a personality that prevented it. He came storming through our door.

"Shit!" Michael said loudly.

"What?" I said, jumping up from a floor pillow.

"All that shit was stolen!" Michael yelled.

"What shit?" I said.

"The shit we've been selling, dude," Michael nervously explained. "Tall Tom and Bambi stole it from the *Whiskey*!"

"The *Whiskey*?" I yelled.

"Yeah, the *Whiskey A Go-Go* in Hollywood! And there are hitmen in town looking for the guys who are selling it!"

The reason the priest needed to talk to Michael was to let him know he and his friends were targets. Michael and I drove over to the apartment where Tall Tom and Bambi were staying and confronted them. Yes, they had stolen it all. For some reason, Tall Tom and Bambi were left alone in the office at *The Whisky* when they noticed the duffle bag behind the door. They grabbed the bag and managed to get out the back door with it. Knowing they would be found in LA, Tall Tom told Bambi that his hometown of San Antonio would be the perfect place to sell it because the guys from *The Whiskey* would never find them there. Wrong! Someone must have known where Tall Tom was from.

No wonder Tall Tom and Bambi didn't care whether we sold their pills and kept the money. They didn't have to pay a dime for them. Father Jim told Michael that there were two guys driving around our part of town in an orange Mustang looking for the dealers of the big, white, synthetic Mescaline tabs. Those tabs were very unique. No one else had them so these guys were on our trail. Michael was told that the guys in the orange Mustang were driving up and down Broadway and knew my car -- my Morgan! -- the only Morgan in San Antonio at the time. Well, that settled it. We were in big trouble. Forget the Narcotics Squad. These were the people to be scared of.

The next day, Tall Tom and Bambi came over to our apartment to talk about the situation. The Bandidos were still looking for Krumb. At this point, finding him was the last thing on our minds. We didn't want to be within a mile of that stuff. Bambi was terrified and quickly made me a proposal. He had an uncle with a farm up in Illinois. He said that if I went with him to Illinois and stayed until all this blew over, he would cover my expenses for the trip -- just for a couple of months. We would stay in touch with people in San Antonio to find out when it would be safe to return. It would be like I was his bodyguard. I looked like I was in pretty good shape back then and stood a good foot taller than Bambi -- but I was no friggin' bodyguard. What in the Hell had I gotten myself into? I'd never even been in a fight! However, considering my options, I said I would go.

Bambi and Tall Tom had driven to San Antonio in Bambi's black MGB so that was the car we would take. I would leave my Morgan with friends. That all changed when, at the last minute, Bambi decided to take his new girlfriend, Julie, with us. I would now have to follow him in my car. Julie was a cute girl with long brown hair, fair skin, and brown eyes. I had never met her before and it was clear that Bambi had only met her recently. Yes, I was about to take off to who-knows-where with a 17-year-old kid who gets too excited, and his 16-year-old girlfriend who was running away from home. It was one of those times when my brain convinced me that I had no choice but to go with the flow --common sense thus put on hold.

I decided to walk over to the Bandidos' house to ask what they thought about my plan. I know, not the best source for quality advice in one's life but that's what I did. Rabbit was there and glad to see me. I filled him in on what was going on. The first thing Rabbit said was that we needed guns. Guns! I had a shotgun at my parent's house that I would sometimes use when I went dove hunting with my Dad, but I couldn't take that in a car with me. No, he said we needed pistols -- serious pistols if we were to protect ourselves from the hitmen. Then Rabbit said he would be more than happy to find us some. He just had to make a call to one of his Bandido friends who specialized in those things. Again, I was going with the flow. It was like watching a movie, but I was the main character and making all the wrong decisions.

I got a call from Rabbit the next afternoon. I was to take money out to a mechanic's shop behind the San Antonio Airport and he would fix me up with what I needed.

I did and he did.

I drove away with a matching set of 9mm, semi-automatic Beretta pistols. I also was given a small derringer with an ivory handle for Julie, per Bambi's request -- as if she would know what to do with it. All this came with an ample supply of ammo in case there was a shootout.

A shootout? Could there really be one of those? This was sounding a whole lot like the story of Bonnie and Clyde to me, but instead of being chased by the law, we had paid killers after us. The Bandidos loved all the drama. This stuff was right down their alley -- literally.

## Chapter Six

With paid hitmen after us, we didn't waste any time getting out of town. I had no money after paying for the guns so I was going to have to rely on Bambi for all food and gas on the trip. He called his uncle in Illinois who said he would put us up for a while. All we had to do now was to get out of town without getting killed. I followed Bambi and Julie out the Austin Highway and on to I-35 towards Austin and beyond. No sign of the orange Mustang.

Bambi decided that we needed to fill up with gas so he took the exit for San Marcos and I followed. We pulled into a Shamrock gas station, gassed up, and we were off again. Bambi had bought some snacks and a soda in the convenience store and tossed them onto my lap before we drove off. I was following Bambi as we pulled back onto I-35 North toward Austin. We had only been on the highway for about five minutes when in my rearview mirror I saw it. An orange Mustang was coming up fast behind me, about four cars back in the fast lane. I felt my heart pounding. I doubted that Bambi was watching. I guess I had his back.

I reached under my seat for the Beretta, unlocked the safety and held it on my lap with my right hand and kept my left hand on the steering wheel. The Mustang kept coming. I was in the slow lane on the right. The Mustang was pulling up on my left. My Morgan was unmistakable. I felt like a sitting duck.

The Morgan didn't have roll-up windows. Instead, it had plastic window panels that were secured with two small chrome knobs. My windows were in place so it was hard to see very well to my left. My tiny rearview mirror on the windshield did not help much, and neither did each little round mirror mounted on the fenders up front -- way up front. You looked at them through the front window. They vibrated so much that they were almost useless.

The bright orange Mustang was not too hard to see regardless of how bad your mirrors were. It came up fast beside me and slowed down. I was ready to exchange fire if I had to. I leaned back as far as I could in my seat so the passengers couldn't see me well and peeked through the corner of the plastic. I saw a guy driving with his girlfriend. It was not the hitmen I was expecting. He was leaning over trying to get a better look at my Morgan. They both had big smiles and he gave me the thumbs-up sign. I smiled back and waved. They went ahead. Little did they know that I had a loaded pistol in my hand ready to use it if I had to. My heart was racing. I put the safety back on, tucked the Beretta back under the seat, and tried to relax. I had a long drive ahead of me. I felt alone, confused and unwanted -- except perhaps by killers. Bambi didn't have a clue. He was too busy playing touchy-feely with his new girlfriend.

---

After our stop in San Marcos, our drive north through Texas was uneventful. I don't know what Bambi and his chick were thinking, but alone in my car, all I could think about was getting out of Texas. Somehow I thought that if we were out of Texas, we would be out of range of the dudes in the orange Mustang. Texas is a big state but finally, we had driven past Dallas and were crossing the border into Oklahoma. We had only stopped one time on the highway for gas. There was a chill in the air and it was getting colder as we drove north.

Compared to Texas, the Midwest states didn't take that long to drive through. I had never even been out of Texas, but I found out what it was like when we stopped for some more snacks in the dusty little town of Ardmore, Oklahoma. The air smelled like petroleum and natural gas. Let's just say our welcome was not one to cherish. We pulled into a Seven-Eleven and went inside. Bambi still looked like Bambi with his long curly hair, flowered shirt, and his fringed jacket. My hair was now a little long and anything over the collar in Oklahoma meant you were a freak -- a no-good *commie hippie* for sure.

All the people in the store stopped what they were doing and stared at us when we walked in. We could have been aliens from Mars and gotten the same look. The cashier reluctantly took our money after we had walked around and collected some food and drinks. There was no smiling going on for sure. It wasn't like they were scared of us. These people just flat hated us. We could see it in their faces. To those people, we stood against everything they loved -- God and country included. The Texas license plate on my Morgan and Bambi's California plate on his MGB didn't help either.

As we walked out the door, goodies in hand, we saw an Oklahoma State Trooper step out of his car. He must have driven up while we were in the store. I wondered if someone in the store had made the call. The trooper was a tall man and his uniform was perfectly pressed and clean. He wore one of those park ranger-style hats like *Smokey the Bear* used to wear.

Our cars were parked next to each other right in front of the store. The trooper walked up to us as we were starting to get in and said, "Excuse me." We turned around and faced him. He had a stern look on his face.

He said, "You boys just passing through?"

I spoke before Bambi could, worried that Bambi might say something out of line and get us all thrown in jail.

I said, "Yes sir."

He responded with, "Good, because we don't like your kind around these parts."

As he spoke he was taking a good look at our cars. I saw no reason for any more conversation. He was expressing the feelings of all the people in the store -- and most likely pretty much all the people in his state. We were definitely not welcome in Oklahoma. As we drove off -- getting over my anger for his comment -- I just had to laugh while thinking to myself that from what I had seen of Oklahoma, why on God's earth would anyone want to be here in the first place? I felt relief when we later crossed the border into Missouri.

We drove through Missouri without incident on I-44 heading towards Illinois. Being alone in my car, I had a lot of time to think and I was wondering what kind of hype Bambi was feeding Julie in his car. I couldn't believe my eyes though when driving through downtown St. Louis; we passed a Morgan dealership. I didn't even know they existed in America, but there it was. Unfortunately, it was a Sunday and it was closed. I slowed down as we went by to see what I could. Bambi kept driving ahead so I had to keep going too. I would have loved to be able to talk with the people in the dealership about my car but this wasn't the time or place.

Crossing the river at St. Louis meant we were now in our destination state -- Illinois. Yet I had no idea where in Illinois we were going. I only knew it was a farm of some kind. If I had gotten separated from Bambi, I would have had no money and no idea where I was headed. I stuck like glue. Plus, there were no cell phones in those days, which meant no number to call to find Bambi if I lost him. That's just the way it was. Our route took us up through Springfield and Bloomington, then up I-39 towards Rockford. We were in farm country -- corn country to be exact.

We were all tired of driving, and when we stopped for gas or food, I could tell that Bambi and Julie were not getting along very well. I really didn't know her. I met her for the first time when we were about to drive out of San Antonio. But I could also tell that she wasn't the most mature girl in the world. She was young. But so was Bambi!

We turned onto State Hwy 38 and drove slowly through DeKalb, Illinois. It was a pretty, little farm town and would have probably been prettier if it had not been winter. This was the first snow I had seen on the trip, but wasn't the first snow that looks so beautiful in photos. The roads were dirty yellow-brownish-gray-white; a mixture of dirt and snow that looked like a giant, spilled Slush. I hated it from the get-go.

We had been lucky so far with good driving conditions. Growing up in San Antonio, I had only seen snow twice, and that was when my parents drove us up to the little town of Fredericksburg in the Texas Hill Country where it sometimes snowed in the winter.

I followed Bambi and Julie through town and past the Northern Illinois University campus in DeKalb. I had never heard of the school but driving along looking at the beautiful lake between the road and the buildings made me wonder if I would ever be able to finish my education. I certainly didn't want to go back to architecture -- maybe something else. I looked at the students walking along the sidewalks carrying their books, laughing, holding hands -- acting like they were going to get somewhere in the world. Me -- I was running from killers -- following this high-strung kid and his high-maintenance, underage girlfriend to who knows where? *What the hell was I doing? And how did I get myself into this mess anyway?* It was certainly something to think about.

We drove several miles out of town, east towards Chicago and stopped. Bambi had pulled over at a roadside phone booth next to an old gas station. I assumed he was calling his uncle, maybe for some final directions. Julie had been helping Bambi navigate with a map, but he had never been to his uncle's house and needed a little more information. Turns out we were only about a half mile away from the farm. We drove on and pulled into a dirt drive off the highway. The drive was lined with evergreen trees and plowed fields in every direction and as far as the eye could see. The farmhouse was a large, wooden two-story structure painted white. An old barn and silo sat behind it, along with a variety of other outbuildings and farm equipment.

Uncle Earle and Aunt Edda Chambers came out the screen door and greeted us on the steps of the large wrap-around porch. They seemed to be happy to see us and we were glad to be through with our driving. It was late in the afternoon and Edda had already started cooking dinner.

They were a nice looking couple. Earle was a bear of a man, heavyset with dark hair. He had his work overalls on and was partially covered in grime. He had worked all day and looked tired. But he was certainly nice to us and glad to see his nephew Dennis, the name Bambi used while we were there. Edda, on the other hand, did not seem too happy to see a young girl with us but kept those thoughts to herself. I could see it on her face. Edda was an attractive woman with brown hair and a good figure hidden behind her plain cotton print dress and white apron. She wore no makeup, which struck me a little strange as I had come from a place where almost every female wore makeup. Edda really didn't need any. She was like the *girl next door,* only grown up.

After our introductions, we were shown to our bedrooms upstairs. I had one to myself, thank God. I had only gotten a few hours sleep on the whole trip and that was at a rest stop about half way up. Bambi wasn't about to spring for the money to stay in a motel. Besides, we were in a hurry to get as far away from San Antonio as we could get –– and DeKalb was it! To me, we were out in the middle of nowhere.

We all sat down for dinner at a big table in the dining room. Earle and Edda had kids but they had already grown up and left the farm. Earle thought that maybe his son might come back to take over but he wasn't sure. They were growing the type of corn used for popcorn. Earle had a big mouth of mashed potatoes as he explained all about the different corn crops. It was the first time I had heard that there were so many different types of corn. Bambi and Julie were slamming down the food and had no interest in corn.

Dinner consisted of a host of comfort food that included meatloaf, fresh corn, mashed potatoes with gravy, cornbread, and iced tea. I hadn't had a home-cooked meal in ages so I savored every bite. Oh, fresh apple pie and vanilla ice cream with whipped cream came last. Geeez, that was good. After we ate, the five of us retired to rocking chairs on the porch to watch the sunset and talk.

Bambi spoke up quickly and asked if Julie could use the phone to call home. He also asked if it was okay to call long distance from the house. Earle said she could use the one in the hall. Julie said she would make it a collect call so it wouldn't cost them any money. Earle liked that. He smiled and nodded his head. Julie came back out after a few minutes and sat down in her chair. She said her parents had been very worried and wanted her to come home. I thought that was a great idea.

Bambi knew it was coming. She must have been talking about it to him while they drove. It was obvious he could care less. It seemed that the decision to take her along was a bit hasty -- and from my perspective, a stupid move on his part in the first place. Earle said he would drive Julie to the airport in the morning if she wanted. Julie thanked him and that was that. She was gone the next day -- not even a kiss goodbye.

One evening we were sitting on the porch after dinner, just looking out over the fields at sunset, when Earle asked us how long we were planning to stay. Bambi and I told Earle that we had no idea and no real plan. How long would it take for things to settle down and for the hitmen to return to LA? Maybe the people who had stolen our stuff were now their targets. Yes, that was a possibility but should we take the chance?

Earle was a welder at a local manufacturing plant just outside of DeKalb. He offered to teach us how to weld and then we could go to work at his plant. Earle said that we could make a good living as welders, but we would have to cut our hair -- as he looked at Bambi. Bambi said it was nice of him to offer but he didn't want to be a welder. I also said no.

Earle looked at each of us and asked, "So what do you two want to be anyway? You gotta do something."

"Uh, I don't know, Uncle Earle," Bambi replied. "I haven't thought that far ahead."

"Maybe an artist," I said.

"An artist!" Earle said. "How you gonna make a living at that? Haven't you ever heard of a starving artist?"

I just looked at him. It was like Bambi's answer was better than mine. At least he couldn't be criticized much for not knowing yet. I didn't have a great answer to Earle's response, but hey, being an artist would be okay.

I just said, "I don't know, sir, but that's what I seem to be good at."

Earle looked at both of us and just shook his head. He had given us the best advice he could think of so he said, "Well, you boys have a lot to learn. If you change your mind and want to try your hands at welding just let me know."

After a few days on the farm, I was getting pretty bored. They didn't even have a TV. I would go for walks in the field and think about my life and where I was -- which was nowhere at that moment.

Using the bathroom in the house was interesting to say the least. There was very little heat in the house and I stayed cold the whole time. I only had my pea coat for warmth so I kept it on. I never knew that so many flies could congregate in one bathroom at a time. They were everywhere, as were an arsenal of flyswatters hanging on the wall. I sat on the toilet every day and swatted flies until the floor was littered with them. Now I feel sorry for poor Edda, who undoubtedly was the one who cleaned up. Bambi and I certainly didn't. We just ate, drank, and slept for free at these nice people's home -- who probably could barely afford to buy food for themselves -- much less for the two of us.

We stayed with Earle and Edda for about three weeks and Bambi was getting harder and harder to live with. He complained about everything. I was embarrassed to be with him. I spent a few afternoons by myself, shooting my pistol out behind the house at a makeshift target. I asked Edda if she minded and she didn't. Earle wasn't there during the day. I had plenty of ammo and, now that we were away from Texas, I didn't really think I was going to be shooting anyone anyway. So I used most of it up practicing. I was getting pretty good at hitting the target.

One evening out on the porch, Bambi announced that we would be leaving the next day. That was news to me. I didn't say anything and acted like I knew. He and I talked later. He told me that he had made a few calls to friends he had in New York City and they said we could go there for a while and they would help us out. That only seemed farther away from where I wanted to be but it didn't sound all that bad either. Bambi suggested that we leave my Morgan at his uncle's house and drive his MGB to save money. His girlfriend left so that made sense. Then he said, "You do the driving and I'll do the paying." I said that was okay and that was it. We left the next morning after a great breakfast. Edda was a wonderful cook. I was going to miss her. I hoped one day to marry someone who could cook like that and still be cheerful to be around. I thought Earle was a lucky man.

    I had experienced a good dose of Middle America –– the Corn Belt, *Where Corn is King*! This was a farm family making ends meet, with the husband working at a factory during the weekdays and working his farm on the weekends. I liked Earle and Edda very much, even with their funny Midwest accents. I appreciated their help and told them so as we said goodbye.

---

    Once again we were on the road –– to New York City! I still had no money and had no idea how much Bambi had. We took a route just below Chicago, through Indiana, then Ohio. These states were so small compared to Texas that as soon as I got used to being in one state we crossed into another. Bambi did a lot of sleeping while I drove, but I did manage to get him to drive through Ohio.

    As soon as we crossed the border into Pennsylvania, he pulled over and wanted me to drive again. It was getting dark. We had filled up our tank with gas so that wasn't a problem. The Pennsylvania Turnpike seemed to have more tollbooths than the other state turnpikes. Twice I had to stop and pay. Each time, I had to wake up Bambi and tell him to give me some change for the toll. Both times he grumbled some cuss words at me and went back to sleep. The clerk in the tollbooth wasn't very happy looking down into our MGB at us. The headlights from the car behind us flooded our interior with light.

The first time I had to get money from him was bad enough, but the second time I shook him and said it again, "We need to pay the toll, dude!"

Bambi squirmed and said, "I've already given them all the money they need. They are just nickel and diming us to death. Screw 'em!" and he went back to sleep.

This time I shook him harder and yelled, "Wake up, damn it!"

Bambi popped up quick this time. He was mad at me for waking him and said, "What now?"

"Damn it all, Bambi, give me money for the toll and some extra for the next toll!" I yelled. "Man, I'm really getting tired of having to ask."

He pulled out some change from his jeans and slapped it into my open hand. I paid the toll and drove on. Now I knew I was in trouble because this kid was getting tired of giving me money, even though a deal was supposed to be a deal. I now only had some change left over for the next toll. No food. No drink.

I was driving through the Pennsylvania State Forest at night and it was starting to snow. A guy from South Texas driving a little sports car on the highway in the snow -- not a good idea. I just tried to keep from falling asleep and running off the road. I don't remember much about that, but the next thing I knew I was waking up in the parking lot of an interstate truck stop.

There was a constant hum from the trucks that were parked nearby. The sun was shining in my eyes through the windshield. I couldn't have gotten much sleep, but I was glad to see the sun for a change. Then I realized that it was freezing cold.

I shook Bambi and asked if he was hungry. He woke up like nothing had ever happened. Evidently he had obtained a good night's sleep. Bambi said that he could use a bite, so we got out and walked into the truck stop where he bought some snacks and sodas for the both of us. Then we hit the road again.

I came back to life after eating some food. Looking around, I could see the tall pine trees I had only seen going by at night. Pennsylvania was really a pretty place, particularly with the snow on the trees and ground. It seemed to take forever to get across Pennsylvania but we finally did. Bambi slept throughout the drive. I wondered if he had taken a sleeping pill or something. The roads were cleared by snowplows almost as fast as the snow fell.

We stopped in Newark, New Jersey, before driving into New York. Bambi decided to call his friends to get better directions. He used a phone booth on a corner and I stood outside listening to his end of the conversation. He was talking to a girl named Abby who he had met in San Francisco. Abby lived with her parents in a tall apartment building in Queens -- Flushing Meadows to be exact.

We drove on through Manhattan, across the river to Flushing and arrived at Abby's apartment. She greeted us on the sidewalk and we all rode the elevator together up to her place. She introduced us to her mother and her little brother, Stanley. Her mother was in the little kitchen area making something I had never heard of before -- potato pancakes. Stanley said goodbye and went out the door.

Abby was just over five feet tall and had long, dark hair. She wasn't all that attractive but she had a great smile and a silly laugh and I thought she was cute. We sat down and had breakfast with Abby and her mother. Her dad had already left for work so I didn't meet him. Abby said she would introduce us to some friends of hers who would help find us a place to stay. Her apartment was out of the question -- probably because her father wouldn't allow it.

I was a bit taken back by our first contact with people from New York. The ones I met in Queens were very Jewish and talked with a heavy New York accent. I had to listen really hard to understand their words -- particularly for this Texas boy because they talked so fast. For the next few days, we kept meeting new friends of Abby's. We were invited on the fourth day to go with them to a *Students for a Democratic Society* meeting, referred to as just SDS, at the Cooper Union Building. We took our seats in a lecture hall and listened to a lecture from three older guys on how to disrupt the upcoming presidential election by demonstrating in our local neighborhoods. That was our first meeting.

A week later at the same place, the SDS hosted two French men and a French woman who had been trained in making bombs and were showing slides of their techniques. I didn't know what I had gotten myself into. When we left, Abby and her friends said they weren't into this stuff at all and just went for the entertainment –– something to do.

Bambi and I didn't really care that much about making bombs, but we did accompany Abby and her friends on the subway to downtown Manhattan for an anti-election rally one day. None of the 1968 presidential candidates, Richard Nixon, Hubert Humphrey, or George Wallace, was the right choice in a lot of people's minds, particularly young, liberal, New Yorkers. We pinned these big, metal campaign pins to our coats. I wish I still had mine. Each candidate's photo was on the pin –– with big red X's across the faces. We were at a rally that was trying to get people to not vote. Hmm –– not the tactic I would have chosen for a democracy –– but it sure was fun being there. The streets were blocked off with thousands of people yelling and chanting anti-vote slogans.

Jane Fonda and her husband, Tom Hayden, were up on a flatbed truck and spoke to the crowd with a microphone. We could hardly hear anything with all the cheering but we didn't really care. We were there because it was a big scene. Young people loved being part of something, and protesting what they didn't like about the politicians was a good start. Nixon ended up winning the election and we all know how that turned out. He had to resign. Racist George Wallace was one of the choices for president. At least California's *Tricky Dick* was better than that guy.

I lost count on how many places we stayed during the two months Bambi and I spent in New York City. Abby and her friends would take turns finding us a place to stay. Some of them had nice homes in the suburbs not too far from Flushing. Wendy and Rita were two close friends of Abby's and went a lot of places with us. They all looked and dressed about the same with their long dark hair and drab, loose-fitting clothes. That was their *thing* -- not wanting to look too feminine. Very different than the girls I knew in Texas.

We would all ride the subway from place to place around New York City, which was a first for me. We stayed at one nice home several times. It belonged to the parents of Abby's friend Larry, who would sneak us into the extra bedroom in his basement after his parents went to bed. He would wake us up very early each morning and get us out of there before the family saw us. Everyone was helpful in putting us up, but I could tell they were all getting a little tired of it. I don't blame them. We couldn't even say how long we were staying. I had left it up to Bambi and he didn't know what he was doing.

One day Abby asked me if I wanted to do some shopping in *The Village*. I said I didn't have any money to do any shopping. She said she would loan me some if I needed it. So off we went on the subway into the City. The shops in Greenwich Village were very cool. Head shops, clothes shops, bakeries, delis -- I loved it! We went into one shop that had second-hand clothes. I was looking at the coats and jackets. There were tons of them. I wanted to find something to go back to Texas with that would just say, *I've been places that freaks from Texas have never ever thought about.*

Well, I found it in a thick, fluffy, off-white and unlined sheepskin jacket. It still smelled a little gamey so it couldn't have been all that old. It only cost ten dollars and Abby said that was fine. I walked out with a new look -- a hippie look. My hair had grown longer and I was finally looking the part. That was important to me. I wanted to be welcomed by freaks and rejected by anyone who wasn't a freak.

In the late 60's, New Yorkers had hash like Texans had pot. Hash, a concentrated form of cannabis, was compressed into small blocks. To smoke it, you would break off a little chunk and put it in a small hash pipe. Hash came into New York Harbor on ships from the Middle East and North Africa. Pot came across the border from Mexico.

It was simple geography. Hash was as rare in Texas as pot was in New York. One evening, after smoking hash at a friend's apartment, Abby announced that they had found us a place to stay where we didn't have to leave every morning. That sounded great.

The new place was a basement apartment in lower Manhattan. We had parked our car in the driveway of one of the friend's house so we didn't have to drive it anywhere. Mike Hershel had rented the apartment but had lost his roommate and said we could hang out there for a short time while he was looking for someone new to share the place. It was a small, dark apartment with some mattresses scattered throughout the four rooms. Everyone smoked cigarettes in those days, including me, and most of the time the place looked like someone turned on a fog machine. I only smoked cigarettes for about two years ––Tarryton's –– but I remember that disgusting odor and taste so well even now.

The music I listened to in that basement apartment was good though. Steve Miller Band's new album, *Sailor,* played over and over again. We didn't go out much. I was starting to feel like a mole. My skin was turning white and my lungs and eyes were burning from the heavy cigarette smoke in the room. I was ready to do something else after the first few nights. But, we stayed there two weeks –– until the day Mike said the fire marshal told his landlord that too many people were staying in the basement apartment and some of us had to go. Come to think of it, we weren't the only ones staying there.

So Bambi and I had to make a decision –– well, I guess he did since I was at his mercy with no money. By this time I was totally sick of him and had had enough, and again, I had no money and was sick of that, too. I suggested that maybe it was time to leave New York. He agreed. The next day we met Abby and some of her friends in Flushing and told her we were leaving. Abby said how much fun she had had with us and that she hoped we would see each other again.

With Bambi riding shotgun, I pulled the MGB out of the driveway after I did a quick review of the map. We were out of New York in no time, heading back west towards Illinois. I drove as fast as I could legally and then some. Bambi cooperated with the gas, food, and toll fees better this time. He knew I had had enough of him and this whole trip he talked me into. I had.

We no longer had our guns with us, since we stupidly placed them on top of a phone booth the first night in Queens for safe keeping. Well, maybe that wasn't so stupid after all. I wasn't the gun-carrying type of guy anyway -- so good riddance -- and I figured that the guys in the orange Mustang had not followed us to New York. The apartment buildings above the phone booth had a clear view of the top of the phone booth and they were probably gone within five minutes.

After a non-eventful drive from New York, we finally pulled into Earle and Edda's driveway at the DeKalb farm. Edda came out to greet us. Earle was at work. Edda was really glad to see us. It gave her a chance to make a nice dinner -- which she did. When Earle got home, he didn't seem as glad to see us. It was more like he was wondering how long we were going to stay this time. Bambi told him that he was heading back to California to his parents' house to try and figure out what to do with his life. I said I was going back to San Antonio where I was from. The only problem was that I still had no money.

I asked Earle if I could make a long-distance collect call.

"Sure," Earle said, "as long as it's collect."

So after dinner, I sat down and called my parents. They were relieved to hear from me. I still had a good relationship with them even though they didn't like my lifestyle. They didn't understand why I took off like I did, but were just happy that I was planning on coming back. I asked my father if I could borrow some money for gas for the trip home. He said he would be glad to wire me some money and asked how much I needed. I wasn't sure, but said I thought $100 would do it. He said he could do that. One hundred dollars was a lot of money back then and would cover all my gas, food, and probably a motel room for a night, if I needed to stop.

The next day I drove my Morgan to DeKalb and stopped at the Western Union office. After showing the nice lady my Texas driver's license for identification, she counted out the hundred dollars in twenties. Now I was ready to leave.

Bambi and I both left Illinois at the same time. We thanked Earle and Edda and both waved goodbye as I followed Bambi out their driveway. When we got to the main highway that divided our routes, Bambi and I waved goodbye to each other, knowing we would never see each other again. We could have said some kind words to each other before we got in our cars, but we didn't.

Bambi was such a young punk. I had been enamored by his cool, hippy look coming from San Francisco, and his giggly laugh when he was fucked up -- but underneath it all, he was just a spoiled kid who needed his momma. Good riddance! The only thing he ever did for me was to almost get me killed. I was relieved and felt good as I turned south towards Texas. Bambi drove straight west towards California.

---

I took the same route south as I had driving up to Illinois the first time and made a few stops along the way for food, drink, and gas. I was alone and happy for the first time in quite a while. I didn't even slow down going through Oklahoma and finally crossed back into Texas.

I made my way down I-35 past Dallas/Fort Worth. It was turning dark and I realized that my headlights weren't very bright. They seemed dimmer than they had been. The next exit was the small Texas town of Waxahachie. I exited and drove into town. When I reached the downtown, I saw that they had a wonderfully ornate courthouse in the middle of the town square. There were only a few cars on the streets. It seemed that most people were home having dinner at that hour.

I saw a motel and pulled in. The headlights on my Morgan were hardly showing by then, so I knew the next morning I would have to find a mechanic -- only this was

Saturday. Nobody works on Sunday in a small town in Texas. Sundays are reserved for church and family get-togethers.

The female clerk at the motel did a double-take when I pulled up in my Morgan. Then another one when I got out in my sheepskin coat, bell-bottom jeans and my leather boots. I walked into the office and she said, "Can I help you?"

"I'm having some trouble with the lights on my car and need to stay the night," I replied.

The clerk was about 20 years old and not bad looking. She hesitated for a moment while she looked me up and down and then said, "That will be twenty dollars for a single."

I don't think she really wanted to rent to me but she didn't know what else to do. I said the price was fine and gave her the money. She gave me a key with a large, plastic tag attached that had a big number printed on it and pointed in the direction of the room. That was the last conversation I had with her. It was like she didn't know if it was proper to talk to people who looked like me.

I pulled the Morgan right up to the door of the room and got out. These were little cottages all tightly tucked together in a U-shape with the drive following the curve in front of them. There was a nice grassy area with trees and a swimming pool in the middle. I opened the door of my room and went in. I took off my jacket and boots and laid down on the bed for a few minutes just to stretch my back out and feel comfortable for a change. It felt great. I thought about how I was going to find a mechanic the next day and how it might be a situation where I would have to wait until Monday when businesses were open.

At that point I thought it might be a good idea to call my parents and tell them where I was. They were always worried about me and a phone call would make them feel better. I looked around and there wasn't a phone in the room, so I put on my boots and jacket and walked out the door to see if I could find one. I noticed a phone booth on the sidewalk out in front of the motel. I opened the folding glass doors, stepped in and shut them behind me.

The sun was going down and the light came on inside the booth. That made it so a customer could read the phone books that hung on a chain beside the big black pay phone. The town was quiet in an eerie sort of way. But at least I was all alone to make my call home. I placed my index finger on the hole with the "O" on it and spun the dial. The operator answered and I told her I wanted to make a collect call and gave her my parent's phone number, PE-52908. She called the number as I listened in. My mother answered and the operator asked if she would accept a collect call from Harry. She said she would and I could hear her call my Dad. They were both thrilled to hear from me. My father was on the phone in their living room and my mother on the phone in the bedroom.

Dad knew everything there was about cars and said I probably had a generator problem if it wasn't my battery. He was worried that I might not have enough money left to pay a mechanic. I was, too, since I might have had to stay another night at the motel. I was about to say goodbye to my parents when I heard someone knock on the glass of the telephone booth. I had been staring at the black phone while I talked and hadn't looked outside. Besides, it was dark by then and there wasn't much to look at. My first thought was that someone wanted to use the phone. I turned and looked over to my left where the knock had come.

Plastered against the glass was a pretty teenage girl's face with a big smile. I heard another little knock and turned to the right -- another girl. I gave a smile back to them and they started screaming like they had just seen a rock star. I told my parents goodbye and that I would call them again to let them know when I would be back on the road home again. Then I realized what was happening outside the booth.

A carload of seven teenage girls had my phone booth surrounded. They looked like they had just gotten back from a high school football game. Two of them still had on their cheerleading uniforms. I pulled back the glass doors and stepped outside. They all crowded around me giggling and poking at each other like they had never seen the likes of me before -- they hadn't. This was *small-town* Texas. Several of them started asking questions at the same time. One seemed to be more vocal than the others, so I answered her first. She asked a string of questions.

"Where are you from?"
"What are you doing here?"
"Are you in a band?"
"What's your name?"
"Where are you going?"
"Uh, no. I'm not in a band," I finally answered. "I'm from San Antonio and driving back home from New York."

That was about as exotic a statement as they had ever heard.

"My name is Harry and my car is having some sort of trouble with its lights," I said.

"What kind of car is that?" one of the girls asked.

"It's a Morgan," I answered.

She turned to the other girls and said, "It's a Morgan!" and they all had a look on their faces like she was speaking another language.

I was tired of standing there next to the phone booth and it was chilly outside, so I said, "Would y'all like to come to my room and hang out for a bit?" They all looked at each other and several of them said, "Yes!" in unison.

Hell, I didn't have anything else to do, so why not? We all walked together to the room. On the way past the office, I could see the girl at the front desk giving the *thumbs-up* sign to this group. I figured she must have called them after I checked in. It wasn't every day that a freak comes to town and stays the night. It must have been the biggest thing to happen to these teenage girls in Waxahachie that they could remember. I was wondering where their boyfriends were. Small town Texas boys were big and strong from working on the ranches and farms -- and I doubted they would appreciate a freak like me flirting with their girls. I was hoping they wouldn't show up to kick my ass.

They all poured into my little room. I sat in the chair and the others plopped on the bed. I said I didn't have anything to offer them. They didn't care. They all just wanted to be part of the event. They passed around my sheepskin jacket and kept asking me questions. They were all pretty cute girls. Two were beautiful. They had that *girl-next-door* look about them –– just a little makeup (an amount their mothers would let them wear).

The girls were really interested in what was going on with the hippies they saw on TV. They even asked if I smoked marijuana. I said I did but didn't have any. They were disappointed. I thought it was weird that these small-town girls wanted to try it, but I was glad I didn't have any. I could just imagine the trouble I would have been in if I were caught by the local sheriff turning-on the town's teenage girl population. It had to happen sometime but not by me!

My thoughts turned to which girl I might be able to make-out with later. But none of them were willing to leave any of them behind. It was as if they were protecting each other from the stranger who came to town. I got the picture and after about an hour of meaningless conversation, I told them I was tired from the long trip and was ready for some needed sleep. They acted disappointed that the fun was over. One-by-one they left the room and made sure no one stayed. They were all so cute and perky in their skirts and blouses –– a far cry from the girls I hung out with in Flushing. I was definitely back in Texas. I was hardly noticed in New York City, but I stood out like a sore thumb in Waxahachie.

I waved goodbye from my doorway as they piled back into their car and left the parking lot. As I shut my door, I had to laugh a little about being treated like a celebrity. Was this my fifteen minutes of fame? I took off my clothes and fell asleep as soon as I put my head on the pillow.

The next morning I drove around town to try to locate some help fixing my car. Even though I didn't need the lights, my car wasn't driving right. About four blocks away from the town square I drove by an old metal building that had a mechanic's sign hanging over the garage doors. It didn't have any pavement, just grass and yellowish dirt that went from the street up to the doors. The shop looked closed, but a small door to the right of the garage doors was open. There was old pickup truck parked nearby. I thought that I might get some information –– maybe even some help.

I stopped the Morgan and walked into the doorway. A greasy-looking mechanic was under a car. I said hello after realizing that he had not noticed me standing there. The mechanic pulled himself out from under the front of the car on a creeper and looked up at me. He was a tall, thin guy maybe in his thirties with brown hair and light-colored skin. He had on blue overalls that didn't look like they had been washed in months and held an oily crescent wrench in his hand.

I said, "Hi, I was wondering if you could take a look at my car."

"We're closed on Sundays and I'm just working on my own car today," he said.

"Yes, I figured you were," I responded, "but I'm driving through town on my way home to San Antonio and my battery or generator is doing something to my electrical system."

He thought for a moment and then said, "Well, let me take a look at it."

He walked out and I followed him. He stopped short when he saw my car.

"A Morgan, huh?" he said in amazement.

"Yep, a '63 Plus Four," I proudly said.

He seemed to really enjoy seeing the Morgan as he walked all the way around it. He stopped at the hood and raised it up from the side. The Morgan's hood was long and narrow with sets of louvers down each side. He looked inside and stared at the engine and the odd-looking set of carbs.

"I've never worked on one of these," he said. "But, I might be able to tell you what is wrong."

"I'd appreciate any help I can get," I told him.

"My car has to come first," he said. "My wife will kill me if it's not running by tomorrow."

"Yes, well..." I started to speak.

"Start it up," he said.

I got in and tried to start the engine. It slowly turned over and then stopped. He frowned and said, "I'll check the battery," and he turned and walked back into the door. He came back out rolling a battery tester and placed the clips on the battery.

"Batteries fine, just needs a charge," he said. "Generator is most likely your problem. It ain't charging."

"I don't have much money," I explained.

"Tell you what," he said, "I'll loan you the tools if you think you can take that generator off and put new bushing and brushes in it. They're cheap. I've got a box of them so I won't charge you anything. You can work on it right here."

"Wow, thanks, man. I'm sure I can do that," I said.

"Yeah, no problem," he said. "Get that battery out and we'll put a charge on it while you are working on the generator. I've got to get back to work."

So I did what he said, rebuilt the generator and put it back on –– the bushings were the culprits after all. By the middle of the afternoon my car was fixed, so I called my parents, checked out of the motel and was back on I-35 heading home. The sunset offered a beautiful display of yellows and oranges out in front of me as I cruised through Austin towards San Antonio. Things were looking up again. It's amazing what you can do when you have to.

———————

Coming back into San Antonio meant traveling down the Austin Highway, a wide four-lane road on the northeast side of town. There were several used car lots, small strip-centers, bars and cheap motels on the Austin Highway. There was one run-down bar tucked just under the Salado Creek Bridge on a narrow access road. I had been in there once with one of the Bandidos and a big, masculine woman in biker clothes wrapped herself around me and said she wanted me. I was out of there in a flash and heard loud roar of laughing and catcalls from the bikers in the bar as I left. I was later told she does that to anyone new that comes in –– just to keep the place for their own kind. Her badass biker husband was her backup.

I was thinking about those bikers as I neared the bridge, then Wham! Something hit the backside of my car! I didn't see anything coming at me. I stopped my car in the middle of the street. It was after midnight and there were only a few cars on the road. Just drunks are driving at that hour –– which is what just hit me –– a drunk biker on a motorcycle to be exact. I got out of my car to see if he was okay. He was about thirty feet behind me. His bike was another ten feet behind him. As I walked back towards him he got up to his feet and without looking up stumbled back to his bike.

"Are you okay?" I yelled.

He didn't say anything. The next thing I knew he had lifted his bike up off the pavement, hopped back on, and took off like a bat out of hell. I stood there a bit stunned, walked slowly back to my car, got in, started it back up and drove on. No one saw it. No cars came by. I had driven all the way from Texas to New York and back without even a scratch. Then on the last few miles of my journey, I have someone hit me. The Morgan had a dent in the back fender that could be easily pounded out so I felt pretty good about what could have been much worse –– I could have killed the guy if he had pulled in front of me instead of hitting me from the side. I guess I was lucky. I guess he was lucky, too.

I drove into my parents' driveway, went up to the porch and rang the doorbell. It was late but they were waiting up for me. They normally went to bed around nine but they were too worried to do so on that night. They gave me big hugs and kisses, and I collapsed on the sofa. Mom had a plate she had fixed from dinner and brought it to me on a tray. I was hungry and finished it quickly, along with a large glass of milk. I was home again, safe and secure. I made my way to my old bedroom and collapsed on the bed.

When my parents built the house, they allowed us to decorate our rooms however we wanted. It was the sixties.

I decorated mine with red shag carpet and drapes, along with a fake zebra skin bedspread and black pillows. It was kept just how I had left it. My parents told me they loved me before I shut my door. That's how my family was. I was blessed to know they would always love me and be there when I needed them, no matter what.

## Chapter Seven

Back to the *nuthouse*. Everyone in Ward Ten had received their meds at the nurses' station and had also finished breakfast. We were all sitting again in the main room. Most of the people around me were resting with their eyes closed when a tall, thin guy came up to me and introduced himself.

"I'm Ken," he said with a small smile.

We shook hands as I looked him over. He was about my age, around twenty, and handsome with light brown hair, blue eyes, and a small mustache.

I smiled and quickly replied, "Nice to meet you. I'm Harry."

"I hear you are the new secretary of Ward Ten," Ken said.

"Yes, that's what Chief decided," I told him.

"I'm the vice president," he said.

"Yes, that's what I hear," I added.

"What are you in for," Ken asked. "Rumor has it you're here for drugs." That turned out to be the big question for newbies.

"Well, sorta," I said. "I think my parents may have had something to do with this."

"They don't let you talk to anyone on the outside for eighteen days. They want to evaluate you without any help from other people," Ken explained.

Being kind of a smartass, I added, "Well, they can evaluate me all they want. Maybe I'll learn something. I don't have anything to hide really. Shit, I'm already locked up!"

"Drugs," Ken whispered. "Do you smoke pot?"

"Sure, you got any?" I was being sarcastic.

"No, but if you're into pot, wait until I tell you about what I've got going on," Ken mysteriously said. "I'm in here to give my operation a chance to thrive without any chance of me getting in trouble. Frenchy takes care of things while I'm gone."

"What?" I said, with a puzzled look on my face.

He leaned over closer, looked around, and continued to whisper. "No one here knows the real truth about me, man. I run a marijuana growing operation in the Hill Country north of town. I have one hundred acres planted now –– but planning on expanding to two hundred next year when I buy this old farmer out next door."

"Really?" I said. "And Frenchy?"

"Oooooh," Ken said with an air of excitement. "Frenchy is my, uh… well, let's just say she takes good care of me. You should see this chick though. She's built like a brick shithouse with long, blonde hair and a body that won't quit. I have her wear those little French maid outfits. Frenchy cooks and cleans and everything –– without any complaints. She was a model in Paris before I brought her over and got her a green card to work for me. That girl's ready to have sex anytime I give her –– *the eye.*"

"Really?" I said, not really believing what I was hearing, but I had to admit that Ken was pretty convincing.

"Ohhhh, yes," Ken explained. "I call her every day to check on the ranch. Frenchy always has questions for me. Lots of employee problems with a large operation, you know. I mainly use *wetbacks* to work the fields –– they don't talk to authorities –– or anyone else for that matter. Have them in a bunkhouse –– you know, like the one in Bonanza, only much bigger."

"Wow," I muttered. I realized that I was only talking in one-word replies. I really didn't know what else to say. I had done some dealing, but nothing like this guy. If what Ken was saying was true, this was the ultimate gig –– the *dream gig* in fact. He went on and on about sex with Frenchy, the John Deere he used for plowing the fields each year to get ready for a new crop, all the money he had stashed away, and many other unbelievably cool perks enjoyed by a rich pot grower. I had heard that these guys existed, but had never met one before.

"Come here," Ken said, gesturing with his hands while getting up from the chair. I got up and followed him. Ken walked over to the nurses' station and talked to one of the nurses through the glass. He came back with something in his hands and walked over to the corner of the room, which was next to the staircase going up to the women's floor. He motioned for me to follow him so I did, wondering what the hell was going on. We walked up to the black pay phone hanging on the wall. Ken put a coin in the slot on the top, picked up the receiver, and held it to his ear. He spun the dial for each number and I watched each time as the dial returned to its original position. I still miss the sounds of those dials clicking away.

Then my new strange friend stopped and waited for someone to answer. I just kept watching, not even realizing how long it used to take back then to dial a phone number without buttons to push.

"Hello, Frenchy?" he said. "Hi, baby, how are things going on the ranch?" He paused as he listened. "Oh, that sounds good. I can't talk long today. I've got a friend listening to me talk right now. Here, say hello to Harry."

Ken handed me the phone and I put the receiver to my ear.

"Uh, hello?" I said with a degree of hesitance.

"Hello, Harry," she half whispered. "Nice to meet you."

"Same here, nice to meet you, too," I responded and quickly handed him back the phone. I didn't know what to say and was a bit freaked out by the fact that she had a beautiful, soft voice and a French accent. Shit! This guy was telling the truth!

"Okay, Frenchy," he said, taking the phone back. "Listen, I'll call you tomorrow (pause). I'm fine. No really, don't worry about me. Okay…okay. I love you. Okay, baby. Bye now." And that was that. We walked back to our chairs. Ken looked over at me with a big grin on his face. I grinned back. I was starting to think I was on an acid trip.

Another day went by. And then another. The same weirdo sleeping next to me tore up his cigarettes again. There was a commotion in the middle of the night because someone got up and hit someone else over the head with a pillow. I again slept with my head towards "Killer," the name I gave to the guy next to me. I kept opening one eye and looking at him, wondering if and when he would jump up and do to me what he was doing to his tobacco.

Hours turned into days. I was only about a week into my stay and my ninety-day sentence seemed like an eternity. No choice. I just had to keep on keeping on. One morning we all woke to several guys yelling something about their shoes. It seemed that this one crazy guy on the other side of the room had gotten up in the middle of the night and stolen everyone's shoes. The shoe bandit had them hidden under his bed, and when the nurse came in, he had to figure out whose shoes belonged to whom in a room full of crazy people. I thought it was hilarious and so did the guy that took the shoes. He was laughing loudly and jumping around the room like a bunny. Priceless.

Patients welcomed any chance for some excitement in Ward Ten. One morning, we had, once again, gone through the same boring routine and were, once again, waiting for the nurse to open the cafeteria doors for breakfast. The men were, once again, lined up at the door looking in. I waited to bring up the rear. Suddenly I heard some of them start to giggle and point into the room. I tried to not pay any attention, but the giggles turned into full-out laughter.

Eager to see what they were laughing about, I got up from my chair and walked over toward the doors. Moving in-between the men, I made it to the window on the door. Just then the nurse walked over to the doors with her keys and opened them. Then she turned around and pushed back the first guys in line. No one moved and the laughter increased. She had an angry look on her face. I poked my head around the corner of the door and there it was –– a big pile of human poop right smack dab in the middle of the cafeteria floor. I busted out laughing, too.

As we waited to enter, the nurse yelled over to the workers behind the cafeteria counter. A man came out rolling a cart full of cleaning supplies and took care of the problem. She scolded the cafeteria worker for not seeing the poop sooner. We all filed in and stayed in a very good mood throughout breakfast. I was having fun and started to actually enjoy myself. David didn't go up to the window when I did, so he finally got his tray of food and sat down across from me.

"I saw you talking to Ken," David said, as he swallowed a sip of coffee from the Styrofoam cup.

"Oh, you mean the vice president," I sarcastically responded, taking a bite of toast.

"You know he's a pathological liar, don't you?" David said.

I looked up at his face and said, "Uh, sure I do." Realizing for the first time that I had been duped by Ken, but not wanting to admit it to David.

"Ken does it to all the newbies, so don't feel bad if you fell for it," he said.

"Well, I fell for it at first," I said, now feeling weird that I had lied about it and trying to cut the lie in half somehow.

"These guys are good," David continued. "They have done it all their lives and have perfected it. Ken's thirty-five, so he's had a lot of practice. He can't make it on the outside -- keeps getting himself into trouble with people -- and they try to kill him. There are just some dudes you don't want to lie to."

"So how long has he been here, David?" I asked.

"He was already here when I got here about six months ago."

"Six months!" I exclaimed. "You've been here six months?"

David acted like I didn't ask that and continued. "They say he commits himself every ninety days. You can do that, you know."

"I ain't doing that," I said. "But why can't you leave?" I asked.

It seemed like a natural question to me since he said his uncle had him committed. He just looked up at me, put his head back down, and shoveled in some scrambled eggs, as if I shouldn't have asked such a personal question. I left it at that and never asked again.

As one would expect, it's weird meeting people in a mental hospital. You never know what you are going to run into. I felt like Alice in Wonderland. Evidently, David wasn't telling me everything either. I just had to let this stuff go, but at the same time maybe there was something about me that wasn't right. I could talk a good game but was I crazy like the rest of them? How does one really know?

Another day went by and then another. The food was awful. Breakfast went by. Lunch went by. Dinner went by. I was really getting bored. Life on the outside seemed so distant. The TV was all the entertainment we had -- with the exception of the card games. One of the men that always played cards in the corner stopped by my chair one afternoon and talked to me for a few minutes. He looked about the same age as my father.

He said his name was Dan. No one bothered to give last names in there. Maybe because they didn't want you to look them up when you got out. Dan was clean-shaven and, although he was in his pajamas and slippers, he still looked like he could have been a banker on the outside. Dan said that he was an alcoholic and had been in and out of Ward Ten several times. He said this was a safe place for him to be to go through detox and he enjoyed the friends he made here. I guessed that the *nuthouse* was a good choice for him. I learned more and more each day. Somehow all this was starting to make sense. I began to better understand that people were in there because of their problems on the outside. That's why we had mental hospitals in the first place...life can be cruel.

Dan walked back to the poker table and I remained in my chair contemplating these thoughts. Then I noticed a female nurse opening the front door of the building. It was dark outside from what I could tell. There were tight-woven, heavy metal bars throughout the hospital. Hardly anyone ever looked out the windows.

All of a sudden, a young black guy who had been sitting in a chair over on the far wall, got up and walked towards the front door. He was the only black man in the ward that I saw. As the nurse was fumbling with her keys and not paying enough attention, he pushed her aside and sprinted out the door! Half of the room got up and cheered for him. I sat with my mouth open. I was in shock just watching this happen right in front of me.

"We have a runner!" the nurse yelled.

Nurses in white came out of nowhere, but this guy was gone. The door was locked behind them as two male nurses rushed out the door in pursuit. A nurse behind the window got on the phone. The last nurse out the door was yelling into a hand-held walkie-talkie.

David walked up to me, sat down and calmly said, "They'll get him."

"In the dark?" I exclaimed.

"Sure, this happens all the time," David said. "He's somewhere on the grounds. This is a big place -- lots of bushes to hide in. But it also has a tall fence with barbed wire along the top surrounding it. It takes them an hour or two, but they always come back with him. Then when they let their guards down -- bam! He's out the door again. Fun, huh?"

"I guess so. Where is he trying to go?" I asked.

"Are you kidding? He doesn't have any place to go," David explained.

"Then why does he try to escape?" I asked.

David leaned over to me and said in a whisper, "He's crazy, man. People in here are craaaaazzzzy. Haven't you figured that out yet?" David paused for a second and then looked me straight in the eyes. "And that includes you and me, man." He leaned back in his chair and chuckled. I knew I wasn't crazy, but now wondered if I was the only one in there who wasn't.

## Chapter Eight

It was evening now in Ward Ten and I was sitting on the edge of my bed thinking about what happened when I returned from New York. I remembered making a phone call from my parents' house. Evidently, I had not learned a thing about staying out of trouble. Tall Tom was over at Wesley's ABC house when I called.

Tall Tom said, "Welcome back. Come on over," and told me where he was. I jumped in my Morgan and took off. It was only about five miles from my parents' house. I walked in and Tall Tom and Wesley were sitting at the table. Tall Tom was rolling a joint and a *Jefferson Airplane* album was playing on the stereo. The house smelled like incense -- to cover up any smell of marijuana, as if people didn't know what was going on there. Wesley went to the kitchen and came back in, handing each of us a longneck beer. We toasted and took a swig. It was an ice-cold Lone Star. Ah, I was back in Texas for sure now!

Tall Tom and Wesley were seasoned veterans of the drug-dealing trade and knew each other well. I knew Tall Tom, but Wesley was new to me. He was about my height with a medium build, short black hair and a small black mustache. Wesley was an experienced dealer and kept his hair short so as not to be noticed by the narcs. Tall Tom told me that he and Wesley were about to rent an apartment together. He said that the guys in the orange Mustang had left a long time ago and the bag of drugs was never found. Tall Tom had been living in his parents' small bungalow near the *Blue Note Lounge* on Blanco Road.

Wesley had been living with several people in an old two-story house off Fresno Avenue just east of I-10 on the access road. It was called the "ABC house" because before a group of freaks rented it, it had been the offices of ABC Pest Control. Lots of stuff went on in that house and Wesley was getting nervous about living there any longer. He thought it was going to be busted any day. Right then, a shady-looking guy walked in the front door without even knocking.

His name was Keith and he was from out of town. He was clean-shaven with short, jet-black hair and wore tight, black leather pants, a black silk shirt, and black cowboy boots. He made runs back and forth bringing pills from LA and taking back pot from San Antonio. I had met quite a few characters, but this guy took the cake. I don't know what he was on but he was pretty weird to talk to with his wild-looking eyes and his sarcastic sense of humor. Keith didn't stay long. He was there to make a deal with Wesley so they went into another room and came back out a few minutes later. Keith said goodbye and was off again.

Wesley grew up in the small Texas Hill Country town of Bastrop --northeast of San Antonio and not far from Austin. Of course, those small Texas towns were full of redneck cowboys and they pretty much hated hippies. That was until someone introduced those boys to smoking pot, for which Wesley took all the credit. Wesley knew people in San Antonio he could easily score from. He hung out at the Teen Canteen near the airport, where high school and college kids would put bands together and play the club. Early rock 'n roll, blues and pop songs filled the place with music; and filled the place with teens who had discovered pot and acid. Wesley made lots of contacts there and became THE dealer for Bastrop and the surrounding area. Wesley used to laugh and say, "Those redneck cowboys put on a good front, but they were sneaking out to the barn with their friends and lighting up." This wasn't the case with all small Texas towns back then but Bastrop had been turned on. I was happy to meet someone as savvy as Wesley.

Tall Tom, however, was his same giggly self and talked a mile a minute while twirling his thin, long hair with his fingers like he always did. Tall Tom had a serious drug problem by the time I got back. I wasn't sure if it was speed or heroin because he did it in private and never said anything about it to us. It was none of our business but we all knew that there was a reason why he was so thin and only ate candy.

Wesley brought up their move, "So man, what would you think about moving in with Tom and me? We could use another roommate. You need a place, right?"

"Yes, I'm at my parents' house right now," I said, "but I don't have any money yet. I've got to figure out a way to get some dealing going -- or get a job, which would mean cutting my hair and taking a drug test. But without having the cash to buy anything to sell, I'm not sure how to do it."

"Hey, don't worry about that," Wesley said. "You and Tall Tom and I will be partners. We have a lot of contacts that you need and you have a lot of friends who buy, right?"

"Well, yes, I suppose so," I said.

"Tall Tom and I have some money to get us going and besides, our biggest supplier fronts us pot anyway. Just move into the third bedroom of the apartment we're looking to rent," Wesley said. "It'll be great!"

"Sounds good to me," I said.

So a few days later I made the move. I didn't have to do anything but take my suitcase of clothes and drive over to the new apartment. Wesley did all the money handling for our partnership. He was a smart guy and did a good job. I always thought that if Wesley had gone to school and gotten his degree, he could have been a success on Wall Street. Plus he had street smarts. He knew when to be where and when not to be, and was an excellent judge of people.

The three of us moved into a furnished apartment on Hillcrest Drive on the city's northwest side. It was a duplex with separate entrances – each on its own side of the house. Tall Tom and Wesley always attracted girls so a couple of them helped us move in and get the apartment ready to live in. None of us cared much about how nice the place was. We just wanted to make sure it was safe to deal there. Evidently, it was. Over the next few months, we did some serious dealing and had a great time in the process. The three of us mainly dealt lids of pot and a little bit of acid.

There was a setup in our dining room with a scale hung from the light fixture over the table to weigh the pounds we would buy, big bowls to break up the pounds and boxes of

Baggies on the table. People came and went at the house. As usual, the lids we made up always weighed over an ounce. Our friends loved them because of their size –– and because they were already cleaned of seeds and stems. The quality was pretty good, too.

We were receiving totally clean pounds pressed and wrapped in brown paper. Our so-called pounds were always much more than a pound, weighing in at about twenty to twenty-five ounces. We paid $15 for each one and made up about twenty big lids from them. Selling at $10 per lid, there was a lot of profit in our little business and our supply would be delivered to our door every week. I felt like a real entrepreneur. It was my first introduction to running a business, if you could call it that.

Tall Tom and Wesley both knew our supplier well. His name was Tex. He was a large Anglo about thirty years old. When I say large, I really mean fat. Tex must have had his clothes specially made, always wearing a pair of slacks, dress shirt and polished black dress shoes. With his short, curly red hair and pinkish-white skin, he reminded me of a big pig. Tex drove an older black Lincoln Continental with *suicide doors*, back seat doors that opened towards the back of the car instead of the front.

Tex had grown up on the west side of San Antonio where many of the old families that immigrated from Mexico took up residence, along with those who were indigenous to the area. The west side was mainly Hispanics; the eastside, Blacks; the south side, middle-class Anglos; and the north side, middle to upper-class Anglos and Hispanics. I grew up on the near-north side in a middle-class neighborhood that was a mix of Hispanics and Anglos.

Growing up as an Anglo on the west side presented some challenges for Tex, but also a lot of opportunities if a kid wanted to be a drug dealer when he grew up. Tex was raised by his grandmother. She and his grandfather owned a corner grocery store on the west side. His grandfather had died when Tex was twelve, so from then on, it was just he and his *Abuela* Irene.

Irene knew everything Tex was up to. He bragged to us how he would take her with him across the border to buy pot. When he came back across, no one suspected that this little 90-year-old lady would be participating in a smuggling operation. She was. His grandmother used to shut down her store and accompany Tex on the trip across the border and back. Irene had closed down the store a few years before so the money Tex made helped her get by.

Tex didn't look like a smuggler either with his short hair and totally un-hip clothes. He was all about keeping his income flowing while not tipping off the law. It was how he made his living and, so far, it had worked for him. It had for years. Both he and his grandmother spoke perfect Spanish, of course, and the families he bought from across the border at Del Rio had close relatives in the neighborhood in which he grew up. *Abuela* Irene had helped many of the families when they were in need and the neighbors kept their mouths shut, even though they knew what Tex was up to.

Tex's best friend was Arturo Sanchez. He and Arturo had been playmates together since they were babies. Then they found themselves dealing drugs together. If Tex needed more pot for a sale, Arturo could always give him some of his.

Arturo was Hispanic with slick jet-black hair that he combed straight back. He had a large black mustache that hung down both sides of his mouth. I only saw him wear black -- black jeans, black western shirt, black cowboy hat and, black boots. His shirts were usually embroidered with flowers, and each of his boots had a sterling silver pointed cap on the ends. You wouldn't have wanted to be kicked by these boots. Arturo rarely smiled and, when he did, you needed to worry because he didn't like to smile.

Tex would drive up into our driveway, open his trunk and bring in two suitcases with about 15 pounds in each of them. Wesley would pay him and Tex was gone -- no dilly-dallying around for him. This wasn't a social call. This was business -- serious business. He rarely said a word to me, just a glance.

One day, Wesley got a tip. Someone said Wesley had been followed by narcs when he left the house. He said we should be careful. We spent the next day looking for another apartment and found it on Ira Avenue, over by Fort Sam Houston on the other side of town. It was in the middle of dealing-country and crawling with hippies and hookers. It was just down from a good head shop and across from Brackenridge Park. Hookers worked on Broadway up and down this strip and all sorts of illegal things went on there. It was the perfect location for us to do our business and have no one notice. We would just blend into the neighborhood. We packed up and moved the next day.

This apartment was more modern than the house we left. It was nestled within a group of about ten. It would have been extremely hard to see which apartment a person was going to from outside the complex. They were two-story, rectangular boxes with limestone rock walls going all the way up both sides with large, glass doors at one end facing a nicely-landscaped courtyard. The space in the living area went all the way up to a vaulted ceiling with a balcony looking down from the three bedrooms upstairs. A red brick wall in the center divided the kitchen from the stairs. Every place we rented was furnished, so it didn't take that much for us to move.

The Ira apartment seemed the perfect dealing place. After we had been there for a week, we received word from friends that the San Antonio Narcotics Squad busted into our last place the day after we moved out. They were on our trail, but we thought we could stay ahead of them by moving.

There were many nights when we went to the *Pusi-Kat Club* to dance and listen to music. The club was in downtown San Antonio and was a nightclub for the new hippie movement that was sweeping the country. Everyone wore hippie attire, of course, but on the upscale side. We were dealers and knew a lot of people. We always chose a table to the left of the band stage to sit with our girlfriends and many people would come by and talk to us. One band that played was the *Laughing Kind* and we knew a couple of the band members. *Lord August and the Visions of Light* also played the *Pusi-Kat*, an early San Antonio band put together by Augie Meyers, who later partnered up with Doug Sahm to create the *Sir Douglas Quintet.*

We got to know *Lord August's* drummer. His name was Pineapple and he gave me a black beaver top hat that he wore often when he played. Pineapple was Hawaiian with long jet-black hair, shiny brown complexion and a plump round face. I never quite figured out why he gave his hat to me. I thought it looked great on him. However, it looked great on me, too! With my shaggy white sheepskin jacket, and my top hat and long hair, I was quite an attraction driving around San Antonio in my Morgan.

Although we were a little more cautious dealing out of Ira, it was pretty much business as usual for us. People came and went; Tex came and went and we did the same. Tall Tom still had contacts in San Francisco and Hollywood where he had lived for several years. The *Whiskey-A-Go-Go* caper evidently didn't concern him anymore because he made arrangements to fly back to LA to score some acid and bring it back to sell. Wesley and I had to laugh as Tall Tom got all dressed up for the flight to LA. He had not been working very hard in the partnership and Tall Tom thought this contribution would make up for it. The price of the acid was very reasonable and more than made up for the cost of the flight.

Wesley gave him the cash and expense money to make the trip to buy five hundred hits of acid at $1.00 each. We planned on selling them for $5.00 each. We drove him to the San Antonio International Airport to see him off. Tall Tom was the epitome of hippie-ness on that trip. He was wearing red and white, striped bellbottom pants; a long-sleeve, blue, silk shirt with white stars; a red scarf tied around his neck and brown cowboy boots. He definitely stood out in a crowd, particularly because of his height and long, straight hair.

There was no real airport security in those days. Tall Tom was flying on Southwest Airlines. We walked him out to where he would board the plane and waved goodbye. Then we walked back down the terminal and turned to go up the staircase to the observation deck where you could watch the planes take off -- a wonderful place to take some acid and go hang out, which we did on many occasions.

As we turned the corner to the staircase, Wesley and I passed a large room full of new Army recruits sitting in rows of chairs waiting to be flown to boot camp. I'll never forget the look on their faces. It was haunting. They didn't make a sound -- they just looked at us as we walked to the stairs.

I thought about what they must have been thinking as we walked by. They were going. We were not. I felt bad for them. They were about to risk their life for a war that couldn't be won. Some were volunteers but many had been drafted and had no choice but to be thrown into a situation where they might have to kill a person in order to save themselves and others. Some of them had long hair like we did. I knew I could have been one of them easily had it not been for the crack in my vertebra from playing football in high school. I never forgot about them.

Wesley and I proceeded up the stairs and saw Tall Tom's plane take off down the runway and up into the clouds, then we headed back to the apartment. Tall Tom was due back the next day. He said he didn't want to hang around California for long. The next day we waited by the phone in our apartment for a call to pick him up, but it never came. He was supposed to come in on an afternoon flight. We thought he might have decided to stay an extra day, or maybe he got fucked up and missed the plane.

That night Wesley and I were watching the local news when they reported on a big drug bust at the San Antonio International Airport. Yes, it was Tall Tom! He was searched coming off the plane, most likely because of how he looked, and they found the acid -- 500 tabs in his carry-on bag. And, yes, he still had on that American flag outfit. He was laughing on TV and flashing the peace sign as they handcuffed him and took him away. It was no surprise that Tall Tom looked red-faced stoned on the television because he probably was.

Unfortunately, my parents also saw Tall Tom on the evening news. The next day my mother was at our apartment door and wanted to talk. Wesley quickly left the room. My mother was obviously upset and assumed that if Tall Tom was dealing drugs, I must be doing the same. She wanted me to come home and start over. I declined and said not to worry, I knew what I was doing and everything would be fine. My mother left in tears just as she had come.

There was no talking me out of my new lifestyle or the easy money I was getting by dealing pot to my friends. It wasn't like I was hanging out on street corners whispering to school kids that walked by. I only sold to people that I knew and Wesley did the same. Tall Tom's dealing habits were another story and we weren't sure how his bust would play out at that point. We certainly were not going to go down to the jail on his behalf. We were hoping his mother would bail him out. She did three days later.

At around 10 o'clock the next morning, I walked down to the *Icehouse,* the name we liked to call the convenience stores in San Antonio, to get a Big Red. We loved Big Red, a locally made strawberry-flavored soda that had a strong flavor and even stronger caffeine kick. We all thought a Big Red went well with smoking pot.

Wesley had left the apartment but I wasn't sure where he went. When I left the *Icehouse,* I walked back up the hill towards the apartment. As I turned the corner where I could see the complex, I saw police cars all over the place. I had a good idea what they were doing. I immediately headed across the street where there were plenty of bushes in which to duck for cover. I watched as they came back and forth to their cars. Some were uniformed cops and some were in suits.

It took them about an hour to complete their search of our place. Nothing illegal was in the apartment at the time, but they knew Tall Tom had been living there. I wasn't sure what to do next. Then Wesley came walking up the street. I grabbed him and told him what had happened. We waited about an hour after it looked like all of them had gone. I had a good view of the apartment and was pretty sure that they had not left anyone to watch the complex. So Wesley and I cautiously returned to assess the damage. They had torn the place up pretty bad. We piled some of our stuff into our cars and left -- once again almost getting busted. This partnership was getting complicated -- and dangerous.

My parents didn't know what to do about what I was doing. They were afraid I would end up in jail and they were right in thinking so. I was just one step away from it. My father had an idea that he thought might work. Even though the war in Vietnam was still raging and kids my age were being killed on a daily basis, he thought it might be a good idea for me to become a soldier. Unbeknownst to me, he talked it over with good old Doctor Dan and he agreed. There weren't a lot of choices then. If I didn't die in a rice patty in Vietnam, at least I would come back a real man. So my father asked Doctor Dan to write a letter to the local draft board, saying that in his professional opinion, my back wasn't all that bad and that they should take another look at me for service to my country.

Tall Tom came back and he, Wesley, and I stayed at the Ira apartment for another week but didn't keep any drugs there. We were just trying to figure out our next move. That's when my father called me to say that they had received some important mail for me. I drove over to my parents' house and he handed me the letter. It was an official notice from the draft board for me to report again to their offices downtown. Of course, he didn't mention that he knew of it and acted as surprised as I was. I had already flunked the draft board physical the first time. Now I had to do it all over again?

I showed up on the day of my appointment like I was supposed to. The draft board was housed in the same Navy armory complex that I had gone with my mother years before to watch government films during the Cuba Missile Crisis. I followed the signs upstairs. All the walls were painted battleship grey. The floors were concrete. It was crowded and there were guys about my age all going through the different sections of the building getting tested for just about everything you can imagine.

I gave the uniformed guy at the reception desk my draft notice and he told me to sit and wait for my name to be called. I turned and joined a group of about thirty or so guys in rows of chairs waiting for the same.

By then my hair had gotten pretty long, which meant they absolutely hated me from the get go. Not that they were kind at all to anyone going through this process, but I had a particularly hard time on that day. Some of the tests were fine but I had a problem when I was told to go into a bathroom stall and pee in the little cup they gave me. I couldn't make myself pee. Finally after a few minutes, and a few times of being yelled at to hurry up, I peed enough to partially fill the cup and came out. They took the cup outside the exit door and said to follow the yellow line on the floor. That led to a line of guys waiting at another station.

When it was my turn, I entered a tiny room with one chair looking out through some glass to the tester on the other side. It was a hearing test. The door to the room was left cracked open just a little so it was hard for me to hear from the start. I had to push this little button when I heard faint, beep-like sounds of different frequencies. Evidently my hearing back then wasn't much better than my hearing now because I flunked the test. The tester came into the room and was furious.

He pulled me out and sat me down in front of a desk off to the side. He was suspicious because of my long hair and demanded to know who had trained me to flunk the hearing test. I assured him that I had not been trained and told him about the open door, so he made me take the test over. This time I passed it, but only barely. I don't know, maybe all that dancing in front of huge speakers at the *Pusi-Kat* and listening to loud music with headphones took a toll on my ears.

After the hearing test, I followed another yellow line to the opposite side of the room and joined about twenty other guys lined up against the wall. We were told to take off our clothes and keep on our underwear. Everyone was in white briefs and looking pretty dumb standing there together. It brought back memories of my high school locker room. Looking down the row I had to laugh at the different looking guys. We came in all shapes and sizes.

The tester came down the row and told each of us to pull down our underwear to our knees. Then he placed his fingers on the side of our testicles and told us to cough. This was how they determined if you had a hernia. It was normal procedure. Doctors did it each year before the sports season in school but that didn't make it pleasant. Next they said to turn around, face the wall and bend over –
– which we all did. They said to spread our cheeks as they walked by each of us and looked at our butts.

Once that was complete, we put our clothes back on and sat in a row of chairs outside a little office waiting for our name to be called. I could see that there was a man that looked like an actual doctor in the little office because he had on a white lab coat and a stethoscope hanging from his neck.

My name was finally called and I walked into the office and sat down in front of the doctor. He had several files on his desk and was flipping through one without looking up. He asked my name and confirmed who I was. There was no small talk. This was serious business to him and he didn't look like he was in a very good mood anyway. I thought that was pretty typical of a military doctor. He looked up at me, placed the file back down on the desk and without saying a word he walked out of the room through the open door behind him. So I sat there for a few seconds wondering what was going on, then leaned over to see if the file he was looking at was mine. It was. He had left the file open and a letter was in clear sight. I turned the letter slightly towards me in order to see it better.

And there it was. A typed letter from dear old Doctor Dan saying that he thought I was now fit for military service. I quickly turned it back and sat back down, just in time for the doctor to walk back in.

He closed my file, and in an angry stern voice said, "Get the Hell out of here, we're never going to take you!"

I was gone in a flash but not after passing about sixty more guys sitting in rows of chairs who had passed the physical with flying colors. They weren't going anywhere except to boot camp. No going home or saying goodbye to anyone. After boot camp, they were headed to Vietnam. I looked into their eyes. Most were in shock. I was in shock, relieved that I wasn't sitting there with them. I was now in a pretty good mood so I hopped back into my Morgan and drove back to the apartment. Things were looking up.

We hadn't seen Tex in about two weeks and were wondering what was going on with him. So we drove over to his grandmother's store. The front door was locked, but the side door was open. We knocked and went in. Tex came into the room to greet us. His grandmother wasn't there. We sat at a small wooden table and told him what happened. He had also seen Tall Tom on the news and was concerned that we weren't being careful. We assured him that we would make sure that Tom wouldn't pull any more of these stunts. He picked up the phone and called his friend, Arturo, who pulled up in his big black pickup truck about five minutes later and came in. Arturo looked at us in disgust.

"You gringos aren't being careful," Arturo said.

"Harry and I are," Wesley responded. "We just have a problem with Tall Tom."

"We don't like this kind of publicity around here," Arturo said. Tex was being quiet and letting Arturo take the lead.

"Did you make sure you weren't followed over here?" Arturo asked.

"Well, we thought we did," Wesley said.

"I don't know," said Arturo. "You have to assure us you can handle this."

"We can," Wesley said. "We're going to look for a place in the country where we won't get so much attention."

Tex made a head gesture for Arturo to follow him outside, so they both walked out the door and came back in a few minutes later.

"Okay," said Tex. "We can work with you still, but one more incident and we're done. And, if you boys ever bring up our names, you are dead meat."

"Fine," said Wesley.

I chimed in, "Not a problem, we'll be careful."

"Then let us know when you find a new place and we'll be back in business," Tex said. Arturo was silent and just stared at us.

We looked carefully down the empty streets for any suspicious parked cars as we left the corner store. Nothing looked out of the ordinary. In those days unmarked police cars were easy to spot. We stopped to get a newspaper then drove over to Annie's apartment to regroup. Annie smoked a little pot but that was about it. She had a decent job as a secretary and was going to school part-time at SAC. She was glad to help us. After spending a few minutes reading the classified section of the *San Antonio Light*, Wesley stood up and said, "This is it! A three bedroom furnished house out Hwy 281 North on 20 secluded acres of land."

"No shit?" I said.

"Yes," Wesley said. "We have to get this one. It sounds perfect." He asked Annie if she would accompany him to the real estate office and act like they were married. Annie spent a lot of time with us, along with her friend, Valarie. Annie was a sweet girl, short with closely cropped blonde hair. Valarie and I became a couple of sorts. She was super cute with lots of makeup. I particularly remember her blue eye shadow. But, she was so thin! She may have been anorexic, but I didn't know much about those things back then. She looked a lot like Twiggy, the iconic model of the 60's -- only with short, black hair instead of blonde.

Although everyone danced with everyone else at the *Pusi-Kat,* Valarie and I always danced together and sat together at the club as if we were a couple. But we never really got romantic. In fact, I don't think we ever even kissed. She flirted a lot with me, flashing her big brown eyes and talking sweetly. It was a strange relationship but I sort of enjoyed having a girlfriend without any commitments.

There were a lot of those kinds of relationships going on back then.

    Wesley thought he would have a better chance at renting the house if Annie was with him and they looked like they were married. Annie was hesitant but said she would go with him. She had a soft spot for us. Annie called the realtor and made an appointment to see the house. We stayed the night at Annie's and they met the realtor the next morning. Annie was nice enough to call in sick that day. I waited at her apartment. About an hour later, Wesley walked in and said, "We got it!" After thanking Annie over and over again, we drove out to the house with what we still had packed in our cars -- mainly our stereo, clothes and some decorations.

    I followed Wesley out San Pedro Avenue, which turned into Hwy 281 once it passed the San Antonio International Airport runways. As we drove past the airport, I thought back to my childhood when my Mom would pack up a picnic dinner -- usually fried chicken purchased from Church's Chicken -- and my family would drive out San Pedro before sunset, pull off where the runway crosses over the road and park our car on the grass. My sisters and I would sit on our Buick's hood. Mom and Dad would sit in folding aluminum chairs, and we would eat our dinner while the airplanes took off with engines roaring overhead. The huge planes seemed close enough that we could almost reach out and touch them. My father loved it most. It was our cheap entertainment during the week and many other families did the same thing.

    Wesley had a hard time finding the turn off the highway to our new rent house. It was just a dirt drive that went through a ranch gate and it was hard to tell that there was even a house back there. It was about 14 miles past the airport and the perfect place to not be noticed, plus the house sat in the middle of 20 wooded acres. We pulled up, opened the metal gate and drove up the dirt driveway to the house at the top of a hill. You couldn't see it from the road since the property was covered with Live Oaks and thick Mountain Cedar trees, typical of the Hill Country north of San Antonio.

The dirt road opened up to a dirt parking area and right up to the front door of the house. The landscape consisted of just natural live oak trees and Texas grasses. There was a lot of rock mixed with the soil and no one had ever planted any additional landscape. The house was made from local limestone with dark green trim and had a brown roof. You could tell it was old. There were a couple of tin outbuildings down from the house and a small stable that didn't look like it had been used in years.

We parked our cars and walked up to the door. It was a heavy wooden door, actually two doors. One opened towards the outside and one towards the inside. That was unusual. Wesley and I walked in and, standing right in front of us, was a regulation size pool table with a bar light hanging above. We were definitely in the right place. The walls and floors were all made of stone. The main living area of the house was about 20 by 50 feet with plenty of sofas and chairs. At the other end of the room from the entrance was a giant rock fireplace with doors on either side. The wall to our left had four double-hung windows. The wall to our right had doors that led to three large bedrooms with a bathroom in-between.

We walked on back. Both doors next to the fireplace led into a large kitchen that was completely furnished with everything we would need. The bedrooms were also furnished. The thing that struck me the most about the place was the fact that every interior and exterior door had heavy black metal L-shaped brackets with a heavy wooden bar that fit into them to secure the door. The front door had two. Every window had heavy-duty, solid wood shutters -- that closed from the inside. They also had the brackets and wooden bars. We wouldn't have to worry about someone breaking in or busting in. They would need a tank to break down that door.

"What's with these doors and windows?" I asked Wesley.

"This place must have been some sort of whore house or illegal casino or something," Wesley said. "Perfect for us, ain't it? I can't wait until Tall Tom sees it."

"Looks good to me," I said. "Let's get our stuff inside and crank up that pool table."

Tall Tom came later. He didn't have a car so Annie and Valarie drove him out. They wanted to see the house, too. By then we were ready to party. We drove down the road to the nearest Lone Star Icehouse and bought some food and beer. It was definitely a house made for dealing!

Our group partied hard for the next few weeks. Lots of playing pool and, with the supply of cut wood stacked outside the front door, we had some great fires in the fireplace. The girls came by some evenings and we all had a lot of fun together. A third girl would sometimes come out with Annie and Valarie. Her name was Sonia. She was really beautiful -- a tall, heavily made-up girl with long, puffed-up brown hair and thick, fashionable glasses. She looked like a model and appeared to be with Tall Tom, although I never saw them sleep together or anything else very romantic. Sonia didn't do any drugs or alcohol. Annie and Valarie just liked to smoke pot with us and occasionally drop some acid. The days went by and we continued our dealing activities and were making pretty good money. It was so easy.

We also spent a lot of time with the girls dancing at the *Pusi-Kat*. We thought we were pretty cool always sitting at the same table as if it was reserved for us -- an illusion of grandeur, of course. In our minds, being dealers made us important, but the real important people were the musicians who actually had a skill. Our special skill was not getting caught by the police.

A lot of people our age had some kind of job, and maybe sold a little pot or pills to their friends. Instead, we were businessmen, full-time drug dealers -- at least for a while. We became very popular at the club. Everyone wanted to get to know us better when they found out we were dealers. This was our reality.

---

Tall Tom, Wesley, and I would drop by people's houses or apartments either making deliveries or sometimes just to party with them. There was a pair of twin sisters we got to know from the *Pusi-Kat* named Elizabeth and Joanie who had an apartment on Cambridge Oval, a circular street at the top of one of the hills in upscale Alamo Heights. Their place was on the second floor of a two-story wooden four-plex. We had partied hard the night before and I had hardly gotten any sleep before we went to their apartment one night. Tall Tom gave me a couple of uppers to take because I was tired and I certainly didn't want to miss any of the fun.

The problem was that I was burning the candle at both ends, not really keeping track of what I was doing and not really caring. After partying for hours at the twin's place, we decided it was time to go home. The three of us said our goodbyes and headed out the door. I went first. The stairs to the bottom floor were steep and not broken up into two flights –– just one long way down. Well, I started getting light-headed as I stood at the top of the stairs looking down. Before I knew it, everything went white and I passed out while standing there and tumbled all the way down to the bottom of the stairs.

I was out cold on the floor. No one knew quite what to do. In those days, calling the police or an ambulance was a sure way to get busted. All the Alamo Heights Police needed was an excuse to come into your place and discover what you were up to. One of the twins called my parents. I'm not sure how they got that phone number but they did, most likely from the phone book. My parents soon arrived, put me in their car and rushed me to the Baptist Memorial Hospital in downtown San Antonio where I had been born nineteen years earlier.

Doctor Dan, who had brought me into this world, met us there. Yes, the same doctor that had written the letter to the draft board. I had spent many hours in his office downtown near Alamo Plaza where he would give me shots or whatever was called for when I was ill. He was a no-

nonsense kind of doctor. Doctor Dan was a friend of the family as well. He and his wife had known my parents from their days at Jefferson High School in 1934.

But on this day, things changed between Doctor Dan and me. It was the last time we would see each other, not that he cared. I certainly didn't. So I was admitted to the hospital and was lying in a comfortable hospital bed with my parents by my side trying to recover. I didn't know what was wrong with me but I had survived the fall down the stairs without breaking any bones.

Doctor Dan came into the room, greeted my parents, and took a look at me. The first thing he did was to shine a flashlight into my eyes. I could see the disgust on his face as he stepped back and proclaimed, "Get this boy out of here! He's on drugs and certainly doesn't need to be taking up any space here."

I guess he saw that my eyes were dilated, not too surprising considering all the pills I had taken over the past few days. My parents were totally embarrassed and I could hear them apologize to Doctor Dan for taking up his time as they followed him out the door of my room. I'm sure he wasn't very happy about having to leave his house after hours to drive to the hospital just to see me in that condition.

So I had to get up out of the comfortable hospital bed, put my clothes back on and follow my parents out to their car. They took me home to their house and put me to bed in my old bedroom. I slept for two days. I guess I was exhausted more than I had realized. When I finally felt well enough, I thanked them for their help and they drove me back to the Alamo Heights apartment to pick up my car. I can just imagine how much they worried about me. Now I very much regret doing that to them.

―――――――

Several days went by. Tex made his deliveries out to the house and felt better about this new location. He even stayed long enough to shoot some pool. We made trips into town to make our deliveries and some customers came out to the house to buy. The money was flowing strong again. Wesley was our business manager and banker and made sure we all had pocket money to spend. Most of the money went to rent, food, utilities, and an ever-increasing inventory of pot.

One day, Arturo made the drop at the house, but instead of the clean pounds of pot we were used to getting from Tex, he brought in two large gunnysacks and said this was what they had this time. If I remember right, each sack held about forty pounds of pot. I had the largest bedroom in the house so we pulled the sacks into my room, out of sight of the living room. The smell was very strong since the pot wasn't in the tight plastic wraps that we were used to. We set up a processing table in the middle of the kitchen and, over the course of a few days, finished turning the first sack into lids.

With money to burn, Wesley heard that the *Bubble Puppy* was playing at the *Armadillo World Headquarters* in Austin on the weekend. The *Bubble Puppy* was an Austin band who, at one point, put out a hit song called, *Hot Smoke and Sassafras*, which made it to number fourteen on Billboard's Top 100 in 1968. So we made plans to drive to Austin. Wesley was friends with the band's lead singer, Roy Cox, and we had heard them play at the *Pusi-Kat* many times.

Wesley and I headed up to Austin on I-35 North and stayed at the house of a friend of Wesley's near the University of Texas campus. Being in a college town made me think of my own education again, or lack thereof. Maybe someday I would go back. But right then, I was having fun doing what I was doing.

We dropped some acid a few hours before going to the *Armadillo*. The band was fantastic as usual and when it was over, Wesley drove us to the house where we were staying. The acid kept us awake for a long time as we sat on the floor with friends and passed around joints. We discussed just about everything under the sun and listened to albums on the stereo. Everyone woke up feeling exhausted sometime that afternoon. The three of us spent another hour or so hanging around the house and then drove on back to San Antonio to the safety of our fortified Hill Country house.

Everything seemed normal when we arrived right before sunset. I had slept all day and I wasn't very sleepy -- but I was tired. Tall Tom hadn't gone with us to Austin and he had a few friends over that night. I stayed up talking and shooting pool until about midnight and then crawled off to my bed and finally fell asleep. Tom's friends had already crashed on the sofas in the living room. It was a cool night, and although the logs in the fireplace were now just embers, they still kept the inside of the house comfortable and warm.

Lieutenant Charlie Dore, the head of the San Antonio Narcotics Squad, was an old friend of my father's. He always bought Buicks from my Dad. Growing up in San Antonio, Dad knew tons of people. San Antonio just wasn't that big back then. After my Mom wasn't able to convince me to change my ways and the military didn't want me, Dad decided to give his friend, Charlie, a call to see what he knew about the people I had been living with. Boy, did Dad get an earful from the lieutenant.

"Is that your boy, Harold?" Charlie asked.

"I'm afraid so," my Dad replied.

"I'm so sorry, Harold," the lieutenant continued. "If I knew he was your son, I would have called you. Listen Harold, we have been chasing that group all over the city for months."

"What?" Dad said, "Our son is mixed up with some serious drug dealers?"

The lieutenant paused for a moment and then said, "These are bad people, Harold. Most of these guys have records and are well-known to us. We knew about your son but until now we didn't know his name."

"What can I do, Charlie?" my father begged to know.

"Well, Harold, since we are friends, I will tell you that we are about to make a bust at their new house out in the country. We followed them out there the other day. We're getting the search warrant from the judge now."

"When is it supposed to happen, Charlie?" Dad asked.

Sighing, the lieutenant divulged the upcoming plan, "It's scheduled for tomorrow morning, Harold."

"What can I do?" my Dad again asked.

"At this point, I'm not sure you can do anything, Harold. It's probably too late. The wheels are in motion. Your son's in serious trouble." Then he hesitated. "But wait, Harold, you may be able to get him committed."

Dad seized on that idea. "Okay Charlie, thanks. I think I know what I can do. I'll call you back later. Thanks for letting me know."

"Sure, Harold," Charlie said, and they both hung up.

My father then placed a call to another longtime friend who was the head of the San Antonio State Mental Hospital. Doctor Blevins took the call. Dad explained the situation to his friend and asked how hard it would be to have me committed for a brief period of time. Blevins said he could make that happen if my Dad needed him to. Dad asked for the favor. It was the only thing my frantic father could think of.

Dad told him that it had to be done right away. Blevins said he would make the call upon hanging up and let Dad know when it happened. The doctor thought he could pull some strings with the Bexar County Sheriff Department, who he worked with on a regular basis. Dad thanked him and waited for the call. The Sheriff deputies showed up at my doorstep the next morning and that's how I ended up in the *nuthouse*!

---

And there I was -- sitting in my chair in the mental hospital. I had a lot of time to think. Years later, I would see the movie *One Flew Over The Cuckoo's Nest* starring Jack Nicholson as Randle McMurphy and Louise Fletcher as Nurse Ratched. I was Randle McMurphy in the lead role and that movie brought back a lot of memories.

I thought about all the people, all my friends, who had been on this dealing adventure with me. I would never see Tall Tom again but I would see Wesley. Wesley would finally be caught and go to prison for a couple of years. After paying his debt to society, he gave up his life as a dealer, stopped all smoking and drinking, and married a girl named Deborah from his hometown. She kept him out of trouble from then on. He moved back to Bastrop and became a small engine mechanic.

I only saw Wesley one more time, several years later, when I sold him an old boat that my father-in-law had given me. That's when he told me that he and Tall Tom had moved to Houston after my episode at the state hospital and that Tall Tom had overdosed on heroin in their apartment. Wesley woke up to find him dead. Wesley didn't want the police to come to his apartment and decided that Tall Tom wouldn't have wanted that either. So what did Wesley do? He dragged Tall Tom's body out to his car the next night, drove down to the Gulf Freeway and deposited Tom's body on the side of the road for the authorities to find the next day. Not something I would have done, but knowing Tall Tom, he would have had a good laugh over that.

## Chapter Nine

Another day in the *loony bin,* and then another. I was actually getting used to it. I had met this guy named Jerry at SAC but didn't know him well. Jerry was a big guy, a bit overweight with a light complexion with pimples, and short light-brown hair. I saw him walking down the hall in front of the cafeteria doors one day. I wasn't sure it was Jerry at first, but then when he turned around I saw that it was definitely him. So I walked up to say hello.

"Hey Jerry, what are you doing in here?" I asked, not knowing what else to say. He looked up at me and smiled.

"Harry, right?" he said.

"Yeah, I know you from Annie and Valarie," I reminded him.

"Oh yeah," he said. "What are you doing here?"

"I asked first," I said. "Just kidding. I think I was saved from being busted -- maybe by my father. Not sure."

Jerry lowered his head and said, "I guess I freaked out or something. I took some acid and, the next thing I know, I'm in here."

"You had a bad trip, huh?"

"I think so," Jerry said. "But I've been in here before. I don't know. They say I'm depressed."

"Being in here is depressing," I said with a little laugh.

Next Jerry talked in a super serious tone. "No, like I was depressed before. They say I may be manic."

"Oh," I said. "So do you know how long you are going to be here?"

"Not really," Jerry said. "But they told me yesterday that they wanted to try something on me that might help. I have bad dreams too. I don't know. I had a rough time growing up and all."

"Man, I had a wonderful time growing up," I said.

Then Jerry mentioned his new treatment. "I'm scheduled for some kind of electric therapy this afternoon. I'll let you know if it helps."

"Well, good luck with that," I said.

"Thanks, man. Uh, I gotta go on down..." he said softly as he hung his head down and walked off towards the hallway that led to the dorms.

"Yeah, I'll see you later," I said.

I saw Jerry later in the cafeteria. He was on the other side of the room eating at a table with some other guys, but he was not talking. Jerry always seemed like a quiet guy anyway. I was sitting with David listening to him rant about his situation again for the umpteenth time.

"So David," I said. "Have you met that guy over there -- the big, white guy?"

"Where?" he asked. I pointed at Jerry.

"Over there at that table with the two Hispanic guys talking," I said.

"No. You know him?"

"Not very well, but I've been around him a little on the outside." I explained. "He said he is having some kind of electric therapy this afternoon."

"Oh, man," he said with disgust. "That shit is bad."

"What do you mean?" I eagerly asked.

"I've seen people afterward. It's like they are a vegetable!" David said. "These people do it all the time here. They wanted to try it on me -- I refused! They can only do it with your consent."

"So what is it, exactly?" I asked.

"It's SHOCK TREATMENT, dude!" David yelled out. "Like they put you on a table, strap you down with big leather straps, hook all these electrodes to your head, and blast you with a buttload of electricity. It causes you to have a brain seizure. That shit has been in use for years, but guess what? They don't even know why it works. Then if it doesn't work -- well, a lobotomy is next!"

"A lobotomy?" I said. "Isn't that something like taking your brain out?"

"No, man," David went on. "But they stick this long ice pick up behind your eyeballs and into your brain. Then they scramble it all around and mess it up."

"You're shitting me," I said. "Is that why some of these people in here are so -- not all here?"

"I don't know," David explained shrugging his shoulders. "I think it's the Thorazine that is making most of them like zombies. Some have heavier doses than others. I'm on a small dose -- just to take the edge off. I get so mad about everything."

"I noticed," I nervously said. "I just hope they don't have anything like that planned for me. I guess I'll know after my eighteen days are up and I can talk to someone on the outside. No one is telling me anything in here."

"They say that shock treatment resets your brain. Like it removes bad memories and lets you start over with new, good memories," David said.

"Oh yeah, like all the good memories you can have after your brain gets fried and you find out you are in a *nuthouse*?" I said.

David was on a roll. "Yeah, well -- since they don't know exactly why shock treatment works, sometimes it backfires."

"Backfires!" I stuttered.

"Yes, you can go into a seizure and never come out of it," David said. "Then you really do end up like a vegetable."

I shook my head slightly and looked at him. There really was nothing left to say. He went back to eating his food and so did I. This entire conversation left me with a strange feeling that I had been watching a *Cheech and Chong* movie.

Later that day, I saw Jerry again. It was time for bed and everyone was filing into the dormitory. He was sitting on the side of his bed across the room from me. He had his head down staring at the floor -- just sitting there in his pajamas. I walked over to him. I don't know if curiosity got the best of me, or maybe I was worried about him.

"Hey, man," I called out, standing in front of him. "Are you alright?"

Jerry looked up at me with a blank stare. My old acquaintance had no idea who I was. He didn't say anything. His face looked empty. His eyes were just blank and I could see that his temples were red. That kind of freaked me out. So I stood there for a minute, thinking that maybe it would just take him a little time to respond. He didn't. I slowly turned around and went back across the room to my bed. I'm not sure if the shock treatment helped him or not. It had sounded like an acid trip may have gotten him in there, but also sounded like he had a lot of other problems from the start.

    Jerry never acted like he knew me the rest of the time I was there, and I never saw him normal again. I turned in and quickly went to sleep. I was used to the routine and no longer afraid. The guy sleeping next to me tore up his cigarettes again, while making angry sounds.

---

    Well, the big day finally arrived. Day 18! -- The day I could talk to someone from the outside. It was only a little more than half a month, yet it seemed like a lifetime, but I signed that paper that said they could hold me for 90 days! If the rest of the days went by as slow as the first eighteen… oh brother. That was going to suck, big time.

    It was after breakfast on day 18 when we were all sitting in the main room. The TV was blaring. People were slumped and asleep in their chairs. The alcoholics had already started their poker game in the corner. Nurses were scurrying about. A black custodian was mopping the hallway. I was thinking about who I was going to try to call on the pay phone that hung on the wall in the main room, also contemplating where I was going to get a dime to use it. Then a male nurse walked across the room and used his keys to open the front door, letting several people inside. Most of the men looked up and then went back to their business. But one of those people who came in was my sister, Beth. Woo hoo! Someone who cares I was there! She looked around the room and saw me sitting there. She came right over. I stood up and we hugged. I could see that her eyes were teary.

    "How are you?" Beth asked.

"I've been better. I AM in the mental hospital if you haven't noticed," I said.

"I know, I'm sorry," she said.

"So who is responsible for this?" I asked, even though I thought I knew.

"Daddy," Beth said. "He didn't know what else to do. His friend, Charlie Dore…"

That tidbit of information was news to me, so I stopped her and said, "Daddy's friends with Charlie Dore?"

"Yes, and also with the head of this hospital. That's why you are here," my sister explained. "Daddy kept you out of jail, Harry, so you should thank him."

"Well, I'm not very happy about being stuck in here," I said, "but I am really happy that I'm not in jail. I really was angry at first, but I know Daddy was only doing what he thought was best to try to save me. So what's next? When can I get out of here? I had to sign a paper that said I would be here for 90 days, Beth."

"Well, you know Daddy," Beth began with a smile. "I am here to offer you a proposition."

"A proposition?" I said, "Okay, what is it?"

Beth went on. "Well, Daddy called Cousin Hugh in California and Hugh talked to his sister, Christine, and her husband, Morten, about the situation. Morten said you could come out there and work for his Architectural Arts firm -- maybe start your architecture career that way."

I stared at Beth for a second, just trying to take all that in, and then said, "California?"

"Yes," Beth confirmed. "You would have to cut your hair. Daddy sold your Morgan and bought you a little Buick Skylark convertible with the money. You can drive it out there."

"My Morgan is gone?" I sadly said. "What about Jack? Who has Jack?"

Jack was my little blonde mutt and the love of my life. She went with me everywhere and never on a leash. There was no need for a leash as she was *street smart,* always knowing how to avoid cars and minding whatever I said. I was praying that I didn't lose Jack.

"Jack is fine," Beth explained. "We got her from Wesley and she's at Mother and Daddy's house waiting for you."

"Thank God!" I said. "I didn't know what happened to Jack and was really worried."

"No, she's fine." Beth said.

I turned and looked at Beth, "Did my house get busted?"

"No," Beth assured me. "Evidently the narcotics squad called off the bust because they thought the element of surprise had been lost."

"That's funny," I said. "No one even knew I had left."

"I guess not," Beth said.

"So if I decide to take Daddy's offer, when would that happen?" I asked.

"I believe right away," she answered.

"Okay, I'll do it," I said. "My hair can grow back if I want." It was a true *no-brainer* and it didn't take long for me to decide.

"Okay, I'll call Daddy and let him know," Beth said as she turned and walked towards the nurses' station window. I watched her walk around to the left side of the station. A nurse unlocked the door for her from the inside. Beth picked up the phone receiver and began talking to someone. I could see her through the glass. I remained seated in my chair and, after a couple of minutes, she came back out and walked over to me.

"You can leave now," she said.

"Now?" I said in shock.

Beth smiled at me. "Yes, they are pulling your belongings, so go on down and change clothes and I'll wait for you."

A nurse came over and told me to follow him. A few people looked up momentarily as we walked down the hall to the little room where I had given up my clothes for the pajamas and slippers. I changed back to my street clothes and came out. Beth was talking with a nurse through the glass and signing the paperwork.

I came up and stood next to her. Another nurse came out with a set of keys in her hand and we followed her to the door. I stopped and looked back around at the scene one last time. Ken was in the corner chair. He glanced up and then put his head back down. He had not spoken to me again after finding out I knew he was a pathological liar. David was reading the paper and absorbed in the politics of the day. The alcoholics continued their card game. A girl was sitting at the bottom of the staircase flirting with a guy through the bars. The TV was blaring. Most of the guys were just sitting there staring ahead or asleep in their chairs. No one said goodbye. No one even noticed that I was leaving. No one really cared.

I would never see any of them again, nor would I ever enter a mental ward again -- at least not by the time of this writing. In some strange way, Ward Ten taught me a lot about people, maybe about life in general. It was an experience that is seared into my brain and, even though I was initially angry about being incarcerated, I don't regret having spent time there at all.

My sister drove us out of the hospital grounds and turned right towards downtown San Antonio. It was like I had just woken up from a dream. I had to squint my eyes from the bright sun after being inside for so long. Beth didn't act like she wanted to talk. I thought about my move to California. The theme song from the old TV show *The Beverly Hillbillies* popped into my head. I sang it to myself as we drove north on South Presa Street toward my parents' house and away from the San Antonio State Mental Hospital.

> *"Well the first thing you know ol Jed's a millionaire,*
> *Kinfolk said 'Jed move away from there,'*
> *Said 'Californy is the place you ought to be,'*
> *So they loaded up the truck and moved to Beverly.*
> *Hills, that is..."*

## Chapter Ten

Beth broke the silence. "So, what was it like in there?"

"You have no idea," I said. "I guess it could have been worse."

"Well, Harry, I hope you can turn things around in California."

"I don't know, Beth. I'll give it a try. I've thought a lot about things while I was in the hospital."

"I bet you did," my sister said.

And that was about the extent of our conversation as Beth drove me to our parents' house. I looked at all the people we passed on the street, wondering if any of them had ever been locked up like me.

I was about to make my second trip to California but under very different circumstances. I was being sent to California to get away from drugs –– to Hollywood! It was a good idea to get me away from my dealing friends, but California was perhaps not the best choice of locations for drug rehab. It was all my parents knew to do at the time. When we got to their house, I went inside and sat down with both my parents and my sister. It was a short conversation because they didn't really want to talk about how I got in trouble. They just said that they thought moving to California to work for Morten was probably the best thing for me. I couldn't disagree. I was glad to be out of the mental hospital, but my real joy was when I opened the door and Jack came running up and jumped into my arms.

After finishing a nice breakfast that my mom had fixed, I excused myself and walked down the hall to my old bedroom with Jack at my heels. My bedroom hadn't changed a bit. I closed the door behind me and plopped down on the bed. Jack jumped up on the bed and licked my face. As I laid there, exhausted from the ordeal, my thoughts returned to what I had been through.

Here I was about to move to California. This wouldn't be the first time I had been to sunny California. The first time was in 1967 when I lived on Lewis Street. My friends, Pete and Gary, wanted to go see what was happening out there. California was *Mecca* for hippies and we just had to go check it out. So we piled into my Corvair Monza and drove to LA -- then to San Francisco. We mostly just walked the streets in Haight Ashbury, bought some souvenirs from a few headshops, and took in the whole hippie scene. Young kids were flocking there from all over the country. Everyone knows the story, *Summer of Love* and all that.

Pete, Gary, and I went into the *Whiskey A Go-Go* in West Hollywood. It had been the launching pad for bands like *The Doors, Buffalo Springfield,* and *The Byrds.* The club wasn't that crowded when we were there, so we sat down at a table and spent the next couple of hours listening to a band that we had never heard of before -- *Country Joe and the Fish.* We loved them. They played the *Fish Anthem* and everyone but us seemed to know the words. *The Fish* later became one of my favorite bands.

While in San Francisco, we went to *Winterland* to hear *The Doors. Quicksilver Messenger Service* opened for them. The whole room...floor-to-ceiling...was painted black with psychedelic patterns in day-glo paint. While most everyone else was dancing, we stood at the edge of the small stage and watched Jim Morrison undulating on the floor in black leather pants while singing *The End.* Hell, I could have reached over and touched him.

The club was using the old-school light show technique, with saucers of oil and water, glass plates and overhead projectors to throw colorful moving images on the wall behind the band. It all pulsated with the music. I could see the guys in the back above the crowd projecting the light show and I thought how cool it would be to have that job.

There must have been a hundred motorcycles parked in front of the entrance. Bikes were all along the street and up on the sidewalks. When the club closed and we came out, I saw that people had already lined both sides of the street leading away from *Winterland.* Our group stopped and wedged ourselves into the lineup.

Then the *Hell's Angels* came out and everyone started clapping. The bikers started climbing onto their choppers and kick-starting their engines. The sound was deafening as each roaring motor added to the sound of the others. These bikers were the real deal -- most with their biker mommas climbing onto the seats behind them. The guys looked very badass and so did their girls. You just stepped back and gave them room. It was a sea of chrome, tattoos, and black leather, plus all kinds of German-style helmets, chains, black boots -- anything to make people afraid of them -- anything to look tough and scary. Performance art... I loved it!

Soon it became apparent why everyone was lining the street outside *Winterland*. One-by-one, the *Hell's Angels* took off down the street in a blast of raw engine sound, each doing a wheelie to the applause of the crowds. Just leaving a place was a big event when it came to the *Hell's Angels*.

We found a cheap motel to stay in for a couple of nights. The Haight Ashbury street scene was so cool. Hundreds of young people dressed in hippie attire roamed up and down the strip. Pot smoke filled the air and we were asked probably a hundred times if we wanted to buy drugs. Anything people wanted could be purchased right off the street. My friends and I thought we were hot shit back in San Antonio, but in Haight we were way behind the times. We Texans needed to somehow catch up.

After a few days in San Francisco, it was time to go home. Our money was running out and back then no one had credit cards to cover any extra expenses. I was proud of my little Corvair Monza that made the trip without a hitch. It was a great car, although it proved to be unsafe later. Pete, Gary, and I returned to Texas with a whole new outlook. Our minds were filled with incense and our eyes with stardust -- *We had been to the mountain*!

———

Goodbye mental hospital, hello California! I arrived in downtown Los Angeles five days after getting my freedom back, having driven there in my dark blue 1965 Buick Skylark convertible with one suitcase of clothes and my trusty dog, Jack. It was sad that a lot of my hippie clothes had been left behind when the Sheriff deputies took me away. I had no idea what happened to them. I especially missed my big sheepskin coat, my black beaver top hat, and of course, my '63 Morgan.

I kept a map of Los Angeles open on the seat next to me as I found my way from IH-10 to the Hollywood Freeway. After exiting on Sunset Boulevard, I headed for my cousin, Hugh's apartment. Hugh was about eight years older than me and had offered to help me get a fresh start. Although we had met years earlier, I barely knew him. Hugh lived in a swank Hollywood apartment on Shoreham Drive overlooking the Sunset Strip. He and Ron owned the apartment complex, which was built in a Spanish Colonial style going up the hillside from the famous boulevard. It was getting dark.

After I parked my car along the steep street next to the complex, Jack and I walked in through the gate to locate my cousin's apartment. The grounds were lush with beautifully lighted tropical plants. I passed several fountains covered with colorful Spanish tile. The complex was a series of buildings all tucked into the hillside with rock walkways winding around the thick landscape. I was instantly impressed. It was a beautiful place.

I found Hugh's building and stepped into the small entrance. There was an elevator door facing me, and an intercom on the wall next to it. I pushed the button and Hugh quickly answered, "Hello!"

"It's Harry," I said.

"Oh, fabulous!" he said. "Come on up!"

The elevator door opened and Jack and I stepped in. Jack looked up at me for comfort, as the elevator started moving. When the elevator door opened up again, Hugh was there to greet us. We hugged and Hugh picked up my suitcase and welcomed me. "Well, this is it!" he said, enthusiastically.

Hugh was as friendly as could be. My cousin really was a handsome man, tall with good facial features, light skin and dark hair combed back Hollywood style. He looked like a movie star to me. My aunt in Texas was always telling me that I looked just like Hugh when he was my age. I have never seen the resemblance myself.

We walked forward onto the snow-white lush carpet in a large living room with very modern and expensive furnishings. A large glass coffee table supported by four white elephants caught my eye, as did a shiny, white, baby grand piano in the corner. The whole apartment was gorgeous, but not as gorgeous as the view through the glass wall of French doors I saw across the room. The lights of Los Angeles were laid out in front of me, framed by the last glimpse of the setting sun over the Pacific in the distance. It was one of those million-dollar views I had heard about but never thought I would ever see.

Hugh acted like he really enjoyed my arrival. I sat down at the dining table and he pulled out a bowl and filled it with water for Jack. Then he sat down for a chat. Hugh let me know that he had a roommate named, Ron, who was gone on business. Hugh and Ron did real estate investing together and evidently one or both of them had a lot of money. Hugh told me that Liza Minnelli lived in one of the apartments in the complex they owned. I would find out that, like everyone in Hollywood, Hugh loved to *name-drop*.

After talking with Hugh for a while, I admitted I was tired from the long drive. Hugh showed me around the apartment and then the terracotta-painted guest room where Jack and I would sleep. He pointed out the new vacuum system that had been recently installed when he and Ron remodeled. It was the kind where you just plug the vacuum hose into the wall to clean the room. It was all so impressive. I went to bed with a whole lot on my mind, but was tired enough to fall asleep quickly.

The next morning, Hugh drove me down into Los Angeles to see the house I was to live in while working under Hugh's supervision at my new job. Hugh drove a baby blue Ford Thunderbird convertible with white upholstery. Like his apartment, his car was gorgeous too. Everything about Hugh was gorgeous -- where he lived, what he drove, what he wore, how he looked -- everything.

It was a revelation to know that my family had people like Hugh in it. He had grown up in Hollywood. His mother had moved him and his older sister, Christine, there when they were young. Their mother, who we called Aunt Ruth, had dreams of she and her kids taking advantage of the entertainment business and all becoming stars. Christine had a talent for singing and Hugh's agent landed him a few supporting roles but nothing big. My family had always said that Hugh didn't make it in the movies because he was so handsome, he would outshine the stars -- so directors didn't like him. At least that's the family story. In reality, few actors actually do make it big.

Hugh proceeded to tell me about his brother-in-law Morten's business as we drove down the hill and what he had planned for me. Morten Lunde owned a company called, *Lunde Architectural Arts* on Sixth Street near downtown Los Angeles -- just a couple of blocks from MacArthur Park. At that time, his was the largest architectural arts company in the world and he even owned his own building.

Morten was once a champion skier in Norway and did some acting in Hollywood. He was a tall handsome man with a good build, blue eyes and blonde hair turning slightly gray. Hugh's sister, Christine, lived with her husband Morten in a large modern home at the top of the Hollywood Hills overlooking the Hollywood Bowl. Morten jogged every morning with his close friend, fitness expert and bodybuilder, Jack LaLanne.

Christine was quite a beauty, with a fair complexion and black hair. She reminded me so much of my mother when Mom was young. Christine also grew up in Hollywood. She did a lot of charity work in LA and was as sweet as she could be. I had not seen Christine in years, and like Hugh, I hardly knew her. I had never met Morten that I could remember.

Hugh turned down Sixth Street and stopped in front of the Lunde Building. It was a long, white two-story building with glass across the whole front. It was a Sunday, so everything was closed. I noticed people walking around the streets. Several men that looked like drunks sat on the curb across the street.

Hugh said, "This is our office," and pointed to the building. Jack was in the back seat and was ready to get out.

I said, "Really?"

Then he turned his head the opposite direction, pointed and said, "And that is the house you will live in temporarily."

I turned and saw a large two-story old house across the street from the office. The house was the second from the corner of Coronado. He turned the car and drove up to the old house. I guessed it had once been a nice residence before downtown finally engulfed it with new buildings. There were others like it down the street.

Hugh parked along the front curb. Then we both got out, and with Jack running ahead of us, we walked up the steps to the door and went inside. It wasn't locked. We entered an entryway with a large wooden staircase in front of us. A hallway down the side of the foyer led to the back with large, wooden sliding doors on either side.

"You have the left side of downstairs for now," Hugh said. "An artist named Chang is the only one living here right now and he lives in one of the bedrooms upstairs. Oh, and you share the kitchen with him, too."

Chang was one of the Asian artists that Morten Lunde brought in for training. Morten set up an office in Japan because the labor was so cheap. He would send them architectural plans rolled up in tubes and they would send back watercolor renderings of the houses also rolled in tubes. Each new artist had to fly to LA for training on how to paint landscapes without them looking like an Asian painting. Their trees and shrubs were the biggest problems. Morten bought the old house so these guys would have a place to stay near the office for several months while they trained. The house was completely furnished with what looked to me like stuff one would pick up off the curb, but it all looked comfortable.

We left the house and Hugh gave me a quick driving tour of Hollywood. Later, Jack and I followed Hugh back to the house that would be my home for the foreseeable future. I carried in my suitcase and placed it on the bed I would occupy. I stood there for a moment and looked around at the tall ceilings, old wallpaper, and hardwood floors. Most of the rooms were covered with oriental carpet. The tall windows had heavy drapes and sheer white curtains – very old-fashioned. But it was that musty smell of an old house that I remember most.

Jack ran all over the house checking it out and seemed to give her approval. Jack was a very flexible dog. She just wanted to go where I went and have a good time. Hugh walked around the house as well, then said he had to go and would see me across the street at the office in the morning.

"Be there at 8:00 a.m. and I'll get you started," Hugh said as he walked out.

I settled into the new house okay. Later that day, I met Chang in the hallway and introduced myself. He was very polite and even bowed as he shook my hand. I thought Chang was Japanese, but later found out he was Korean. He was a very quiet man, soft-spoken and ultra respectful. It was my first experience with an Asian person so he was a little strange to me. He had short, dark hair and usually wore a dark suit and tie when I would see him, which wasn't that often.

There was a convenience store down the block, so Jack and I walked on down so I could buy a sandwich and a drink. When we got home, I sat at the top of the wooden steps and finished them off. I had bought a little bag of dog food and put that out for Jack. She was more interested in what I had and would eat her food later.

Part of my first evening was spent just sitting there watching all kinds of people walk by. A drunk man stumbled and fell across the street. I got up thinking maybe I needed to help him but sat back down when I saw that he got back up and stumbled forward. There was a liquor store at the corner across the street from the house where these guys were buying their booze. They would come out with a bottle in a small, brown paper sack and make their way down the sidewalk alone. Since MacArthur Park was only two blocks away, I assumed that some of them were heading there. Most looked like they were homeless and probably slept in the park along with many others. The park was known for it.

    I had a lot on my mind at that point, wondering what my life was going to be like from then on. But I had Jack with me and that gave me comfort. We were in it together, for better or worse, and she trusted me to take care of her. I crawled off to bed when I felt like I could finally fall asleep. Jack jumped in bed with me and curled up at my feet. Except for my time in New York, Jack and I had been together ever since she had been given to me as a puppy in 1968, and she stayed with me throughout my adventures. Now she was my only company. I really wished she could talk.

# Chapter Eleven

Hugh was the manager of *Lunde Architectural Arts,* which took up the first floor. Another man managed the Architects on the second floor, so Hugh didn't have to deal with upstairs issues. I got dressed a little before eight the next morning, told Jack to stay in the house, and walked across the street to the office for my first day at work. I hadn't worked in a job for a while but it felt good to make a go at it. I was ready for whatever was to come and had a positive attitude as I opened the large, wooden front doors and walked into the reception area.

The Lunde receptionist greeted me with the typical, "May I help you?"

I told her who I was and she smiled and buzzed Hugh. He came out right away and greeted me. I followed him through the doors to the right of the reception area and into his little, glass office where I sat down across the desk in front of him while he shuffled some papers and looked at a calendar.

Guys would walk by with mugs of coffee, cracking jokes and acting friendly. Hugh would stop some of them and introduce me. I didn't see any women because there weren't any. But I could tell this was going to be a nice place to work because all these guys had smiles on their faces and acted really glad to meet me. Almost to the man, they said that if I needed any help, just let them know. Hugh walked me around the first floor and introduced me to all the artists and told me how the company worked. It was an amazing assembly line of about 30 artists, each with a specific role in creating architectural renderings for clients all over the world.

Every room in the building had a purpose, starting with placing the blueprint on a table that tilted and photographing it to put it in the perspective of a rendering. Morten invented that system and it saved a lot of time. That created a tracing that was then moved to another room where it was transferred to a large, white illustration board. The artists in that room drew the building in pencil, put in the basic colors of the building, and then painted in the background sky and the basic colors of grass, sidewalks, driveways and streets. All the colors used came from plastic squeeze bottles, all mixed perfectly by an elderly Japanese lady named Akiko who had them on trays and ready for the artists when they came in each day. Akiko had been doing that job for twenty years. Many of the artists had been there from the beginning. I was amazed by the level of planning and organization Morten had developed. I thought he was a genius.

The basic renderings would then move to another room where artists would put in the landscape. The last artists' room would complete the rendering of cars, people and any other detail that were needed. Then each piece of art would move to the photography studio where they would be photographed in black and white and in color. The studio had its own color processing equipment. Prints would be created per each order and sent to the mat room for mounting, packing, and shipping. Henry Ford, himself, would have been proud of Morten Lunde's assembly line! And it was all done before the introduction of computers.

Morten's office was upstairs from the Architectural Arts business. Nine architects, plus their support staff, worked upstairs. They specialized in office buildings and country clubs. While I was there, the company worked on a major renovation to the Wilshire Country Club -- one of Morten's distinguished clients and favorite hangouts. I quickly found out that Morten's name around the office was ML.

Hugh gave me a short briefing on my new job responsibilities and told me I would start my training in the mat room. He said everyone who comes to work for ML has to spend at least a month working in the mat room. ML's theory was that everyone needed to know the process from the ground up.

When we got to the mat room, I was introduced to Rich Dubose. Rich was about my age and had a big, white-teethed smile contrasting with his short, black hair and his large black mustache. Rich wasn't just working in the mat room for his month of *boot camp*. Because he wasn't an artist, he was simply hired to work in the mat room full time. Rich was tall, handsome and very friendly.

Hugh said he needed to get back to his office and left me with Rich, who was to show me how to do all the mat room duties. Rich had grown up in Hollywood and was, because he had gotten his girlfriend pregnant, newly-married. Rich went right to work training me to cut mats, laminate large photo prints to board, and pack them for shipping.

It was called the mat room because all the renderings and photos produced had to have a mat cut and framed around each piece for display. ML had a large, heavy table made just to the right height. There also was a custom-made, heavy, flat, metal bar made with a handle for moving it about. We used that to lay on the mat board and make a cut with a special angled tool that cut a perfect window within the mat board. Every detail had been worked out years ago and renderings were shipped out like clockwork. After a long day working with Rich, I said goodbye to the receptionist at the front desk and walked back across the street to the Coronado house. Jack was glad to see me and was eager for her dinner as I pored her dog food into her bowl. She knew I would always come back home to take care of her.

Besides working for his brother-in-law, Hugh had another way of making a living. He would partner with friends, such as Ron, to buy and restore properties, then either rent them or sell them for a profit. He rented one of his houses in Laurel Canyon to Cass Elliot of the *Mommas and the Papas*, but she had moved out. One day, Hugh and I drove up there to check on that house because mud would slide down from the hill above into the backyard and driveway after a heavy rain. Hugh pointed out Frank Zappa's complex as we drove up Laurel Canyon Boulevard towards the house. Hugh's rental didn't have much land with it, but took advantage of all it did have. The one-story house featured dark red brick with hand-hewn timbers, giving it a look like maybe Heidi's grandfather might live there. It had a high-pitched roof and high-vaulted ceilings.

We stepped inside and there wasn't a stick of furniture in the house. No telling what it looked like when Momma Cass lived there. The inside walls and ceilings were all natural woods and the paned windows let in a blast of light that cast great shadows across the dark-stained wooden floors. The fireplace in the living room was beautifully done with river stones. I could definitely see why Cass liked it. I looked around and thought about the good times she and her friends must have had there. Hugh said she had a lot of dogs that slept with her in her bed.

Hugh checked out the hill above the house and said he would have to get a crew to remove some of the mud next week. He wanted to get it rented again as soon as possible. We drove back down into Hollywood and I thought about how hip Laurel Canyon was, with narrow winding roads going up to little flats and houses, all tucked together among the heavy landscape and rocky outcrops. Many of the little houses just hung out over the hillside.

As we were getting back into Hugh's car, he stopped and pointed up the hill behind us where a row of houses filled the hillside on the street above Hugh's.

"*Canned Heat* lives in that one," Hugh said.

"Really?" I said, after bending my head down to see the one he was pointing to. I loved their music and thought that was cool.

Hugh and I became closer in the months following as we got to know one another better and occasionally spent time together after work or on weekends. Hugh didn't get high and I was fine with that. I started to get into a routine at work and enjoyed the break from my previous life in San Antonio. *So far so good -- was my optimistic thought -- This California thing might just work for me after all.*

---

One day at work, Rich invited me to join him and his friends, Billy and Jerry, on a camping trip to Big Sur. I didn't even know what Big Sur was. He didn't get along with his wife as well as he did with her younger brother, Billy. Jerry, whom I later found out was called Motorcycle Jerry, was our age and owned a motorcycle shop in LA. They both had light complexions with slightly long, light-brown hair. All three of them liked to wear hip, mountain-man clothes –– flannel shirts, blue jeans, and expensive leather hiking boots. Rich also liked to wear white long-johns with blue-colored farmer overalls. I just wore whatever I had, usually jeans and a T-shirt, along with my leather boots.

    They all piled into my car early on a Saturday morning and off we went up the California coastline on Highway One. Jack went too, riding up on the collapsed convertible top behind the seats. Jack enjoyed the wind on her face and always wanted the best view. She went everywhere with me except work

    Highway One from LA to Big Sur was the most beautiful road I had ever been on. We were almost at Big Sur when Rich said, "This is it!" and told me to pull over to this little dirt area to the right of the road just before a long concrete bridge. We got out of the car and walked onto the bridge. It was about two hundred yards long and spanned a deep canyon and creek that came out of the mountains with cliffs going all the way to the surf. A waterfall came out of the cliff on the other side of the bridge from us and fell probably 100 feet, right on the beach at the edge of the water. I had never seen anything quite like it before.

    We gathered our camping gear, locked up the car, and started up a grassy footpath that traveled along the side of the cliff and up into the canyon. The small river flowed far down to our left and the tree-covered hill went up to our right. Rich said the hike was about a mile or so to get to the place we were to camp. After about two hundred yards, we descended down the dirt path to the creek. Our legs brushed against the bright green ferns that carpeted the ground on both sides of the path. The path crossed the creek back and forth through the most beautiful green-moss forest imaginable.

    Large tree trunks that had fallen across the creek were used as bridges, worn smooth across the tops from all the hikers who had taken this path before us. The farther we went the more beautiful and lush it got. Huge trees and giant ferns surrounded us. The creek gave a constant sound of running water. It was like a small river as its cold water flowed strong through the forest -- occasionally pouring over rocks in small waterfalls. The hill went up on both sides.

    We finally reached our camping spot. No one had told me what to expect. Rich liked to surprise me and somehow felt it was his role to introduce me to the things his home state of California had to offer -- the things he loved. As we made the last creek crossing over a log, we heard several voices say hello.

    Getting closer we could see that there were about forty or fifty people gathered around the campsite. These were gentle people, all with long hair and all dressed like hippies. I thought that was cool. Talking with them, we discovered that some of them had earned college degrees but had chosen a different path than many graduates. Tents and blankets dotted the hill of grass and ferns that rose from the creek's edge and up the mountain on either side of us. Large trees provided speckled shade. Except for a few boulders jutting out from the hillsides and along the water, everything around us was bright green. A large black cast-iron pot sat on a fire in the middle of the clearing surrounded by a mix of people who were preparing food.

    These were not your typical Yellowstone Park campers. Many of these people were living up in those hills to avoid the draft. They objected to the U.S. involvement in Vietnam and were hoping it would all just blow over so they could go home. A few of them were older hippies who enjoyed living there regardless of the draft. Anyone and everyone seemed to be welcome there. It was a very friendly crowd and joints were lit regularly and passed around to those sitting close.

    Insects don't like redwood forests, so we could just lie down most anywhere on the ground without worrying about being bitten. There were a few other dogs there and I loved that Jack had the chance to play with them.

All four of us slept in our cheap sleeping bags out in the open night air without tents. We were taking the chance that it wouldn't rain, but Rich did bring pieces of clear plastic to put over us. I felt a little unprepared when I first got there, but as it turned out I didn't have to worry.

Darkness and cooler temperatures came quickly when the sun dropped behind the hill. The campfire was already blazing and people were bringing food down from their makeshift tents. All the food was put into the cast iron pot to create a stew. Smooth logs surrounded the fire where we all sat to enjoy its warmth and the dinner to come. Lanterns began to glow along the hillside and threw an orange cast of light on everything along the stream and hills. There was a long piece of black sky that ran along above the river and we could see stars. Looking up, I must have seen a million stars at one time. We were out in the middle of nowhere so there was no light from the city to hamper our ability to stargaze. It was so beautiful.

The stew consisted of whatever people had brought at that time. Many people were only there for the weekend so, upon leaving for home, they left any surplus food for the people to use who were living up there. The conversation around the campfire was brisk and interesting, from the war to politics and music. The joints people passed around stimulated the conversation and there was a lot of smiles and laughter. Soon we had music to go along with the fabulous campfire.

Guitars came out of nowhere and people started jamming -- not any songs I knew -- just freestyle. Someone would start a rhythm beat and another would play a few simple chords, then off we would go on a set that could last for an hour.

People like us who didn't have an instrument kept the beat with sticks on logs or metal spoons on pots. The music went on into the night -- only breaking for a bowl of stew served in various vessels such as metal coffee cups. It was an amazing place and an amazing time to be alive. Rich did me right inviting me to join him and his friends.

We made the trip several times, but as time went on, the old man who owned the property tried his best to stop people from trespassing. Once in a while, he would come down the creek path with a shotgun and chase everyone off. Some people just went deeper into the mountains, for the trail went for miles up into the wild. Campers told us that there were many large waterfalls up higher. The river went on for miles but we were perfectly satisfied to stay where we were. During my employment at Lunde, I went to Big Sur at least three times with Rich and his friends, returning each time to the city renewed and ready to get back to work.

After a few months in the mat room, I was promoted to help an artist named Kenneth Ko in a portion of the art department that handled extra projects –– like pen and ink renderings of houses. That was something I could do. My architecture schooling helped a lot.

Kenneth's favorite singer was Don Ho, who had become wildly popular in Hawaii. My new coworker was proud to say that he had all the Hawaiian signer's albums and knew all his songs. I liked Kenneth a lot and he seemed to like me.

Finally a job I could feel good about. Maybe I was embarking on an actual career working at the studio. Guys were being hired fresh out of art school to work at Lunde. I knew that someday I would have to get my degree in order to be taken seriously at a place like this. But I had dropped out of architecture, so I wasn't sure what I would eventually do. If becoming an architect wasn't in the cards for me, then maybe being an artist would work. It was something to consider.

---

One day Hugh came up to my desk and asked if I wanted to go with him to a Hollywood party. He had a lot of friends around town since he had grown up in Hollywood. Like Hugh, many of them were in the entertainment business and those people loved to party.

So Hugh picked me up in his T-bird and we drove up into the Hollywood Hills to the party. We pulled up to an incredible house and Hugh said, "We're here!" He knew I would be blown away. The house was literally designed to look like a castle on a hill. We found a parking place down the street. There were lots of cars parked already and people walking up the street to the house. We passed through an ornate metal gate at the base of a winding rock set of steps that led to the entrance of the castle.

Hugh didn't knock. We just followed people on through the huge front doors and into a crowded scene of shoulder-to-shoulder people. Everyone had a drink in hand. Rock music was blaring throughout the house and people were dancing in every room that I could see. If they weren't dancing, they were hugging and kissing on the cheek. Many people wore costumes and I wondered why because it wasn't Halloween! No, it was just Hollywood!

We started walking through the crowd and people would come up to Hugh to say hello and give the expected kiss. Hugh introduced me to everyone as his cousin from Texas. I remember one lady, very made up and wearing a mink cape, seriously flirting with me after we were introduced. She was right in my face with her big red lips and fake lashes. Hugh pulled me away and told her I was too young for her. They both had a big laugh. She turned, looked me up and down, smiled and walked off with her cocktail held high. I felt like I was ten and didn't belong there at all. It happened again with another rich-looking drunk woman. We didn't stay too long but I did get a good glimpse of what a real Hollywood party was like. I was getting hit-on by a slew of Mrs. Robinsons. Wow!

---

Since I had studied woodworking in my junior high school shop class, I had a pretty good handle on making things out of wood, but maybe not the best judgment to go along with that skill at age twenty-one. So, I will now admit to a really stupid thing I did while working at Lunde that year. What was I thinking? I guess I wasn't.

ML had a woodworking shop on the next block down from his company. It just had a front door and no windows. It was a long and narrow space with tall ceilings. The workspace was just a few doors down from the corner liquor store. Hugh told me that I could use the shop if I liked. The company only uses it every once in a while. I was bored and needed a project. He said he didn't think ML would mind and gave me an extra key to the shop door.

I went down that night with the key and looked around. The place was full of sawdust with plenty of power tools, and complete with a heavy-duty table saw and drill press. Hand tools were hanging everywhere. Racks along the back of the shop held lots of scrap wood. Sheets of plywood leaned all along the right wall. I thought that it would be cool to build some large speaker cabinets for my apartment. So not having a large budget I bought two twelve-inch speakers from the Radio Shack down the street and started plans for my custom speaker cabinets.

The speakers would be four feet tall, four feet wide and about eighteen inches thick but the sides needed to be at an angle so that the speakers would fit into the corner of a room. One big twelve-inch speaker with a built-in tweeter would go right in the center of the cabinet and I would use acoustical padding on the inside to make the sound better. I decided to use plywood instead of solid wood to keep the weight low.

I made my frames out of two-by-two's over the course of a few nights then went about making the plywood enclosures. I made the top, bottom, and front panels that held the speakers out of thick plywood scraps and then started looking around the shop for thinner plywood for the back and sides. There were so many pieces of plywood everywhere I didn't think ML would miss any of it. I wasn't going to use that much.

I was lucky enough to find two four-by-eight sheets of good, quarter-inch plywood that looked like it would be nice when stained and finished. It took two weeks to complete it all working a little each night. When I finished, the speakers looked and worked great. That was the good news.

The bad news was that I had them sitting in the shop while the final coat of stain dried when ML came by the shop to look for something and saw them. He never said a word to me but did a good amount of complaining to Hugh for letting me use the shop and his wood. The plywood I used was the spare paneling that he had saved when he built the lobby of an office building he owned. I had no idea.

Hugh called me into his office the next morning when I got to work and said I had to give up the keys to the shop. I apologized and he said ML would get over it. I should have gone up and apologized to him personally. Missed opportunity to do the right thing –– again.

---

One day, Hugh told me that I could start using the company VW Bus. No one else was driving the bus and it was parked in the lot next to my house. The bus wasn't decorated with the obligatory painted peace signs and paisley icons, but it still seemed like a hippie bus to me. I loved driving it up and down the Sunset Strip. It was supposed to be used to run company errands but I would also drive it on the weekends just for fun.

Leave it to the Germans to do things differently than we do in America. Back then, car manufacturers in America gave us big ole warning lights on our dash to tell us that something serious was wrong with our car and that we better take care of it right away. That's my excuse.

I had been seeing this tiny, little-blue light, only about one-eighth of an inch in diameter, light up on the dash above the steering column of the bus. First, it would light up intermittently, hardly catching my eye at all. Then it just stayed on and I just kept going about my business, not really thinking much about what it could be. *How important can such a little tiny light be anyway?*

So I was driving the bus down the Hollywood Freeway, going the speed limit, running an errand and minding my own business, when I heard a noise, then a clunk and then a lot of noise. The bus slowed down and vibrated as I saw, in the tiny rear view mirror, all kinds of auto parts bouncing on the road behind me. Some of them were big. Oh shit!

Yes, that tiny little blue light was the warning light for the oil pressure. The bus was out of oil, something that never occurred to me to check. It wasn't my personal vehicle. It was the company bus. Did I have the responsibility to maintain it? Well, no one else was driving it so I guess I did. I had blown the engine. I managed to pull over and then walk to a nearby store to call Hugh. He had a tow truck come and haul the bus away. It was the last time I saw the bus or drove it. The only time I drove a company car again was when ML asked his secretary to have me to drive his big, black, Lincoln Mark III to get it washed for him. I never heard another word about the bus, nor did I apologize for my stupidity like I should have. Hugh just kept protecting me and I will just chalk that up to a family that loved me. He was always upbeat, generous, and fun to be with.

One day, Rich was called up to ML's office. Only this time ML gave him a job to do for him. Rich was to paint ML's two large office doors. ML wanted them to be painted a light, warm gray to match his office décor. He had the paint custom mixed and it had to be just the right color. When Rich went into his office, ML proceeded to tell him exactly how he wanted it done.

ML explained to Rich, "You will have to put the paint on thick and then use long smooth strokes from top to bottom so I won't be able to see any brush marks when it dries."

Rich came down and told me of his assignment. I was so glad it was him and not me who had been chosen for this important job. I wondered if Hugh was protecting me again. As my friend started painting the doors, ML would walk by and say, "I can see the brushstrokes. Strip it and start over!" Rich spent a week painting those doors over and over until ML was finally satisfied with the work. Rich had painted those damn doors six times before he got it right. Morten Lunde was like that about everything. Hugh was my savior at Lunde. Being ML's brother-in-law, Hugh knew his ways very well. Others were not so lucky. ML could make a grown man cry. You did best by just doing your job and staying clear of him.

---

I had a lot of time to myself while living in the Coronado Street house. While sitting in my living room listening to music, I would think about some of the things that happened before moving to California. There was a girl who I met after graduation from high school and before my drug-dealing days. I just couldn't get her off my mind. Maybe it was loneliness. It helped for me to look back on a happier time when I fell in love.

San Antonio was host to a world's fair in 1968. It wasn't a whole world's fair but only a partial world's fair. Most people don't recall ever hearing about the fair. It was called Hemisfair '68 and was limited to the America's -- North America, Central America and South America. City leaders at the time worked together to purchase and clear a large portion of downtown San Antonio in order to create the fairgrounds. The centerpiece of the fair was the Tower of the America's, complete with observation decks and a revolving restaurant and bar on top. The fair was touted as a way to revitalize a run-down portion of downtown San Antonio and to bring attention to one of America's most beautiful cities -- and it did just that.

The fair only lasted six months but lots of San Antonio business people got together to support the fair. Many thought it was a way to make some money from visitors and put together a business. Others just liked the idea of owning a piece of the fair and invested in small businesses, not really caring about profits, but just to be a part of it and have some fun with the other investors.

One such business was called *The Yellow Rose of Texas*. It had eight booths dotted around the fairgrounds. There were about 25 of us working for the little company and most were girls. The boys had to wear white shirts, white pants and black and white saddle oxfords. The girls wore multicolored, striped, disposable paper dresses, which were to be the next trend in 60's fashion and convenience. They weren't. Summers in San Antonio were hot. After a few days of wearing them, the girls could just throw them away and grab a new one from their booth.

    On the first day of the job, I was assigned to Booth Number One and was told to help decorate the inside. It was a small rectangular building about fifteen by thirty feet with glass on two sides and white pegboard walls on the other two. Racks displayed the paper flowers on a stick and shelving fixtures in the center of the room held stacks of paper dresses and other colorful items made from paper. My job was to take boxes of big paper roses and stick the roses into the holes on the pegboard walls, making a solid wall of yellow and red color. My partner on this first day was a girl who had also been assigned to work in Booth Number One, a beauty named Brenda Miller.

    Unlike the other girls who worked the smaller booths around the fair, Brenda was given a bright solid-yellow paper dress. That dress, plus her short black hair, great figure, and bright white smile made her something special. It was love at first sight.

    She and I hit it off right away as she handed me the paper flowers and I placed them on the walls. It was like some kind of chemical reaction. Beauty and personality -- Wow! I could tell she liked me as much as I liked her, so I invited Brenda to come over to the Lewis Street house on a Sunday when neither of us was working.

    Brenda still lived at her parents' north side home and was a bit taken back when she entered our apartment. I could see her looking around the room and wondering if she had made a mistake in coming over. I introduced her to my roommates and we all knew right away that she was very straight. Brenda had not even considered the idea of smoking dope or taking any drugs. I wasn't sure whether I wanted to get involved with a girl that didn't do what I liked to do. I was well on my way to a life of hippie-ness and she was stuck in the fifties. Yet I was extremely attracted to her.

I asked her to take a walk around the college campus and just talk -- away from my apartment and roommates. For some reason, I wanted to get inside her head and see what made her tick. We spent several hours walking, sitting, and talking that afternoon. I did most of the talking. Brenda was a great listener and maybe a little naive. I remember sitting on a short brick wall telling her about the archway of the building in front of us and how it was built. I was full of architectural information since I was taking those classes then. I don't think she cared about that, but I had her attention regardless.

Brenda's beautiful blue eyes stared at me the whole time. I didn't know what else to do but keep talking. She was also taking classes at the college that surrounded our house on Lewis Street and would stop by between classes to see if I was home. I knew she must have been interested in me to do that. I liked that she wasn't critical of how I lived and didn't seem to want to change me. That was a good thing because I would have run from the first sign of it.

I was petting Jack while I sat there in my Coronado Street living room thinking about Brenda. Jack made me feel less alone. She had jumped up on the sofa next to me and put her head on my lap. I thought about when I was given Jack as a puppy. Brenda went with me when I picked her up.

Louie was one of the guys who worked with Brenda and me at *The Yellow Rose of Texas.* He was the nicest person -- a Mormon who had moved to San Antonio from Utah. Louie was a handsome guy with short dark hair and a friendly smile. He had a new litter of puppies and was trying to give them away. Brenda went with me to take a look. She thought Lewis Street could use a dog. She was right. They were all blond and were to become medium-size dogs with pointed noses and long hair. We picked one out and I drove us back to the house in my Corvair Monza.

We named her Jack after the Rolling Stones song, *Jumping Jack Flash*. Lewis Street now had its mascot and Jack would stay by my side for the next seventeen years. She became a legend among my friends and everyone loved her.

The best story about Jack was when I was sleeping in one morning while students were walking by our Lewis Street house on their way to classes at SAC. We weren't really concerned about security in those days so we would just leave our front door open, except for the screen door, which we usually kept latched. We must have left our lid of pot out on the coffee table in the living room because Jack grabbed it and ran out the front door with it while we were asleep.

I'm not sure how long Jack had the pot out there but when I woke up I saw some of it on the floor. My eyes followed the trail of pot to the screen door. I jumped out of bed, quickly pulled on my jeans and ran to the door. What I saw wasn't funny, although we laughed about it for years after that. The pot was scattered all along the front sidewalk and students who were walking by were pointing and laughing. Running back into the house, I grabbed the broom and dustpan and went out to sweep it up. It seemed almost a sure thing that we were going to get busted. We just knew that this humorous event would be shared around the school that week. We got rid of everything in the house for about two weeks but nothing happened, so we just went back to our same old daily routines.

Brenda and I continued our romance throughout the run of the fair but we didn't exactly date. She and I enjoyed taking walks around the SAC campus. Sundays were best because the college was closed and we had the whole campus to ourselves. Brenda and I laughed and flirted all the time at work and she dropped by Lewis Street on a regular basis. We would also join a few of our fellow workers after work behind the Falstaff Pavilion on the Hemisfair grounds to have a few beers and enjoy listening to music on the back patio. I never really had enough money to take her anywhere, plus I wouldn't have been able to buy a drink since I was only twenty and still under the age limit for drinking, although the Falstaff people never asked me for an ID.

I didn't really think there was a chance with Brenda, but I couldn't seem to get that beauty off my mind. All I knew was that I was doing a lot of partying. My circle of friends was widening as friends-of-friends came to hang out at Lewis Street, listen to music, smoke dope, and drop acid. It was my first hippie pad and lots of fun.

Hemisfair was the best job I had ever had, but it had to come to an end because it was designed to be only six months long. No more days of driving the little electric cart around the grounds delivering paper flowers to the booths and flirting with the girls. On the last day of the fair, when the closing ceremonies ended, I had to leave my cart at the main booth and walk out of the fair for the last time –- alone. There were literally tears in my eyes. I was out of a job, a job I would sorely miss.

When the fair ended, we all went our separate ways. I didn't see any of them again, with the exception of Brenda. But I was heading one way and she was heading another. Neither of us could imagine being part of the other's lifestyle. Brenda transferred to North Texas State University in Denton to major in Music. NTSU was in the Dallas metro area about 5,300 miles from San Antonio. NTSU's *Lab Band* was known for its excellent music. Brenda went there to study classical piano so we basically lost touch.

I came home from my new job at Lunde one day and found a letter from Brenda. A mutual friend of ours had told her where to write me. Most of my letters came from my parents. In those days talking on the phone long distance was an expensive luxury. Letters were slow, but welcome when they arrived. My parents would send me self-addressed postcards in order to better their chances of getting a letter back from me.

It had been a year since I last saw or heard from Brenda. She was now living in Dallas with a roommate. She had also changed since I knew her at Hemisfair. She too had gotten the hippie bug, wearing bell-bottom blue jeans and attending rock concerts. Her letter told how she understood me better now and wanted to know if I might come to Dallas and go to a concert with her. She said that her group was friends with the band *Grand Funk Railroad*. I wrote her back a nice letter saying how my life was now in LA and I had no plans to go to Dallas, but I was interested in seeing her again. I just didn't know when or how.

    Meanwhile, I was getting a bit lonely working all week at Lunde and hanging out with Rich and his friends on the weekends. Rich was married but I hardly ever saw his wife because she worked most of the time. His friends were not the type to attract girls either so they seemed satisfied just to hang out with each other. Billy was still in high school and Motorcycle Jerry spent most of his time at his shop covered in grease. Although I had fun with them, it just wasn't doing it for me. Shit, I hadn't planned on abandoning girls all together.

## Chapter Twelve

While looking through my little black book of names and addresses one afternoon, I came across phone numbers from some of the friends I made while visiting New York City with Bambi and thought they would be fun to talk to. Anyone would have been nice to talk to at that point. I saw the phone number for Abby, so I gave her a call. Her mother answered the phone and told me Abby now lived in Hollywood with friends and gave me her number. I dialed her number and sure thing -- Abby and Wendy lived just up the hill from Sunset on Gower. She was only ten minutes away.

Abby was surprised to get the phone call, but happy to hear from me. When she found out I also lived in Hollywood, she invited me over. I hopped in my car and drove a few miles to her apartment. It was some kind of homecoming. She and Wendy had several other friends over and we all talked late into the night. Plans were made to get together again and we did several times. I would not have picked Abby out of a crowd to say I had to have this girl. But she and I just hit it off so well -- like old friends. One thing led to another and we made love one day in her apartment when the others were gone. After being lonely for months, I was ready for that *loving feeling*.

Abby was pretty much the same as I remembered her in New York, short and cute with long, straight black hair that hung down over her shoulders, the way most of her friends wore theirs. She had a small waist and large breasts and always wore dark colored, loose T-shirts with bell-bottom jeans. None of the hippie girls back then wore bras and Abby was no exception. It wasn't really a big deal.

I remembered Wendy from my time in New York also. Wendy was an attractive lesbian and very smart. Her hair was long, blonde and straight. Of course, they all had very heavy New York accents. They really enjoyed using their accents and laughed about it all the time. I had a Texas accent, and while I was in New York, we enjoyed making fun of each other. I thought their accent was cool and wasn't aware until then that I even had an accent.

Abby started coming over to my Coronado Street house a lot and we made the trip together with the boys to Big Sur again. We were starting to do everything together. Some evenings, she and I just enjoyed sitting on the curb in front of my house and talking with some of the homeless men. To our surprise, some of these men were educated and had held good jobs before alcoholism ruined their lives. We sat and heard so many stories, just one after another. One morning while walking across the street to work, I saw a man stumbling around the corner of the building looking like he was about to fall. I stopped and went around the corner to find that he had fallen and cracked open his head on the sidewalk. I went in and had the receptionist call for help. Later that day she told me that he had died –– another victim of alcoholism.

Some of the men who passed us on the street were talking to themselves. Some had the *DT's* as they call it, thinking ants are crawling on their bodies or worse. It was really sad. We didn't know any alcoholics that were our age. Our crowd seemed pretty normal … just smoking dope, drinking a couple of beers, and taking some acid once in a while. We really weren't worried about doing any damage to ourselves. The alcoholics knew they were doing damage, but their brains wouldn't allow them to stop on their own. The self-destruction was evident.

We had known people who had become hooked on heroin, speed, or coke, but we had not thought that much about alcoholics and the destruction drinking could do. These guys would buy a cheep bottle of booze from the liquor store on the corner and carry it out in a brown paper bag, stopping to unscrew the top and take a swig as soon as they stepped out the doorway. There were plenty of them to talk to and they welcomed the conversation. I learned a lot from them: *Nice to meet you –– don't want to be you.*

―――――――

Before we were reunited, Abby and Wendy had made friends with an older black man named Cap. He lived in an apartment about a mile down Hollywood Boulevard from Abby and Wendy's apartment. He was a great cook and had been inviting them to dinner at his place once a week. He seemed lonely and enjoyed their visits. Abby asked Cap if they could invite me along and he said that would be great. He wanted to meet their friend from Texas they had talked about.

Cap lived alone in the upstairs of an older four-story apartment building. We met Wendy there and he greeted Abby and I at the door with a big smile. He was a friendly guy -- super smart and a gracious host. The meal was vegetarian, but tasted great. He poured us some decent red wine and the four of us had a great conversation over dinner. As we were leaving, Cap asked if we wanted to join him on the upcoming chanting session.

Abby and Wendy said, "Of course!" at the same time.

I chimed in after them with the same response, although I had no idea what they were talking about. Driving home, the girls said that this was something I didn't want to miss. I asked when we were going and they said it was always on the last Friday of the month and it was coming up the next week.

On that day, we met Cap at his apartment and all squeezed into his little yellow VW Bug and off we went. He had the music playing something that sounded like reggae, which at that time I didn't even know existed. He drove us all the way to Venice. We pulled up to a small house on stilts right on the beach. There were a lot of cars on the street so we had a hard time finding a parking place. We climbed the wooden stairs, knocked on the door and entered when a nice looking lady opened it. The living area was full of people sitting on the floor and talking. There was hardly any furniture but there were plenty of pillows and small rugs. The chanting session was about to begin and we got there just in time.

The group leader greeted us with hugs and asked us to be seated. I could tell Abby and Wendy had been there before and Cap was evidently a regular. Looking around at the people I knew something was different but I didn't know exactly what. There was an altar or shrine on the wall in front of the group. It was a large wooden three-panel box with hinges that was open to expose a variety of interesting stuff on the inside. Incense and candles were burning on either side. Different fruits and unidentifiable things were sitting within the box. The box was sitting on a table covered with one of those India tapestries we all had purchased from Pier One Imports at one time or another. More tapestries covered the windows.

The leader asked if everyone had a chant book and passed out this little blue booklet to those of us who indicated that we did not. The book's cover had some little type on it that said, *Nichoen Shosho – Book of Chants.* The leader began explaining that the group would be chanting from the book and, that if we chanted often enough, our wishes and desires would come true. I was still a bit puzzled about what was going on. He explained that Nichoen Shosho was an ancient Chinese belief centering on chanting and that it was not a religion. So we were not really chanting to a God or deity. We were just chanting into the universe for good things to happen to us.

Several people came up to the front of the room, one at a time, and gave testimonials about how chanting had changed their lives. Most of them had been chanting for money and sure enough, some had money mysteriously come their way. A distant aunt died and left one of them a chunk of money. Another hit the jackpot playing a slot machine at a gas station while driving through Nevada, and so on and so on. About six people went through this explanation for the group. Everyone clapped as each sat down. The leader returned to the front and thanked the people for their stories.

The last thing I remember the leader saying before the chanting started was that people who chanted didn't need any drugs and how, if you look at someone who chants a great deal, you will see a visible aura about them -- a glow that surrounded an obviously happy person who loves life and is benefiting from the things they chant for. I realized that Cap had that glow. Wendy and Abby mentioned that about Cap, too.

Cap appeared to really be enjoying life, didn't take any drugs, and was always happy when we were with him. As the leader was speaking, I thumbed through the little blue chanting book and realized that it was in a language I had never seen before. There were words that represented sounds and no one in the room knew what any of the words meant. The book started with the phrase, *Nam neo ringea kio*. This was the phrase we started to chant when the people were all through speaking.

The chanting started rather quietly with the volume going up and down like a slow moving roller coaster. Everyone stared at the altar as they sat with their legs crossed on small rugs on the wood floor. It sounded to me like the hum of a million bumblebees. That one chant lasted for about an hour, and when we were through, we said our good-byes and drove back to Hollywood. I don't remember what I was chanting for but it didn't matter because that was the last time I went with them. I thought this was great for all those people who believed in it, but with my Christian upbringing, I just couldn't buy into it.

I thought although it may have worked for them, somehow I didn't think it would work for me. It was one of those experiences in LA that makes you realize how different people are -- different lifestyles, different beliefs, different religions. There seemed to be something for everyone that lived there. I didn't know if Abby or Wendy ever joined Cap again for chanting, but I told Cap I thought the whole deal was groovy and thanked him for including me.

---

Since the traffic in LA was horrible, I decided to sell my car and buy a motorcycle. So I sold my Buick and bought a bike from Motorcycle Jerry. I had never driven a motorcycle before. Jerry drove me up to a neighborhood in LA that had wide streets and no traffic and taught me how to drive it. Michelle, my biker momma girlfriend from Texas, would have been proud.

I drove it over to the California Department of Motor Vehicles and got my special California motorcycle license. I had to drive it around a course of orange cones in their big parking lot and pass a written exam to get the license. I didn't have a helmet since they were not required. My motorcycle was a 350 Honda that Jerry had souped-up for himself. It had Triumph racing carbs, scavenger exhaust pipes, high-race cam, etc., and was in perfect condition. I would drive it over to Billy's apartment up in the hills where we would smoke dope and listen to *Jethro Tull*, Billy's favorite group at the time. I remembered how hard it was to go up the steep hill to Billy's dead-end street and try to turn the bike around to go back down without falling over.

I drove it for a couple of months, but had to take it in to Jerry's shop several times for a tune up. Finally Jerry got angry and said I wasn't driving his bike fast enough to keep it in tune as it required a high RPM to satisfy all those upgrades he put on.

Well, I didn't like to go over the speed limit and didn't like to take chances with it. I drove it fairly slow up and down the Hollywood Hills most of the time, and once in a while on the freeways. So, Jerry just kept taking the fancy stuff off of it until it was pretty much stock again. But it ran well and was dependable after that.

Those guys loved to hike and get out of the city, so we continued to go to places like Big Sur and up into the mountains above LA. Sometimes I would follow them on my bike with Abby on the back holding Jack.

Being an artist, I painted the gas tank of my motorcycle with an American flag design. I thought it looked way cool. Lots of people were doing things with the flag image. I saw it as a way to be patriotic in spite of the fact that I didn't agree with our participation in the Vietnam War. I was pro-America, not pro-Richard M. Nixon.

One day Abby got on the back of my motorcycle and we headed off to Santa Monica to see a movie we had heard was good. I parked my bike near the front door of the theatre and went in. The movie was *Easy Rider,* considered an important classic that launched the careers of several superstars. Dennis Hopper and Peter Fonda were the hippie bikers and Jack Nicholson was the straight guy looking for a road trip.

The ending was really dramatic because after all the fun they had had in New Orleans, a redneck in an old pickup pulled a shotgun from under his seat and blasted them off the road. Like the rest of the crowd, Abby and I exited the theatre in shock, but maybe even more so because as we approached my bike, we realized that my painted gas tank looked just like the one we had just seen Peter Fonda die on. This fact wasn't lost on the other people coming out of the theatre either. They started to gather around my bike as we got on it and drove off. I never looked at my motorcycle quite the same way again.

---

Abby and Wendy lived upstairs in a garage apartment. I would ride my bike up the hill, turn left, and drive down the driveway to the back, then park next to the wooden staircase. Their door was at the top of the stairs to the right. Another pair of girls shared the apartment to the left. One of them was named Emily. She was tall and extremely cute with short, curly brown hair. If I hadn't hooked up with Abby before meeting Emily, I would have definitely fallen for her. But unlike what people probably thought of us hippies, we didn't just swap around so easily.

Emily's roommate, Janet, was a skinny blonde and not attractive at all. She had some sort of sickness that was never explained. Janet looked like a walking skeleton with dark sunken eyes and cheeks. I felt sorry for her. Emily and Janet were from Columbus, Ohio, and were in Hollywood to find their fortunes and have some fun, although I never saw Janet having any. Emily could hardly do anything that Janet approved of. As far as I could tell all Janet did was complain. She never felt okay -- ever.

Emily brought home a guy she had met walking on the street. He needed a temporary place to stay while he looked for a job. Janet was not happy when Emily offered him their couch for the night. Emily liked that he sang and played the guitar and thought he was pretty cute. But, it had been three weeks since she told him he could stay the night, and he was still there. He would buy a newspaper every day and search the *classifieds* to see if there was a job opening he could qualify for. Emily was too nice to ask him to leave. Janet felt like it was Emily's duty to tell him since Emily was the one who agreed to let him stay. Emily came next door to Abby and Wendy's apartment to talk about her problem while I was there. She was visibly upset.

Emily said his name was *Sunny*, not *Sonny*, as he liked to correct people. He was tall with a good build and a light complexion -- a handsome guy with long, curly blond hair. Sunny usually wore a solid-color tank top with tight blue jean bell bottoms with about an inch of a woven pattern of color sewn along the bottom. Sunny wore a thick, brown leather belt with a large brass buckle. Attached to his belt was a leather pouch that held a pack of cigarettes, along with his driver's license and money. The pouch had long leather fringe along the bottom that came down to his knees.

Sunny played a beautiful Martin acoustic guitar and sang his original songs to anyone who would listen, no matter where he was. We spent a lot of nights sitting around either Abby's or Emily's apartments listening to Sunny play his guitar and sing. He considered himself a great songwriter, musician, and singer just waiting to be discovered. He was a perpetual optimist always thinking things could be and would be better.

His songs were good but his voice stunk because he was never in tune. He acted like he sang well and we never mentioned it to him. Everyone knew he was off-key, but it didn't matter too much to us. Any live music was better than no live music. His guitar was always in tune and he was an accomplished musician. We couldn't join in with him because we didn't know the words to anything he sang. They were all original songs. It was his deal and his deal alone. He was the entertainment and we were the audience.

Sunny would get upset if anyone talked while he played. He would ask everyone in the room if they wanted to hear a song, as if someone would have said no. If people started talking while he was performing he would stop playing until they stopped talking, then start again. He was always saying that he had a new song he wanted to try out on us.

Emily begged us to help her get rid of Sunny. She originally thought she and Sunny would hook up but the chemistry just wasn't there. Janet was getting more and more upset by the day and was ready to move back to Ohio. Emily was desperate. She didn't want to lose her close friend and she didn't want to move home either. I never quite figured out Emily and Janet's relationship. It was as if Janet had some kind of power over Emily. Or maybe Emily had been handed caregiver duties without wanting them.

Soon I had saved enough money working at Lunde to find a place of my own. Cousin Hugh helped me find a small flat at 2067 Ivar, not too far up in the Hollywood Hills. That was the first time I had heard an apartment being called a *flat*. It wasn't a term we used back in Texas. Hugh talked to the landlady and vouched for me. Hugh was a smooth talker and could do just about anything that required his good looks and social graces.

The flat was on the side of a hill looking across at the famous Hollywood Sign. It had a balcony patio made of stone with a faded red and white striped canvas awning. The patio had comfortable furniture with matching striped cushions and a great view.

The Hollywood Freeway cut through the houses and trees below at about where the hills started flattening out. From there, it was rolling hills and tall palms all the way to the Pacific beaches. I walked about a hundred steps from the street down the side of the apartment building on narrow concrete stairs to get to the flat. The tiny one-room apartment had a sleeper sofa and a bed tucked into an alcove in the wall that was across from sliding glass doors to the patio. I loved the flat so I moved in right away.

    Emily quickly took advantage of the situation and begged me to ask Sunny if he wanted to temporarily stay at my flat. I asked him and he loved the idea. Sleeping on the sofa at Emily and Janet's apartment was getting old, and he was really tired of Janet's complaints. Sunny grabbed his guitar and a bag of clothes and came over right away. I was the only one working at the time and Sunny just wrote songs and played his guitar most of the day. He was looking for a job and said he would soon be able to find his own place. He never would.

    Over time Abby and I became a lot closer than I had expected. I really enjoyed her company and wanted to spend my time with her. She was a sexy, little nineteen-year-old with a lot of spunk, but I was getting the picture that she and Wendy may have been lovers when I arrived on the scene. For some reason that didn't really bother me. I was trying to keep an open mind –– like a good hippie.

    Wendy never really acted like she liked me much. She may have been jealous of where Abby and I were heading or knew we were just wasting our time. I never heard anything come out of Wendy's mouth that wasn't sarcasm. Regardless, Abby and I became a couple, and from then on Wendy only tolerated me. Abby moved into my flat with Sunny and me, although it was a bit crowded and Abby and I didn't have any personal space. Sunny had yet to contribute to the rent. Weeks went by and finally, Sunny and Abby both found jobs. Sunny went to work for Studio Instrument Rentals and Abby got a job packing boxes for Frederick's of Hollywood. All three of us were working and splitting the expenses. For a couple of months, we had some great times together in that little flat and got along exceedingly well.

    Wendy got a new roommate named Rita. She was also from Flushing and grew up with Wendy and Abby. Janet never did well in Hollywood so she talked Emily into moving back to Columbus. We would never hear from them again.

———————

One afternoon, Abby and I decided to drop some *Sunshine* and asked Sunny if he wanted to join us. He had done it before but wasn't experienced at it. About an hour or so after we took the acid, we were all flying high. But Sunny wasn't having the fun Abby and I were having. Abby and I were sitting on the sofa *tripping out* on things around the room of our flat, talking a lot and doing a lot of giggling. Sunny crawled up into the bed in the wall and closed the curtain. He was getting paranoid and talking nonsense about our flat being a coffin. We heard him say he must be dead-- not where you want to go with your thoughts while on acid. Since Sunny wasn't doing well at all with his trip, we decided that what he needed was to get out and walk around. We were determined to enjoy our acid trip and maybe that would help Sunny change his attitude.

So we walked down the hill from our flat on Ivar, and through the pedestrian tunnel under the Hollywood Freeway, to Hollywood Boulevard where there were plenty of people walking around. It was a fun street to walk down at night and we enjoyed watching the street people coming and going. I'm sure plenty of them were tripping just like us. If they weren't tripping, they at least had smoked a joint. No tourists were in that area at night either -- just a lot of freaks of all shapes and sizes.

Walking down the sidewalk seemed to help get Sunny off his bummer. We burned some energy walking and did a lot of laughing at what we thought were ridiculous things that we walked past … things that wouldn't have been funny had we been straight.

Once walking around got old, we headed back up the hill toward our flat in good spirits but still tripping on the acid. There was a long night ahead of us since an acid trip usually lasted about eight hours or so. In order to go home, we had to pass back through the tunnel under the Freeway, which was about a hundred yards long and illuminated by orange-colored lights every ten yards or so. It was about 11:00 p.m. and there was no one in sight when we walked down the middle of the street approaching the entrance to the tunnel.

Upon reaching the entrance, we could see the opening at the other end of the tunnel. After we walked a few feet into the tunnel, Sunny said he thought he saw someone's head peek out from the other end.

We stopped and waited for a few seconds, all watching the other end but saw nothing. So we went on, thinking Sunny was seeing things. We had almost reached the end when, all of a sudden, cops in dark blue uniforms stepped out in front of us from both sides of the opening.

It was like an ambush of sorts and we didn't understand it at first. We had done nothing wrong and didn't have any drugs on us. Abby and I stayed calm, thinking we would get through this harassment fine, but Sunny was crazy nervous and started acting strangely. I looked over at his face and it was red and his eyes were open wide. Hell, he looked like a madman. I knew things don't exactly look the same when you are on acid, but I also knew none of this could be good.

There were about ten uniformed cops in the group. All except one looked young. The older one had on a different uniform and appeared to be the supervisor. We were stoned on acid, so their faces looked like some sort of Halloween masks, contorted and plastic looking. I tried not to look directly at them. It became apparent that these guys were in training because they went through a predetermined list of questions for us.

"Can I see some ID?" one of the young ones asked.

Abby and I had our driver's licenses, but Sunny didn't have anything on him.

"Where are you going?" another one asked Sunny.

Sunny didn't know if he should tell them or not and could hardly talk.

"Uhhh, I'm not sure," Sunny said, trying to think of something else to say.

"We live up the hill on Ivar," I said. "We've just been out for a walk and heading home."

"Do you have any drugs on you?" another one asked.

"No, we do not," Abby said. "Why are you hassling us?"

"Just answer the questions, young lady," he rudely replied.

Abby was probably older than he was. So there we were, stoned on acid and being harassed by a group of police academy trainees. The supervisor looked on as each one took his turn asking us ridiculous questions. Sunny was getting more and more nervous and acted like it, too, so they started focusing on him.

Abby and I kept calm. I told them Sunny wasn't feeling well and we wanted to get him home where he could get some sleep. They kept asking us what was wrong with him. He was sweating, red-faced, and getting worse by the minute. His *bummer* acid trip was coming back. He couldn't even speak.

Finally, the overzealous trainees had asked about all the questions they could think of and, after consulting with the supervisor to see if they had left out anything, we were allowed to leave. We walked on past them and up the hill. I looked back and watched them divide back up into two groups taking their places on either side of the tunnel once again.

That's how it was in Los Angeles in those days. The police were training to be mean and the LA County Sheriffs were just as bad. I felt that they had no right to treat citizens that way, but they hated us for being hippies.

We spent the last few hours back at the flat trying to calm Sunny down and explain to him that nothing important happened. It was just cops being cops. He was worried that they would follow us to the flat and arrest us. We were no longer having any fun. Sunny climbed into the wall space and closed the drapes that covered the front.

Abby and I pulled out the sofa bed and lit some candles. We could hear Sunny whimpering and talking to himself from behind the curtain. Every once in a while, we could understand what he was saying and just had to giggle to each other because it was so ludicrous. It took several more hours for the acid to wear off enough to sleep, so we made love and tried to enjoy ourselves. Everyone got through that night unscathed. Sunny would never take another acid trip, preferring to just drink a few beers and smoke a joint.

Everyone was finally able to sleep about the time the sun was coming up. Tomorrow was another day. We finally figured out that Sunny wasn't going anywhere so Abby and I started looking for another place to live that could handle Sunny. We just couldn't kick him out. Both Abby and I had actually become fond of Sunny. From then on it would be the three of us. He became like a brother. That is how things were in those days. People living with people off and on, coming and going, for better or worse. It all seemed normal then and nice people attracted nice people. We three were like family and cared deeply about each other.

---

A funny thing happened while we lived in the flat on Ivar. I had been buying just a little pot to smoke but had a chance to buy a larger quantity through a guy that Abby had met at work. Frederick's of Hollywood was known for their sexy lingerie, which I thought was pretty funny because Abby wouldn't have dreamed of wearing them -- just too feminine for her taste. She was tougher than that.

I gave Abby $50 to buy a pound of plain old Mexican pot from the guy. I thought I could go ahead and sell some of it to friends in order to pay for the amount I was smoking. That was pretty common back then. I knew we were taking a chance buying from someone I didn't know, but Abby said he was cool. Abby came home from work with the pot in a clear plastic bag and rolled up tight. She had the plastic bag in a small brown paper sack, which looked like it might have been a lunch bag.

During that time in LA, pot had gotten very scarce and it wasn't very good. The lid I had bought prior to this guy's pot was coated in sugar that had crystallized into little, white chunks spread between the dried leaves and stems. No buds! Just plain trashy stuff that really wasn't worth much, but it was all we had to smoke. I was told the

Mexicans were coating it with cola to try to hide the smell from dogs. That was ridiculous. Dogs can smell through just about anything.

Cannabis lovers today wouldn't be very happy living back in the *good old days*. A few buds came in our lids but they were mixed in with all sorts of leaves, seeds, and stems. We referred to thick stems as *logs* and would always remove them from the lids we made.

The cost of lids stayed at ten bucks for years, regardless whether they had all the junk in them or not. People got excited if the lid they bought was fairly clean and had a lot of buds. That was a special shipment from somewhere and people wanted to buy from that dealer again if possible. But the stream of pot wasn't always that reliable. The guy they got their last stuff from may not have gotten that good stuff again.

Growing pot in Mexico was pretty simple back then. The process was not all that sophisticated. Peasants grew it up in the mountains where they would harvest it, press it into bricks, stems and all, and use their network to move it up to the border to smuggle. Mexican pot farmers were paid by the kilo and they didn't want to waste anything that gave it weight, so everything went in. Dope smokers weren't in a position to complain or be choosy at that time.

The one thing about pot back then was that it was cheap enough to smoke about as much at one time as you wanted to. You shared anything you had with your friends just like they did with their friends. Joints were passed freely. Often, when we rolled a joint and passed it to the next person, it didn't always make it all the way around. So we would just roll another one and pass it on again. Sometimes several people would light one up at the same time and start passing it around. So just as you took a big hit from one and passed it, another one was coming your way. This would come to an end when people were too stoned to remember to pass it.

Sometimes people used pipes, but usually just rolled a joint. Water pipes and bongs were found in some people's house but weren't very mobile. You couldn't walk around with one in your pocket to smoke in the park. Pipes looked suspicious, too, outside your home. A hippie-looking guy driving around LA smoking a pipe would definitely have been stopped by the law.

    We sometimes got a little crazy when there was a big bunch of pot at a party. People liked to show off by seeing how large a joint they could roll. Big, oversized joints were called *blunts* and took all sorts of shapes and sizes. Sure, they were a big waste of pot because so much would burn that wasn't inhaled, but pot was cheap and these big monster joints got a lot of laughs. Some joints got really long when we glued rolling papers together. Others were short and fat. I liked the ones that took the shape of an ice cream cone, big and fat on one end, and a normal joint opening at the other that you drew the smoke from. The room would fill with smoke. It was crazy. Smoking pot was as much of a social event as it was something to make you high. Maybe that's why I didn't see that much wrong about buying and selling it. Everyone was always happy to see the dealer come by to enjoy a smoke together.

    When I got the bag of pot from Abby's friend at work, I was too busy to stop and try it. Abby just brought it home and gave it to me. I thought maybe she had tried it. After our experience with Sunny, we decided to just hide our stash in the little crawl space on the side of the building, just up the steps from the door to the flat. I thought we would smoke it the next evening after work to see how good it was.

    So the next morning, I woke up, came out my door, and started walking up the little concrete steps alongside the building to check on my stash. Lo and behold, there was my pot all strung out along the steps, torn plastic, paper sack, and all. I couldn't figure out what had happened until I saw three neighborhood cats lying around on the steps with the pot. I reached down, picked some of it up, and smelled it. It wasn't even pot. It was catnip!

    I spent the next few minutes busting my butt to clean it all up before my landlady saw it. It made me think of the time Jack scattered my lid all over the Lewis Street sidewalk. Abby talked to her friend at work and he apologized profusely and returned all the money we had given him. We all had a good laugh and no harm was done. That was Hollywood for you. It was so easy to get ripped off if you weren't careful.

---

    It wasn't long before the landlady that owned our flat realized that I had two other people living with me. She lived in the house at the top of the steps where we parked and the long steps going down the side of the building went right passed her entrance. Since Hugh had set up our rental, she gave him a call and told him that I had broken my lease and had to move out by the end of the month. He called to let me know. Hugh didn't make a big deal out of it. He had met Abby and Sunny and understood my situation. But being a landlord himself, he also understood my landlady's concern. That was fine. We would move out. I was going to miss my patio view of the Hollywood Sign, though.

    Someone had told us that the Silverlake area had some very reasonable places to rent. It was about halfway between Hollywood and downtown LA. I had passed through it driving the Boulevard to downtown, but never turned to explore it. Silverlake was majorly hilly with a lot of trees and winding streets. It was easy to get lost but eventually you would find yourself back on a major road. We checked the classified ads and found several places to look at. Rentals in the LA paper were listed by area.

    The first place we found seemed to fit the bill. It was a large house up a hill from the street. The address was 850 Tularosa, Apt D. There must have been a hundred narrow steps leading up to the house. They were made of concrete and stone and would make several turns before reaching the entrance. The two-story house was made of roughly-textured stucco and it needed some work. But it also looked like a house where hippies would live. All the exterior stucco walls were painted different colors, including the steps. It was perfect for us. We found a pay phone and made a call to the landlord. He met us there within the hour. The house had four large apartments. There were two upstairs and two downstairs all coming off a central entrance and staircase. The inside walls of the house were brightly-painted stucco, too. It was a *hippie haven,* for sure.

Max, the landlord, arrived in a big, pink Oldsmobile convertible. He was older than us, obviously gay, a fast talker, and had long, frizzy, black hair that stood high on his head. Max didn't care who or how many people lived in his rentals, as long as he got his money on time, and as long as there weren't any complaints by the neighbors. He let us know that he wasn't about to spend any money fixing anything that went wrong either. At least he was honest, and the rent was cheap enough. Max owned rentals all over town and spent his time trying to keep them rentable and rented. We paid him the deposit and first month's rent. We moved to the upper left apartment within a few days.

Right after we moved in, Sunny met a nice girl named Kathy and asked her to move in with him. There were three bedrooms in the apartment and it was furnished with cheap, but heavy-duty furniture. Sunny and Kathy took a bedroom in the middle of the apartment and Abby and I took the larger one at the back of the apartment. Kathy was from the Midwest. She was young and had just moved to California by hitchhiking. Girls did that back then. Kathy had that country girl look with her long, cotton, flower print dress and sandals. She wore her long, reddish-brown hair in a single braid down her back and her fair complexion was dotted with light freckles. I remember her as being sweet and a little shy. Kathy was perfect for Sunny. He quickly fell in love with her.

An older man named Greg lived downstairs from us with two women and a daughter who was about eight. Greg was an author of paperback books –– which made him seem like a scholar, however his books were sleazy romance novels. He had a wife named Jane and a seven-year-old daughter named Mindy. Jane was a teacher. Karen was his mistress who shared his bed when he felt inclined. Coming from a conservative state such as Texas, which was always several years behind the culture of a state like California, this relationship was a bit disturbing to me. Their daughter, Mindy, was the one that would suffer.

But I was in LA and things were different there. Besides, it really wasn't my business. I saw Jane crying on several occasions and I couldn't figure out why she stayed with him. Jane talked to Abby and me about how hard it was for her when Greg decided to have sex with Karen. Jane and Mindy would sit in the living room watching TV and cry together. Karen was unsympathetic. She was getting what she wanted. All three of them were well-educated. I just didn't get it, but they lived a lifestyle that was all about him. It was as if Greg had some weird power over them. It was certainly nothing I could ever see myself doing to my wife and child. Somehow he was getting away with it. California!

---

Three long-haired guys shared the apartment across the hall from us. Two of them had jobs and we rarely saw or talked with them. One was just hanging out most of the time and dealing small quantities of pot and pills. His name was John Paul. I remember him calling himself one of the *Three Musketeers*. He dressed that way, as well, with a plumed hat, goatee, and mustache to match. He always wore tall, fringed leather boots. John Paul spent his evenings hitch-hiking up and down the Sunset Strip meeting new people, selling pot, and picking up girls. He would bring some of those girls back to his apartment for the night, have sex, and never see them again. They didn't seem to mind. There seemed to be plenty of that going on in Hollywood. John Paul showed up several times at our place with girls that we had never met. Some of them were very interesting to talk with.

One such girl was radically different than others. This one was short and fragile looking with pale skin and lots of freckles. Her red hair was pulled back with two thin braids that hung on each side of her head. She wore the hippie-style clothes that most girls were wearing at the time -- a long cotton dress with sandals and beads. But something was wrong with her, and Abby and I had a hard time putting our fingers on exactly what it was. We tried to have conversations with her and had difficulty understanding the broken sentences she muttered. Her voice was soft and had a high pitch to it. Abby and I decided that John Paul had either brought home a *nutcase,* or she was really high on something. We had been exposed to a lot of weird people living in Hollywood and most of the time we just laughed it off. Now this one was in our house.

    This new girl wouldn't look us in the eye as she spoke and instead stared off into the distance. John Paul would try to crack jokes to get her to laugh but she wasn't falling for them. She just went on about her life on a desert farm and said she had come to Hollywood to get away from it all. She talked about some bad things that had happened out on a ranch where she had been living, but didn't elaborate on just exactly what they were. It was hard to understand her words because she talked so quietly. I became frustrated with the conversation and decided to walk away and find someone more interesting to talk to. Abby put up with them for a little while longer and then found a way to end it.

    John Paul left with her and we never saw her again, at least not in person. We remembered her telling us her name was Squeaky. It wasn't long after that night that we saw her picture on the TV. Yes, we had been hanging out with Squeaky Fromme, the same girl who was part of the infamous Charles Manson Family and the same Squeaky Fromme who tried to assassinate President Gerald Ford a few years later. The murders were all the media could talk about and it had only been a few hours since we had been talking with her in our apartment. Some of the strange things she had said that night all of the sudden made perfect sense to us.

    John Paul choked on his coffee when we told him. He said they spent the night together and he had taken her back down to the Strip and dropped her off at the same corner where he had picked her up. His habit of picking up girls ended that night. He never again brought another strange girl over to hang out.

The story of Squeaky was a sad one. Her real name was Lynette Fromme, born only about a month after I was in 1948. She had performed in a popular dance group as a child, appearing on *The Lawrence Welk Show* and even at the White House in 1959. Lynette graduated from high school in California and was kicked out of her house after an argument with her father. In 1967, she went to Venice Beach and was said to suffer from depression.

Charles Manson was mentally ill. Charley, as he was called, was the victim of a horribly cruel childhood and had just been released from federal prison when Squeaky met him. She liked his philosophies and they became friends, traveling with a few other people who felt the same way. Eventually, they moved to a ranch near Death Valley, California.

Manson's sick and hypnotic manipulations of his followers resulted in the Tate/La Bianca murders in 1969. Squeaky was not one of the murderers, but stuck with Charley, protesting outside the courtroom during the trials with several others. They all carved X's into their foreheads proclaiming Manson's innocence and preaching his apocalyptic philosophy to the media. It was a dark time in America.

Squeaky showed up in the news again in 1975 when she went to Sacramento, California, to plead with then-President Gerald Ford about saving the California redwood forests. She dressed in a red robe and armed herself with a pistol. Squeaky stood only an arm's length away from the president when she pointed the gun at him and pulled the trigger. The gun failed to fire and no one was injured. Squeaky was quickly arrested by Secret Service and received a life sentence for the attempted assassination.

In the end, she never stopped professing total allegiance to Charles Manson. The rest of the country considered him a homicidal maniac. Manson later died in prison. The book *Helter Skelter*, by Vincent Bugliosi, tells the true story and its gruesome account of the murders. Squeaky Fromme was released on parole on August 14, 2009, and moved to New York. I don't think I'll be contacting her to catch up on old times.

---

Painting is one of my hobbies so I decided to paint a mural on mine and Abby's bedroom wall. Picasso had done a painting of two nude females running on the beach and I decided to paint that. It was helpful to recreate a work of a master to understand how they did it. It came out great, but I'm sure it eventually was painted over.

Sunny came home one day complaining about a traffic ticket he had gotten that day. It was a beautiful, warm day and Sunny was walking down Hollywood Boulevard when he decided to take off his shirt and jog. He was on the sidewalk when he approached an intersection where a small side street crossed the boulevard. There were no cars coming so he just kept on jogging across. A sheriff deputy on a motorcycle saw him and pulled him over on the sidewalk.

Sunny confessed to jaywalking and the cop wrote out the ticket. When he got home we all had a big laugh because the cop had written "5 mph" in the box for how fast the suspect was traveling.

I continued my work at Lunde and Sunny still had his job at Studio Instrument Rentals in Hollywood. Studio Instrument Rentals was a good place for Sunny to get a start with his career because he was around professionals all the time. The business was founded by two brothers. Rock 'N Roll historians would know them by their stage name *Jan and Dean*. It was a recording studio, but had several rehearsal studios where groups could just come and practice in a good, acoustic environment and not be bothered. The store also rented out musical equipment for bands playing in the area. They let Sunny drive their white company delivery van home and back. He loved working there and never complained, although he really never got his own music off the ground like he thought he could.

Abby and Kathy spent their days in the new Silverlake apartment just hanging out with friends and cooking great meals. Kathy knew how to crochet and was teaching Abby, who said she was going to make me a cap. I was enjoying my job and thought I might have a future there. It was a very happy existence until one day when I received a call from someone out of my past.

## Chapter Thirteen

Abby answered the phone and yelled to me. I was in the back of the apartment. It was mid-morning on a Saturday.

"Harry, it's for you!" she yelled. I picked up the receiver in the bedroom.

"Hello?" I said in my normal answering tone.

A man's voice on the other end said, "Hi, Harry! This is Tex."

"Tex? Tex who?" I asked.

"You know, Tex from San Antonio," he quickly replied. "Tall Tom? Wesley? You know –– Tex."

I was taken back for a second and didn't know what exactly to say. I did, however, remember who he was.

I said, "Oh, Tex," as if now just realizing who he was. "Where are you?"

"I'm in LA just like you are!"

"Really? How long have you been here?"

Tex began talking nonstop. "I've been here for several months. I talked to Wesley the other day and he said you were out here, too. Just had to do some telephone research and there you were! Wow! Thought I would give you a ring and see if we could get together for a drink or something…for old times sake."

"Uh, sure that would be great," I said hesitantly.

"So, where do you live?" Tex asked.

"Silverlake," I quickly answered.

"Well, Harry, I don't have a car so would you mind coming to pick me up?"

"You don't have a car?" I said.

"No," Tex said.

"Uh, where do you live?" I asked.

"Not that far. I have a small apartment in Burbank. You just have to get on the Hollywood Freeway and exit at Burbank Boulevard."

Tex went on to give his address and, before I knew it, I had agreed to drive to Burbank to pick him up. Now I had to

177

break the news to Abby and borrow our neighbor's car. I hung up the phone and Abby said, "Who was that?" She followed me down the hall to our bedroom and we talked while I got dressed to leave.

Sunny and Kathy were already gone for the day. There was a free concert in a nearby park and they walked down to the Boulevard to hitchhike to it.

"It's this guy I knew in San Antonio. A guy named Tex," I said.

"Oh, so what's he want?" Abby asked.

"I don't exactly know. This could be a big connection though." I said. "Remember me telling you about the guy who smuggled marijuana across the border with his grandmother and supplied Wesley, Tall Tom, and I with pot when we were dealing in San Antonio?"

"Yeah, I remember," Abby replied.

"Well, I just barely knew him but he has asked me to come pick him up so he could come over and visit."

"That's cool," she said, "I'll ride with you. I gotta get out of this house and do something. I'll go ask Greg if we can borrow his car." About ten minutes later, Abby came back with the keys and we left.

When I abruptly left San Antonio to move to LA to *get away from drugs,* I thought I would never see or talk to Tex again. He was just our supplier and looked more like a businessman than a hippie. He wasn't someone I wanted to hang with.

Abby and I picked him up at his apartment in Burbank and after hugs and introductions; the three of us drove back to Silverlake. Tex brought along a suitcase. Abby stared at me with a look that spoke for itself. She didn't want another roommate. Sunny was enough. I glanced back at her and shrugged my shoulders. I just went with the flow.

Tex loved our apartment and pulled out a large roll of joints from the oversized pocket of his slacks. That roll probably had a hundred joints in it. It was held together by a big rubber band. He carefully pulled one joint out of the roll and handed it to me.

"You still smoke, don't you, Harry?" Tex asked laughing. That was an easy answer for me. "Sure, fire that baby up!"

We smoked and had some lively conversations, mainly Tex recalling the old days in San Antonio and relaying all that to Abby. She and her friends dealt small quantities in Flushing before moving to LA, so Abby loved hearing about how things worked in Texas. Didn't seem to be the old days to me. It had not been that long since I left San Antonio.

Sunny and Kathy came back to the apartment before the sun went down. I introduced them to Tex and they went off to their bedroom to shower before dinner. Abby and I started cooking a stir-fry dish and invited Tex to stay for dinner. I was hungry and that seemed like a better choice for the moment than driving him home. Tex kept us up talking for hours after dinner. He asked if he could sleep on the sofa and I thought that was a good idea so I didn't have to drive all that way at night. The next morning, we started talking again over a cup of coffee. Tex had something on his mind and it finally came out.

Tex began talking in earnest. "I have a plan that I think you are going to like. I'm on hard times right now and you know my ability to deliver and make you money."

I quickly responded. "I quit that when I moved here, Tex."

"Sure you did, Harry," he said.

"I actually have a job," I said. "I just get a little pot here and there to smoke."

"This place doesn't look like you are doing so good to me," Tex said sarcastically. "If you would just listen to me, I think I can change your mind."

"What are you talking about, Tex?" I asked.

"Here's the deal, Harry. You know all that good stuff I used to bring you and your partners," he said. "Well, I still have those contacts and now, living in LA, we have a much larger market to sell to. We could make a fortune together!"

I thought for a moment and then responded. "I don't know, Tex."

"No one around here will even look at me sideways," Tex said. "I can't seem to get anyone to trust me because I don't know anybody – and I don't look like you all do, either."

Tex pulled out another joint and lit it up. From the day he walked into our apartment, I rarely saw him without a lit joint in his hand. Tex was so fat that when he put his big roll of joints in his pocket it basically disappeared. He went on with his plea.

"I need your help in order to make something happen," he said.

"I don't think so," I said, "I'm pretty happy with what I am doing now. I don't think taking that level of risk is in my future, Tex."

"Let me tell you more. Just hear me out," Tex implored. "The stuff I used to get came from the border town of Del Rio. Recently, it all came to a halt when Joe went to the Mexican jail for heroin possession."

"Heroin!" I said, "I don't want anything to do with that stuff.

"No, that was just Joe's thing. The rest of his family is straight," Tex said.

"What does Joe have to do with me?" I asked.

Tex got going again. "Just let me explain more."

"Okay, go on," I said.

"Joe's wife, Maria, was part of the smuggling operation right alongside Joe," Tex said, "but without any cash or transportation, there isn't much she can do now. She and Joe have seven kids, and they live in a small Mexican village called Villa Fuentes just on the other side of Eagle Pass. That's where I would go to score the pot I used to bring you guys."

"So?" I said.

"So, before I left Texas for LA, I drove down to Mexico to talk to them. Maria assured me that if I could come back down with some transportation, she would front me fifty pounds of pot and said I could bring them back the money when I sold it. That would get all of us going again and we could start making some real money."

I understood now. "So all you want from me is to go back down there and help you get the pot?"

"You're getting it now," Tex said.

It was time to explain my current transportation situation. "Man, I don't even have a car right now. All I have is my motorcycle."

Tex kept talking about the trip we needed to make. I kept resisting. This went on for a week, and Abby and Sunny had had about enough of Tex. My old San Antonio pot supplier wasn't planning on leaving. In fact, he never even went back for anything else. Then I wondered if Tex even had anything else, or even an apartment. I finally came to the realization that Tex had moved in with us without even asking. The big man also had a pistol in one of those pockets. He would pull it out and fool with it in front of us. Tex never threatened us with it, exactly. I think it was just a reminder to us that he was armed. We certainly were not. Everyone in the building became scared of Tex and wanted him gone.

Sunny never forgave me for letting Tex move in. He and Abby pleaded with me to get rid of Tex. But that was easier said than done. I talked to Tex about him leaving, but he made it clear that wasn't his plan. This went on for another week. Sunny's girlfriend, Kathy, moved out and moved on, saying Tex kept looking at her breasts and making sexual comments and she didn't like it. We never saw her again and I know Sunny blamed me for it.

When I told Tex about everyone's feelings towards him, he would just grin and say, "The only way you are going to get me out of here is to go with me to Mexico. Just trade your motorcycle for a car and we can get out of here."

Of course, looking back I had other choices. But at the time, it seemed that my choices were limited. Calling the police was not on any respectable hippie's mind when a problem arose.

One evening, Abby and I talked about the situation while lying in bed.

"Well, Tex is very threatening, Abby." I said, "I really don't know if Tex means it or not. It's like a game to him. If we call the cops, he might go to jail for a short time but then come after us when he gets out."

"So, what are we going to do, Harry?" she asked.

"What do you want me to do?" I asked Abby. We just laid there quietly for a minute, thinking and staring at the ceiling of our bedroom.

Then I made a decision. "Okay then, Abby. I guess I'm going to Mexico with him."

"I'll start looking in the paper first thing in the morning for a car, Harry," Abby said. "I'll just grab Greg's newspaper in the hallway and give it back to him later."

Abby checked the classifieds and didn't come up with anything. When Tex woke up, I informed him that I would go with him to Mexico. Word got around the building that I needed a car. One of John Paul's roommates knew a guy who wanted to trade his car for a motorcycle. He had a 1959 Ford Fairlane convertible that he said ran very well. They got him on the phone and he said he would drive over and show it to me. He was interested in trying out my motorcycle too. This guy's name was *Junkie John*.

"Oh great," I thought, "I'm getting a car from *Junkie John*, so I can go buy marijuana from *Heroin Joe*. What had I gotten myself into?

Sunny was worried that I chose to go to Mexico with Tex, but at that point, he was just glad that Tex would be gone. Everyone else felt the same way. I said that once Tex got money from selling the pot, he would leave us alone and I would make sure that things got back to normal for us.

Junkie John arrived at the apartment the next morning driving the Ford Fairlane he wanted to trade. We all went down the steps to the curb to see the car. He was the typical hippie with long, brown hair and a beard. The Ford was off-white with a tan top and interior. I thought it was pretty cool.

After introductions, Junkie John said, "Why don't we just switch vehicles for the day? You drive the car around a bit and I'll test drive the bike. At the end of the day, we'll meet back here and, if we agree, we can make the trade."

"Okay, man," I said. "That sounds good," and we shook on it.

So off Junky John went on my bike. Two male friends of Abby's from Flushing were coming to town and needed picking up that day. So Abby asked if we could pick them up where they would be turning in the car on Sunset Strip. I said that would be fine.

Abby's friends, Allen and Brian, drove a car from New York to LA for a company who had advertised for cross-country drivers. A lot of people back then would drive these cars from one side of the country to the other basically for free. The guys already had a place to stay, but would have had to take a cab if we couldn't pick them up. They called Abby from the company's office down on the Sunset Strip about noon when they got in and we left right away in Junkie John's car to pick them up. The Strip was only a few miles down Sunset from us so it wasn't that big a deal.

I loved the Ford and so did Abby. She was tired of riding on the back of the bike and we couldn't take Jack with us places very easily. We drove to the address they gave us. Allen and Brian were on the curb with duffle bags for luggage. They both looked very New York –– Navy P-coats, T-shirts, and bell-bottom jeans were the uniforms of the day for most kids from the East Coast.

"Hey, need a ride?" Abby yelled out the window when we were pulling up.

"Sure," Allen yelled back. They were really glad to see Abby. It had been a couple of years.

Allen was heavyset with short, brown hair and a light complexion. Like most New Yorkers, he rarely got any sun. Allen wore small, hippie glasses, the kind John Lennon used to wear. Brian had short, black hair with a little mustache and was taller than Allen. They both seemed like really nice guys. Most of Abby's friends were. They threw their duffle bags in the trunk and hopped into the back of the car. I needed to turn the car around to go the other direction and that wasn't easy on the *Sunset Strip*.

Sunset Boulevard runs along a high rim on the edge of the Hollywood Hills. The hill makes a sharp drop down on one side towards the ocean in the distance. I was looking for the best place to make the turn-around when I started smelling smoke. It was coming from under the dash in front of me.

I made a quick left turn at the next intersection and drove down the hill. I pulled over to the curb as soon as I saw an open spot on the next block and we all piled out of the car. Allen opened the hood and flames came up with a loud woofing sound. We were trying to figure out what to do when, all of the sudden, a red Mustang stopped in the middle of the intersection. A guy jumped out with a fire extinguisher and put the fire out in only a few seconds. It all happened so fast. We thanked him and he drove off. I was relieved that the whole car didn't burn to the ground. We were standing there looking at all this white stuff covering the engine and not sure exactly what to do next.

Well, *next* came quickly. Two large fire trucks came roaring up to the intersection where the Mustang had been and blocked all cars from passing. Two firemen came over to our car and asked what happened. I told them the story of the car catching fire and the guy in the red Mustang stopping and putting out the fire. I thought that would be the end of it. Then the questions came.

"Is this your car?" the fireman asked.

"Well, no," I said. "I'm test-driving it because I'm thinking about trading it with a guy who is test-driving my motorcycle right now."

"May I see your registration?" he asked.

"Registration? Uh, I don't know. It might be in the glove box," I said.

"What is the person's name that does own the car?" he asked.

"His name is John."

"John who?" The fireman wanted to know.

"I don't know," I said. I didn't want to say his name was *Junkie John*.

As fate would have it, the registration was not in the glove box and the fireman said, "Well, I'm going to have to call the Sheriff's office so you guys just sit tight."

It didn't take long for two LA County Sheriff Deputies to come driving up on their motorcycles. They immediately acted like assholes, slamming us all face-first against a rock retaining wall where our car was parked. They asked the same questions and we had the same answers. Then the deputies forced our arms behind our backs and put on the handcuffs. Police cars drove up and we were taken to the police station just a few blocks away from the scene of the crime.

The officers on the inside were a lot nicer than the ones on the streets. A detective listened to my story and had us sit in the lobby while he took off my handcuffs and asked me more questions. Still, they were in the process of booking me for Grand Theft Auto! I had never even been in a jail before, much less booked into one. After all my dealing days, I get caught for stealing a car?

The detective asked me to sit next to his desk while he figured out what to do.

"When is this John guy supposed to be back to your apartment?" the detective asked.

"We are supposed to meet back at the end of the day," I answered.

"Why don't you call your house and see if he is back yet," the detective suggested as pushed his desk phone towards me.

I dialed our house number and Sunny answered. I explained the situation to Sunny and he said Junkie John had not returned yet. I called back several times over the next couple of hours. As we sat in the lobby together, I assured the others that everything would turn out okay once Junkie John returned with my bike.

Junkie John finally showed up at our house at the end of the afternoon and read the registration numbers to the officer over the phone. It was registered in his name and the numbers were right so they told us we could go.

We left the station and I had to pay a taxi to take us home. Junkie John's car was in the police pound and, the next day, we returned with him and I paid $70 to get it out. Junkie John was somewhat of a mechanic and got the engine cleaned up and running again. The fire was put out so quickly it didn't burn anything important. He tightened up some bolts and the car was okay to drive again. He determined that it was just some leaking gasoline on top of the intake manifold that had caught fire.

Two days later, I met Junkie John at the California Department of Motor Vehicles and legally traded the car for the bike. Tex said that we should put the car in his name since he knew his way around Mexico better than I did. He said that he spoke Spanish and could get us through the border without any trouble if the name on his license matched the registration on the car. I didn't think anything of it. The car wasn't worth much anyway when compared to the amount of money I was going to make upon our return. The plan was now in place for a quick trip to the Texas-Mexico border!

What Tex needed in order to execute his plan was a car, which we now had, and travel expenses, which we didn't have. I wasn't the only one who listened to him talk about how if only he could get to the small border town in Texas, he could return with fifty pounds of pot dirt-cheap and everyone could benefit. So several of our friends pitched in money to finance the trip and get in on the rewards upon our return.

---

One of our friends who pitched in money was Ray Jackson. I had met Ray one day at Jerry's motorcycle shop. Ray was a handsome guy with short, dark hair and a good build. He drove an old Indian motorcycle and had a good job in medical sales. He would come by the house and we would take a ride on our bikes together. Ray didn't have any cash on him but he gave us one of his credit cards that we could use for emergencies if we had to. Others, like the guys who just arrived from New York, put up cash. Abby and I put in a few hundred dollars that we had saved. Sunny even pitched in some cash and that was surprising since he was very tight about spending his money. I thought that his contribution was less about making money and more about getting rid of Tex.

Abby was still working at Frederick's of Hollywood, so I felt okay leaving them as they would be able to pay the bills and buy food while I was gone. It shouldn't have taken more than a week to do the whole thing.

After trading for the car, I walked into Hugh's office and told him I was quitting the job at Lunde. It wasn't the best job, but at least it was a job. However I couldn't see that. I had to get rid of Tex, but honestly, I had visions of making big bucks with Tex.

Hugh gave me a puzzled look and said, "Well, okay. What are you going to do?"

"I'll be fine, Hugh," I told my cousin. "Thank you for all your help while I was working here. I'm going to do some traveling for awhile and I'll catch up with you when I get back."

"Okay," he said. "I'll tell Morten."

I didn't want to tell Hugh the truth so I just said, "I'm leaving in the morning so please just put my last paycheck in the mail, okay?"

"Sure," Hugh said. "Let me know if I can help you."

"I will," I said, as I walked out of his office and out the front door of Morten Lunde and Associates for the last time.

At that point, I was blinded by the opportunity of making money and wasn't afraid of a little more adventure. Lots of people around me had money, but Sunny, Abby, and I had not finished college and were struggling with minimum wage jobs.

The pot being sold in California was expensive and of poor quality. I thought I could bring better pot to town and unload it quickly just with my friends and never have to be worried about being busted. It was a perfect plan, except maybe the part about being with Tex.

With a full tank of gas in the car and money in our pockets, Tex and I drove out the LA freeway towards Texas. The drive to Texas takes about twenty hours depending on stops. I did all the driving. My hair was still short since I had been working at Lunde. Morten didn't like long hair. I took clothes that looked about as straight as I could find. Tex said he didn't want me looking like a hippie when we crossed the border.

After staying the night in a small motel in Las Cruces, New Mexico, we finally reached the Texas border city of El Paso. The car was holding up well so everything was a *go*. Tex talked constantly about how much money each of us could make now that we had a partnership again. I didn't remember that Tex and I ever had a partnership, but I let him go on with his planning. We continued our journey through West Texas on I-10, which seems to just go on and on forever. When we reached the town of Sonora, instead of continuing on to San Antonio, we turned south on 277 towards Del Rio and checked into a motel for the night when we arrived.

The next morning, we had breakfast at the motel's cafe. Our final destination was the Mexican town of Piedras Negras, just on the other side of the border from the Texas town of Eagle Pass. Tex said it would be best if we reached Eagle Pass in the evening. He didn't want to be recognized and the cloak of night would be better. So we stayed most of the morning in the motel, watching TV and talking about the future. I was getting tired of talking about the future, but played along just to get along. I hesitated to get into any arguments with Tex and liked that he was so optimistic since I had always been an optimist myself. Of course that had not always served me well. We left the motel at dusk.

We had only driven about half an hour out of Sonora when I heard a loud bumping sound. It was a flat tire. I pulled the car over, got out, and looked at the tire. It was blown and would not be able to be repaired. There was the spare tire, but as soon as I lifted it out of the trunk, I could tell that it didn't have any air in it. Tex and I agreed that it was useless to even try to use the spare. Ugh! I should have checked it before we left.

There we were sitting in the dark out in the middle of nowhere. Cell phones didn't exist in those days so we couldn't make a phone call. We hadn't seen a car on that lonely road since we left Sonora and Tex informed me that there wasn't much chance of seeing one for the rest of the night.

"Not much traffic on this road at night," Tex said. "You better start walking."

"Walking?"

"Yeah, walking," Tex said a second time.

I could hardly believe my ears. "Walking where?"

"Back to town," Tex said with emphasis.

"You mean Sonora?" I gasped.

"Well, where else?" Tex said. "Maybe you can get back in time to find a gas station still open that can come out here and fix this thing."

"And what if I don't?"

Shrugging, Tex said, "Well, what do you think your choices are?"

"I don't know," I said. "I don't even have a flashlight."

"That don't matter," Tex argued. "Even if you don't find anything open, you can still check into a motel and get someone to come back out here in the morning. Think of the time it will save us. Instead of walking tomorrow you can get this done now. Besides, there will be plenty of moonlight so don't worry about it. Just get your ass going."

"Okay, okay," I said. "I guess I'll be back when I'm back." I got out and began my journey.

I wasn't exactly sure how many miles we had traveled since leaving town that evening. I started with a fairly brisk walk and soon began to pace myself. The terrain was so flat all I could see was the sky in all directions. I was walking on a narrow two-lane highway that was as straight as a board into the distance. There was no reason to make any curves since there was nothing in the way that had to be avoided when they planned it – just sand, cactus, and scrub brush with maybe an occasional mesquite tree.

My mind wandered while I walked. I was thinking about what I was doing and why. Was I crazy? Going off like this with a dangerous older man like Tex? I hardly knew him. He could be a murderer –– Hell, he probably was. But I was in too deep now. I should have thought about this before I agreed to pick him up that day. All I needed to do was focus on reaching Sonora and finding help.

I heard something like a howl in the distance. It hadn't really occurred to me that there might be other dangers out on that dark road. The sun had completely gone down now and the moon that Tex said would light my way was nowhere to be found. It had yet to rise. The temperature was dropping and I wasn't wearing a jacket. After all, this was spring and LA had been warm for weeks. But there was a chill and I was starting to feel it. This part of Southwest Texas was a desert -- hot during the day and chilly at night. I was lucky to have on at least an undershirt under my cotton shirt.

A sound came from somewhere off in the distance. I decided that it must be a coyote howling. Then there were more. I wondered if they ever attacked people. I didn't remember hearing that, but how many people are out in this land alone at night to find out? I thought about growing up in Texas and remembered other things that could get me -- like mountain lions, bobcats, and snakes. Snakes come out at night to hunt after basking in the sun during the day and cats hunt at night.

I could barely see the road ahead but did see a glow from the town in the distance. I wondered how far a person could see lights at night when the only thing visible is the horizon. It seemed to me that someone could see a very long way.

*What if I can't make it to Sonora tonight?* I thought, while I walked quickly along. What am I supposed to do, lie down in the rocks, sand, and cactus on the side of the road?

I told myself to just keep walking. That's all I could do. It was a dark clear night and the stars were shining brightly across the open sky. Then I heard a vehicle. It was quite a way off and the sound it made on the road indicated that it was getting closer -- traveling fast, heading towards me. Then I saw the lights. The only thing I could think of was to put myself in a position that the driver could see me and take my chances that he would stop and render aid to a person in trouble.

The vehicle got closer and closer. I wasn't sure the driver would stop, but he did. Seeing me only at the last minute waving my arms like I needed help, he slammed on his brakes and stopped in the middle of the road just about a fifty yards past me. It was a pickup truck. It's taillights turned to white backup lights, which lit the road between us. He had put the truck in reverse and was backing up towards me. The driver had to make a quick decision whether to stop or not and luckily he decided to stop.

"Where's your car?" the driver asked, hanging his head out of the window looking back at me as I walked towards him. He was about 50 years old with a dark tan and lots of wrinkles in his face. He had a lit cigarette hanging out of his mouth that he puffed on as he spoke.

The man could see me better now and acted relieved that he had made a good choice to stop since I didn't look like the kind of person who was going to rob him. He looked like a rancher. Growing up in Texas, I had seen his type a million times. He wore a faded blue denim shirt with a light colored straw cowboy hat. I couldn't see but he probably had on blue jeans, a western belt with a big buckle, and boots.

I quickly explained what had happened. "My friend and I had a flat a few miles up the road so I started walking back to town to look for help."

"There's no one open to help you there at this time of the night," he said. "I can give you a ride but you're not going to get that tire fixed anytime soon. Get in."

I got into the other side of the truck. It smelled like a combination of fresh hay and cow shit. It definitely had been used on a ranch. We drove off towards Eagle Pass and our Ford. He didn't say much after that but asked how far I thought our car was from where he picked me up.

"I don't know how far I have walked but I really thank you for stopping," I said.

"Don't mention it," he said. "It's not safe for someone to be walking out here at night. Lots of things can get you out here. The border's just beyond those mesquite trees in the distance."

I squinted my eyes and looked in the direction he pointed. The moon had started its climb and I could make out silhouettes of a few scattered scrub trees in the distance.

"Of course, there are the wetbacks. They probably wouldn't kill you," he said. "They would just take whatever money, food, and water you had. But there are other dangerous things out here, too."

Just as he was about to describe the other things, he stopped in mid-sentence and said, "Is that your car up ahead?"

"Yes, that's it," I said, relieved to end that conversation.

I couldn't see Tex at first but as we got closer Tex sat up and looked back at us driving up. His skin was so white that his face almost glowed like a headlight as our lights hit the car. Tex was opening the door as we stopped. He got out and greeted us with a big smile.

"Hi," Tex said to the driver. "Thanks for your help. We got a little tire problem here."

"I'm headed to Del Rio if you want a ride," the rancher said. "That's about all I can do for you boys. Y'all can stay the night there and come back out here with a truck from the gas station in the morning. I'm sure they'll come out and fix it. These things happen a lot out here."

"That would be great, thanks," Tex said, as he climbed in.

"You better take what you can of your things with you," the man said. "You may not have much when you get back here tomorrow."

Tex climbed back out of the truck and we both went over to the car, opened the trunk, pulled out our two suitcases and put them into the bed of the pickup.

We thanked the rancher again for his kindness and checked into a motel in Del Rio for the night. The next morning, we walked down to a gas station that had a mechanic's garage attached to it. Most stations did in those days. Not much was going on that morning in Del Rio so he agreed to give us a ride back to our car. He had one of those self-contained trucks with everything needed to put air in our spare tire and get us back on the road. We paid for the work and drove back to Del Rio. When we got back to town, Tex saw a tire place and said our car needed a new set of tires if we were to continue on the trip. We used Ray's credit card to pay for them. We had become short on cash by then and were starting to use Ray's card for all our gas. We saved the little cash we had left for food only.

Once the new tires were on, we gassed up and drove to Eagle Pass and across the international bridge into Mexico. We drove straight through town and into the small village of Villa Fuentes. The streets were dirt and only a few people were walking around. I was driving and Tex gave me directions through the village. We first came to a house where Tex said the family lived. It wasn't much to look at, but it was one of the better houses in the barrio.

"Something's wrong," Tex said. "They don't look like they live here anymore."

"Didn't you talk to them about fronting you the pot?" I asked.

"Well, I never really talked to them," Tex explained. "I tried to call them but it never went through. I figured they changed the number and you and I would just have to come down and talk to them in person."

"Uh, huh," I said, not believing how stupid I was for trusting him. I wanted to throw a fit, but held back.

We sat there in front of the house for a few minutes then Tex got out of the car and went up to the door of the house. I stayed in the car and watched. An elderly Mexican woman in a cotton dress and apron opened the door and I could see that they were talking. There were no smiles and hugs that I could see, so I couldn't tell what was going on.

Tex returned to the car, got in and said, "Drive on."

"What?" I said.

"They don't live here anymore," Tex said. "They moved to the other side of the town."

After a few turns and about a mile of dirt streets we arrived at our destination. Tex was quiet and didn't share any information with me. I was just following directions at that point.

"Pull over here," Tex said.

I stopped the car in front of a small adobe house within a neighborhood of similar structures.

"Stay here," Tex said. "I'll go up and talk to them first."

Tex got out of the car and walked up the dirt yard to the front door. I watched from the car. The front door opened and out came an attractive Mexican woman who gave Tex a big hug and welcomed him in. Tex pointed back to me and I could see her looking past him at me in the car. She quickly waved her arms as if to tell me to come in also. I got out of the car, walked up to the house and was also greeted with a hug.

"I'm Maria," she said.

"Harry," I responded.

The three of us were still standing in the doorway when her kids started coming up from behind her greeting Tex with hugs on his legs and looking at me, wondering who I was. In the past, Tex usually always drove down with his grandmother.

We all walked into the little house. The floor of the house was dirt just like the streets, yard and everything else I saw there. I was trying to be friendly while glancing around in dismay about their living conditions. She and Tex were talking in Spanish with an occasional English word mixed in. Maria had smooth dark skin with long black hair going down the back of her neck. Her clothes were simple but not ragged. She looked more sophisticated than someone I would have expected to find in a house like that.

Maria and Tex soon realized that I was not able to understand their conversation and changed to English so I could be included. The kids dispersed. We moved from the small, front room to the small kitchen and the three of us sat around a little round table. I could see through another door into the only other room in the house. It was the bedroom and had mattresses covering most of the dirt floor. A number of kids were in there playing on the beds and keeping themselves away from the business we were conducting in the kitchen.

Tex and Maria had already talked in Spanish, so I had to catch up with what was said before I was able to understand. Tex started off and told me that Maria had said that her husband, Joe, was in jail charged with heroin possession.

"I told Joe not to mess with that stuff," Maria said. "He wouldn't listen to me. We were doing great, living in a nice house with a TV and had plenty of cash. Joe got careless and drew the attention of the *Federales*. I think it was something political. Somebody wanted him arrested, but we're not sure whom. Could have been several people. Doesn't matter now." She stopped talking and looked down at the floor.

"So, how long is he in for?" Tex asked.

"Years," she said. "We don't know how long. That's how it is in Mexico. A person like Joe has no rights!"

"So, what happened?" Tex said.

"One night, we were all in the house when the *Federales* broke through the front door and came in with their guns drawn yelling to get down," Maria said.

"Did they hurt any of you?" Tex asked.

"Just Joe. The *Federales* knew who they were looking for. Those uniformed thugs pulled Joe from the house and dragged him across the yard into their truck. Then they came back in and searched the house."

Maria started talking a mile a minute. "They took everything we had! All our money! All our drugs! Anything and everything of value."

"That's horrible," Tex said.

She kept going. "The kids were all crying and so was I," she said. "They took more than fifty grand and left us with nothing. By the grace of God, my cousin had this little house for us."

Tex took this information very seriously. "I was hoping you could front us some marijuana," Tex said.

"I would if I could," Maria said, "but now I have nothing to offer you."

"I understand, Maria," Tex said. "Is there any other way to get some?"

Maria thought for a few seconds before speaking again. "There is one way, Tex." She was looking first at Tex and then turned her head and looked at me. "Fernando."

Maria and Joe had a son named Fernando. Fernando was a twenty-three-year-old, strong and handsome young man who had grown up in the trade with his parents. He was the oldest of their children. They all lived together until Joe went to prison. The house was too small for Fernando's needs so he was living with a girlfriend when we visited Maria. Tex knew Fernando well as he had helped him many times loading and unloading pot. They treated Tex like he was family. After all, he grew up with their relatives in the states. They would have loved to see Tex's grandmother, but she had passed away, which was the reason Tex had moved to Los Angeles.

Tex had the best of both worlds. Being Anglo, he could find the Anglos who had money to spend on one side of the city and sell them pot from his friends on the other side. With his short hair and large physique, no one suspected him of being a smuggler.

Maria told us to come back in two days and she would have Fernando ready to drive with us into the interior of Mexico. There we would buy pot at the same price that they bought it for. Tex had never driven down to their supplier in the mountains and knew this was a golden opportunity.

Tex and I drove back to Eagle Pass that day, but not across the border bridge that was just a couple of miles away. He said we had to drive on the Mexican side back up to Del Rio and cross there. That way, he explained, the border guards wouldn't notice us crossing so many times. The dirt road up to Del Rio was scattered with potholes, but we made it by dark. After crossing the border, we drove the miles back down to Eagle Pass and checked into the same motel from the night before. Tex told the girl at the motel counter that we had so much fun in Mexico we decided to stay another night.

When we got into the room Tex said, "Okay I didn't plan it this way but this is the only choice we have."

"It sounds like we have to buy the pot," I stated, "and so where are we going to get the money for that?"

"Give Abby a call and see if she can raise money tonight," Tex said.

"Tonight?" I said.

"Sure, Harry. I bet you guys have friends who would put money into a deal where they could get a pound of pot for $20. We'll owe Maria $10 for each pound, so we can pay them back what we spent and still come out with plenty of pot to sell ourselves. What else would we do at this point? What would you suggest we do?" Tex asked.

I didn't have a real answer to that last question so I picked up the phone in the motel room and made a long-distance collect call to Abby. She answered the phone right away and told the operator that she would accept the charges. It had been several days since she had heard from us and was concerned.

"Why haven't you called?" Abby said. "I've been worried sick."

I started apologizing immediately. "I don't know. I'm sorry, we've just had a lot of trouble and I didn't think about it."

Abby sounded relieved. "Well, I'm glad you are okay."

Tex was listening so I couldn't tell Abby exactly what I was thinking. Tex had lied about getting the pot fronted to us. Regardless, I had to continue to make something happen out of this fiasco.

"Here's the deal, Abby," I explained. "Tex was lied to. There is no pot to be fronted so we are going to have to drive deep into Mexico with the son of the suppliers to get it from the source."

"So...?" Abby said, in a not-so-happy voice.

"So Abby, we need money to buy the pot now. But the good news is that we can give people an unbelievable good deal on what we bring back if they want to invest more."

Several seconds of dead silence passed before Abby spoke again. "So what do you want me to do?"

"I want you to call some of our friends and see if they are interested in investing," I said. Again, Abby hesitated before answering.

"Okay," Abby said. "How do I get you the money and when do you need it?"

I took a deep breath and blurted out what needed to happen ASAP.

"We need it right away. Like tomorrow!" I began. "You can wire it using Western Union. They have an office here in downtown Eagle Pass. If you give them cash, they will give us cash about an hour later. They do it all the time."

"I know, I know. But by tomorrow?" she said. "This is no small thing to do."

"Yes, Abby, but I don't have another plan. I don't know what else to do. I have to see this through."

"I'll make some calls and see what I can come up with," Abby said. "Some of the people who are here now might be interested. I'll ask the others in the apartment, too. How much did you say you needed?"

"As much as you can get," I said. "We're trying to get fifty pounds if we can. That's about the limit the Mexican woman said her son can carry by himself. The pot will cost us $500.00 and we'll have more traveling expenses on top of that."

"Okay," Abby said. "I'll call you back tonight and let you know."

"Okay, babe," I said. "We'll be here," and I hung up the phone.

Tex sat up from the bed of the hotel room where he had been listening and said, "So, she's raising the money, I assume?"

"Yep, she's trying," I said. "As much as she can in one night, man. We will call again in a few hours."

We called back later and Abby said she had raised five hundred dollars between everyone she talked to. It would have been more, but they couldn't promise to get her the cash she needed by the morning. After a quick breakfast at the cafe, we checked out of the motel and drove to Western

Union just after 9:00 a.m., the time they opened for business.

It took about thirty minutes, but they finally called us up to the window and handed us five hundred dollars. With cash in hand and Ray's credit card, which was now our primary source of paying for our expenses, Tex and I headed back across the border to Maria's house. Fernando was standing in the front yard when we arrived, as if he had been waiting on us for hours. Maria came out of the house to greet us. Her kids were playing a few houses down the dusty dirt street.

"Hola, Amigo!" Tex called out to Fernando.

"Hola, Tex!" Fernando called back.

Tex introduced us. Fernando flashed a big smile and addressed me in perfect English, so I knew he had at least gone to school. Fernando appeared to be a nice and friendly guy. He stood about five-foot-nine with short, black hair and a thin mustache, and looked to be in excellent shape. I figured that we were about the same age –– in our early twenties.

Maria told us that Fernando knew exactly what to do. He had done this many times before with Joe and stressed there was nothing to worry about. When we got back with the stuff, they would help us get across the border and wouldn't even take a cut on this trip. Maria just wanted Tex to get back into the business with her family so they could prosper again. She had no idea how long Joe would be held in the Mexican prison.

We drove off with Maria and her kids waving goodbye from their yard. This time our car was heading away from the border on a paved two-lane highway that went off into the distance from the village. Tex pointed out the bullfighting arena as we passed it. I had been looking at the broken down cars on the streets, trash scattered everywhere, houses needing paint, and dogs that looked like they were starving. Everything seemed to be covered in yellow dust. This was Mexico.

I drove the car, Tex rode *shotgun* and Fernando rode in the back seat. Fernando had put a footlocker into the trunk before we left the house and I figured that it was for carrying the pot. It was a two-lane paved road with grass creeping in on both sides. After driving for about ten miles, we came upon a small guard station. A wooden board with faded red and white stripes kept cars from proceeding without showing papers to the guard first.

By then it was late in the afternoon and the sun was going down in the distance. The little guardhouse was in silhouette – black against the yellow-orange sky. As we approached a guard came out the door with a flashlight in his hand. He wore a uniform and hat that reminded me exactly of what I had seen Nazi officers wear in the movies. Another guard followed him out and, when we stopped in front of the gate, one of them came up to the passenger window and the other walked around the back of the car. Tex spoke Spanish to them in a friendly voice and Fernando kept quiet.

I could barely see their faces since the only light was from our headlights on the car and an oil lantern that was hanging on the porch of the station. They had no electricity that far out. When I did get a glimpse of their faces, I could see that although Tex was talking very nice, they looked extremely serious and concerned about what we were up to.

Tex whispered to me, "Watch this."

Neither of the men had yet to say anything to Tex. He handed him the registration for the car, his driver's license, and a folded $20 bill.

The guard looked down at his hand, saw the money, and nodded at his partner who was shining a flashlight onto the $20 bill. He handed the papers back to Tex without looking at them and opened the gate for us to proceed. No smiles. No thank you's, just an open gate into the real Mexico. We pulled through and kept driving into the warm night air. There was little traffic on the road that night, but occasionally a large truck would roar by us heading towards the border. I wondered how many of those trucks were carrying pot. We drove another half hour and came upon another guardhouse.

"Checkpoint Numero Dos," Tex said softly, as I slowed the car down to stop.

The same routine transpired and, driving through the gate again, I realized that these two identical encounters with the guards were all part of this unspoken dance between the Mexican police and drivers in Mexico. When we drove off, I asked Tex about the Mexican police.

"So, how does all this work in Mexico?" I asked. "The guard stations are out here in the middle of nowhere. How do these guys get paid?"

"They don't exactly," Tex explained. "They're all paid by the public directly. In fact, the police in Villa Fuentes have to pay to get the jobs!"

"What?" I said.

Tex motioned to the backseat. "Tell him, Fernando,"

"These guards are not paid at all, amigo," Fernando told me. "They get the money from the cars. Poor people don't have to pay much. Gringos, well that's a different story. Twenty dollars is the going rate for Gringos. The guards will mess with you and your car until you figure it out. They won't ask you for money. In our town, someone who wants to become a policeman saves his money, and maybe with his family's help, gets enough to buy a position in the local police force. Villa Fuentes only has two policemen and they both had to pay off the mayor to get the job."

"So why would someone buy a job?" I asked. "There can't be that much money in it."

"No, there's not a lot of money in it, but it is regular money," Tex said.

Then Fernando started talking again. "And there are not that many ways to make a living in a small town like that. If you're not born with money, like all the rich families that live up the hill, then you are either a cop or a criminal. I didn't want to be a cop so here I am, working to feed my family and help all our relatives survive who live up in the mountains."

"Wow," I said. "Man, it was different where I grew up in San Antonio."

"Si, amigo," Fernando went on. "I went to school in Del Rio so I know about that. I just don't know how to change anything here. My family sent me to a good school but when my father was taken, I had to return to take care of them. My mother can't do it by herself. We don't know if my father is ever coming back. No way I could leave them."

"Hey, man, I didn't mean anything..." I began, trying to apologize for comparing my life with his.

"I know," Fernando said. "Esta buenos, amigo."

We all got quiet for a while and just kept driving, but I had no idea where we were headed or exactly how far we had to drive.

We traveled on a fairly flat terrain coming from the Rio Grande Valley, and then started climbing steadily. It was dark and the sharp curves in the road made me nervous. We would enter a village, slow down, and without seeing a living soul, drive on through and out as if it wasn't even there. Town after town went by as we drove south, deeper into the central mountains of Mexico.

We drove all night. Or, I should say, I drove all night. It started feeling like I worked for Tex. He had that attitude from the day we left California for Texas and it was starting to get to me. Tex treated Fernando that way, too, but he had known Fernando ever since he was a baby and would always treat him like a kid. I wasn't a kid, nor was I Tex's friend. We were just business associates, so to speak. And I was on a dangerous and risky adventure with this guy.

I kept telling myself that when this crazy trip was over, I was going to parlay my new Tex and Mexico pot source into a big business for Abby, Sunny and me. Tex could stay in Texas and I could meet him halfway between Texas and California to exchange pot for money. Then I could sell it for big bucks back in LA to my friends. A perfect plan! I thought to myself. I could do that for quite some time and get away with it. It sounded like *the good life* to me.

We finally reached our destination -- a place where I could stop driving and get a night's sleep. Aguascalientes, Mexico. It means *hot waters* in Spanish, which was ironic because I felt like I was in *hot water* at that moment.

The city most likely had some natural hot springs nearby. The main road going through Aguascalientes was paved, as were a few of the other streets. It looked like it could be a fairly large town. It was dark and only a few people were walking along the streets. All the homes and businesses were closed and boarded up for the night. We watched one lone taxi cross our street in the distance ahead.

Fernando's voice rang out from the backseat. "Turn right on the next street!"

I made the turn. The road changed to dirt quickly and the Fairlane created a big dust cloud behind it.

Fernando told me where to pull over. "This is it. On the right. The yellow building. It's a hotel."

I stopped the car on the side of the hotel. Fernando went inside and quickly came back out.

"Up these stairs," he motioned.

We locked the Fairlane and dragged our things up the stairs to the second floor of the hotel. The stairs were on the outside of the wooden, two-story building and our car was parked at the foot of the stairs, on the dirt street. I couldn't see well in the dark but it looked like someone was curled up and sleeping under the stairs.

The next morning, Fernando told us he had to be gone for a couple of days to talk to people in the mountains. Tex and I couldn't go this time. We agreed and stayed back as he walked off down the street. Fernando didn't talk a lot and used facial expressions much of the time to show how he felt. Today his look was serious. No big white smile coming from under his thin, black mustache. Tex and I both told him to go ahead and we would wait for him at the hotel.

"Good luck, amigo. Stay safe," Tex said in a low voice.

---

Tex and I waited for two days. During the day, I roamed the blocks near our hotel, never wanting to get too far into the rest of the town. I obviously needed to be available if Fernando was to return all of a sudden. It was a very quaint town from what I could tell. There were mostly homes of poor people along the streets but I was sure that behind some of the stucco walls and heavy wooden doors, there had to be people with money. I never saw another Anglo person in the town during our stay, but I did see a gringo couple drive by in a Toyota Land Cruiser one afternoon. The couple looked like they were on an African Safari. They didn't even look my way and didn't slow down.

So there I was sitting at the top of the stairs watching the street scene below. Tex was in the room taking a nap. An old woman was selling live chickens under a big tree nearby. She had them hanging upside-down from the tree. I looked at those chickens hanging by their claw feet. I thought that buying live chickens would be good assurance that they were not spoiled, but felt sorry for the animals.

There was not one person selling tourist items like those sold in the Texas border towns. There were no tourists in this town to sell to. Aguascalientes felt different. It was better than the border towns I was familiar with. It was a real Mexican town with people just going about their business. I had a lot of thoughts going through my head while I watched the woman sell two of her chickens to another woman who walked up.

All of a sudden, Fernando came walking around the corner of the hotel. I saw him before he saw me. "Hola, Fernando!" I called out.

"Hola, Harry!" Fernando answered as he continued to walk towards me.

He looked hot and tired but he was not a complainer so I didn't expect any. Climbing up the stairs, Fernando stopped to look around the streets before reaching the top, pulled back the screen door wide enough for me to enter behind him and we went inside. Tex rose from his nap, covered in sweat, but excited that Fernando had returned so soon. We had no idea how long we would have to wait for him.

Fernando spoke first, "Okay, here's how it's going to work, Tex. I have arranged for us to drive up into the mountains. We will have to go all the way to a small village at the top. That's where we will get the stuff."

Tex smiled before speaking, "When do we leave?"

"Tonight!" Fernando said. I was happy to hear that.

After waiting for two days, I just wanted to get this over with and get home. This one week to Texas and back had turned into several weeks, and we had been charging way more than expected on Ray's credit card –– money that had to be paid back. Mexico was cheap but I was still anxious to get home. Spending time with Tex had gotten really tiresome. I just wanted to be with Abby and Sunny again – like it used to be.

Soon we were driving out of town in the direction of the higher mountain range and away from the main highway. The road was narrower than the one we came into town on and not paved. After a few miles, the road narrowed to one lane. We never saw another car and just kept driving up higher and higher. The sun was going down behind the mountain as we drove. Fernando initially gave directions but once we were on this road, there were no directions needed.

"Just stay on this road, Harry," Fernando said.

After about two hours, we rounded a turn and came to a little village at the top of a hill. Our car stirred up plenty of dust as we slowed down. There was only one building where the dirt road widened. It reminded me of an old saloon, a place maybe I had seen in a western movie, or better yet, maybe on an episode of *Zorro*. It was dark and the entire scene was bathed in warm light coming from the arched openings on the front of the building. There were two old cars parked along the street but it appeared that the normal transportation to the saloon was on horseback since about six horses with saddles were tied out front.

I pulled up and stopped across the street from the saloon and away from the horses. Fernando gave me instructions from the backseat. "Turn off your lights. They don't like them. You guys stay in the car. I'll go inside."

The building didn't have any doors – just stucco arches. The yellow dust from the road went straight into the saloon. I could see a long, wooden bar with people leaning on it when I looked into the saloon from our car. Everyone was standing. There were no bar stools and no electricity up in the mountains, so the inside of the saloon was lit with oil lanterns hanging on the walls. One hung in the middle arch to light the entrance and the horses. Candles lighted the mirror and bottles behind the bar. It was all a warm yellow light that I thought was beautiful enough to paint. But we had other business on this day.

Fernando got out of the Fairlane and walked through one of the arches. He was in the saloon about ten minutes before coming out. A man followed him out and turned past the horses without looking our way. We sat in the car quietly and watched as he became a dark shape in the night and disappeared.

Fernando got back in the car and explained, "We'll just sit here for a few minutes, then drive down the hill.

"Okay," Tex said. "Just tell us when."

As we sat in the car waiting, Fernando told us what he had heard in the saloon.

"My uncle said that the *Federales* had just arrested several growers here about a week ago. There was a big shootout right here in the street. Several people were killed. Lots of bad things have been happening lately. No one is sure why the *Federales* are coming now. They used to leave us alone and worry about other things. We need to get out of here fast once we pick up the pot. The locals don't like you two coming here. They think you will bring trouble. My uncle is cool though. Everything will work out okay. Don't you worry."

We drove down the hill when Fernando said it was time and pulled over to a small, wooden house. I gave Fernando five $100 bills to pay for the pot. Everything was dark. Fernando got out, pulled the trunk from the back of the car and carried it into the darkness of the house. Moments later he came back out carrying the trunk on his back. He dropped it into the open trunk of the car, slammed it shut, and got back into the car.

"Let's go!" Fernando said, and off we went into the night back down the mountain. We finally made it back to the hotel where we had stayed the night before. Fernando went in the front of the building and came back with a room key. We got our things out of the car and carried them up the stairs again. Fernando pulled the trunk from the car and carried it on his back up the stairs and into our hotel room.

Fernando opened the trunk and showed us the contents. It was packed tightly with compressed kilos of pot that had been wrapped in clear plastic and taped. Even though it was tightly packaged the distinctive odor of fresh-cut marijuana filled the room. We all stood around the trunk as it sat open on the bed. Looking at each other, we all shook hands.

"Muy bueno!" Tex blurted out.

Fernando and I looked at each other and just grinned.

I spoke up next, "This is what we came here for. Finally, something is going right for a change."

"I told you it would be okay, right? Right?" Tex said.

"Yeah, yeah, so far so good," I agreed.

We woke up early and headed out of town. I saw a lot more of the countryside since it was daylight for most of the drive back to Texas. There were three checkpoints to cross again, only this time we were carrying fifty pounds of pot with us. Fernando said not to worry and that he would do it like he and his father always did, so that eased my mind.

As we started up a hill, Fernando said, "Pull over at the top, Harry. The checkpoint is about a mile ahead."

I stopped the car at the top of the hill like he said. We could see in both directions and no other cars were in sight. Fernando got out, walked to the back and pulled out the trunk. He slung it over his back, holding the handle over his shoulder with his right hand, and started walking into the brush. Turning back to us, Fernando yelled, "Drive on through and stop the car one mile past the checkpoint. I'll find you, amigos."

We did what Fernando said and drove on to the checkpoint. Tex handed the guard the customary $20 dollar bill and we pulled through. I stopped the car when the odometer read one mile. It was an hour of nervous waiting before Fernando came out from the mesquite trees, cactus, and tall dry grasses. He was sweating but didn't complain. Putting the trunk back in the car's trunk, he wearily climbed into the backseat.

"Let's go," Fernando said, and I put the pedal to the metal.

We repeated this technique three times until arriving back to Villa Fuentes at the end of the day. Maria heard our car and met us at the door. I was tired from the drive but Fernando had to have been totally exhausted. That wasn't a light trunk he carried on his back. I was impressed with the shape he must have been in to do a fast walk carrying that much weight through the brush.

"Tex," Fernando said, "I will meet you guys tomorrow night in the abandoned base just like we used to do, hombre. Si?"

"Sure," Tex said. "No problemo. It will be just like old times, amigo!"

It was turning dark already and Tex said we had to drive on the Mexican side again so we wouldn't be noticed crossing at Del Rio.

I was ready for some rest but didn't want to screw up things after all we had been through. Taking fewer chances sounded like a good plan. So we drove north out of town up to Del Rio, then back across that bridge and down to Eagle Pass on the U.S. side.

Checking into the same motel, Tex and I got some much needed sleep. We watched TV in the room all day and had to pay for an extra night since we didn't have anywhere else to go between then and nightfall. Once it got dark again, Tex and I drove out of the motel back in the direction of Del Rio.

About a mile out of town, Tex said, "Turn right up here where that old pavement comes out."

I watched closely and saw what he was talking about. Slowing down to a crawl, I turned into a partially paved street that had grass growing into it from both sides. Mesquite tree limbs poked themselves into the street and hung down from above, scratching the side of the car. Weaving our way through this obstacle course of pothole-filled pavement, we came to an intersection. Our headlights were all that lighted the area. It felt eerie and strange. It was extremely dark.

"Turn right here," Tex whispered. "Then go down to the end of this street, take another left and park right there. Fernando will come out of the bushes when he gets here."

As we waited, I asked Tex what this place was. He explained that it was an abandoned Air Force housing area. The homes had been torn down but they left the streets. Eventually, the plants would take it over and we were seeing that process about halfway through the job. We waited and waited. There was no moon that night. An hour went by.

"Hard to see without the moon out," Tex said. "I wonder if he got lost?"

"Well, I don't know," I said. "Do you normally have to wait this long?"

"No, that's what's bothering me. Something's wrong," Tex said. "The river isn't that far away. Fernando should be here by now."

"How long should we wait?" I nervously asked.

"No longer. Let's go. I don't like this." Tex said looking over at me.

I turned the car around and headed back to the entrance. I pulled out onto the highway and drove towards Eagle Pass. We turned into the motel parking lot and went back to our room. We didn't sleep well that night. Fernando and his family were extremely trustworthy according to Tex. That was comforting to me, but still something went wrong.

"Maria and her family wouldn't rip us off after all this," Tex said. "It's just not in their blood. They are good people. It had to be something else."

We took a chance and drove back across the border again to Maria's house. She and Fernando were both there waiting for us.

"I got lost!" Fernando quickly explained. " I couldn't see. It was too dark."

Tex let Fernando know that we were not upset. "That's what we figured."

"I will try again tonight," Fernando said. "I know what I did wrong. I will be there on time tomorrow night, Tex. You don't have to worry."

Again we drove up the Mexican side to Del Rio and back down to Eagle Pass and waited for the sun to go down. I did the same routine, pulling into the abandoned Air Force base and stopped at the designated spot. Again we waited and waited… and waited. Again Fernando didn't show. It was too dark.

"Why are we doing this a second time if there wasn't going to be moonlight again?" I asked.

"Oh shut up!" Tex said. "You're not helping anything by complaining. We are going to have to talk to Fernando again and figure out a new plan. But we can't keep going across this border and we have worn out our welcome crossing at Del Rio, too. Let me think for a minute."

As I let Tex ponder about our dilemma, I pulled out from the entrance again and on to the highway. I was about one hundred feet away from the entrance when suddenly bright red and blue flashing lights burst on behind me. Not knowing what else to do, I pulled over on the side of the highway. It must be some kind of cop. We didn't have anything illegal with us and I was driving fine, so I didn't think we could be in that much trouble.

The headlamps from the police car filled our car with light. I sat in the driver's seat and waited for the officer to approach the car. I could see him walking up in my rearview mirror. Tex sat calmly and didn't say a word. My window was rolled down and I pulled my wallet out to show my driver's license. I wondered what they would think of it being from California. Suddenly I felt a hard, cold, metal object pushing into the side of my left cheek.

"Put your hands on the steering wheel!" the officer shouted.

He opened my door and kept the gun to my head. The other officer did the same with Tex from the other side. A second car drove up fast and two more officers got out with guns drawn. The first two officers pulled us out, slammed us against the side of our car, and put handcuffs on our wrists behind us. Then shoving us forward, they placed their hands on our heads and pushed us into the back seat of two different patrol cars. I watched as they opened up the trunk and searched our car. After about an hour one of the officers came back to the car I was in.

"Get out," the officer said.

I did and he turned me around and took off the cuffs.

"You drive," he said to me and pointed to my car. "Follow us back to the station." Tex remained seated in their car.

Upon arriving at the border station, an officer took me into a separate room from Tex, did a body search and told me to sit down. After about twenty minutes, a detective in a suit came in and talked to me separately.

"Tell me, Harry," looking down at my driver's license, "What are you doing with this character? We know who he is and we know what he does. But we don't know you. How did you get mixed up with him?"

"I guess I made a big mistake," I said.

"My advice, son, is to get about as far away from this piece of shit of a person as you can. We can't charge you with anything this time, but everyone knows why you boys are down here. California, huh? I don't want to see your face anywhere near this border again -- understood?"

"Yes sir," I told him. "You won't see me again."

"Good," he said. "Now get with your friend over there and get the hell out of here."

Tex and I walked out of the border station, got back in our car, and headed to San Antonio. We just lost a hard-fought round in a dangerous game of smuggling. Or, did we win the game by not getting caught? I was such a novice and had no business playing the game at all. I had no idea what the next step would be, but Tex did.

He and I drove into San Antonio and pulled into a motel out on Fredericksburg Road on the other side of town from where my family lived. We checked in with Ray's card again, after filling the car up with gas at the gas station nearby.

We just sat there silently contemplating what to do next for a while with the TV on. He was on the bed and I sat in a chair. Then Tex said, "Give me the keys, Harry. I'm going down to the grocery store. We need a few beers to help us figure out what to do."

I pulled the keys from my pocket and tossed them over to him without a word. By that time, I was really sick of being with Tex and getting rid of him for a short while was a welcome relief. His *know-it-all* attitude was wearing me down and obviously his expertise at smuggling wasn't all he had said it was.

I missed Abby and my friends in LA and here I was in San Antonio, only a few miles from my family, stuck with this big, fat jerk in a cheap motel room, broke and without a plan. I sat there watching TV. An hour went by. Then another hour. Then another. I finally came to the realization that Tex wasn't coming back. He never did.

## Chapter Fourteen

Since my Ford Fairlane was conveniently in Tex's name, it couldn't even be reported stolen. There was one positive thing that would result from him stealing my car and leaving me stranded in the motel -- Tex was finally out of my life. I could go back to LA without him and somehow make everyone happy again. Surely he would never contact me again since he had stolen my car.

My parents didn't know that I was in San Antonio instead of Hollywood when I called them to come pick me up. It was just before the Christmas holidays so I told them that a friend in California was coming through Texas and offered me a ride. Mom and Dad drove over and picked me up within the hour and were thrilled to have their only son home for Christmas. I was still in shock from my smuggling boondoggle and was so glad to be with my family. They were very proud of me for starting a new life in California.

It had been over a year since I was sent to Hollywood to get away from drugs. Boy, did I blow that plan. After settling down at my parents' house, I finally made the call to Abby and told her what had happened.

"What the fuck!" Abby yelled out. "We're screwed!"

"I'll figure something out," I said. "It looks like I'm stuck here for the holidays."

Abby had an idea. "Why don't I come to Texas for Christmas? I'd like to meet my boyfriend's parents anyway."

"Wow. Okay. How are you going to get here?" I asked. Abby always had an answer for every situation. "Don't worry about it. I'll fly. Sunny will take care of Jack and I have enough money."

"Well, okay," I said. "Call me when you know when you are coming."

Abby called the next day to tell me her plans and was on a flight the day after. I borrowed my little sister's maroon

Buick Skylark and picked Abby up at the airport. It was so awesome to see her again.

Abby was a fast-talking little *pistol* of a New York City Jewish girl from Flushing. My parents were Southern conservative Christians, but treated everyone kindly regardless of their faith. My Mom and Dad were a little taken back by Abby, but wouldn't dare criticize her. They were rarely critical of me, even when they should have been. Abby and I slept together in my old bedroom, which my parents couldn't have been in favor of. Not a word was uttered about it though.

Even though Abby was Jewish, she loved the Christmas holidays and gladly participated in our family gathering. I had three sisters, two older and one younger. Being the only boy was a good place to be. My family would all agree that I was a bit spoiled growing up. All of my family loved each other and that love spread to my girlfriends. Abby was a very different girlfriend, but they still extended that kindness to her when we were together and I loved them for that.

After Christmas passed by it was time to figure out what to do next. I called Sunny to let him know everything was good and we would be home soon. He had spent Christmas with his family in Torrance where he grew up. Abby and I knew that we owed our friends back in Hollywood a lot of money and no telling how much had been charged to our friend Ray's credit card. We needed to do the right thing. But, how?

Abby and I were hanging out with some of the San Antonio people I was friends with before I started dealing. But that wasn't getting us anywhere. We had a big problem. I told Abby that if I could just get back down to Eagle Pass maybe I could somehow get the pot, sell some of it to my San Antonio friends for expenses, and we could make it back to LA and make things right. I felt like I at least needed to try. So a new plan was hatched.

Since I had borrowed my little sister's car a few times already, there didn't seem to be any harm in borrowing it one more time. I felt desperate and left San Antonio late in the afternoon without Abby. I didn't need to put her at any unnecessary risk. My little sister thought we were going to my friend, Gene's house that evening, so I dropped Abby off there and drove all the way down to Eagle Pass. When I got there, I hoped I was crossing the international bridge into Mexico for the last time.

The sun was low in the sky and things looked very still as I quietly rolled slowly through Villa Fuentes. Turning on the dirt street, I pulled up to Maria's house. It looked even more like a shack to me then.

I got out of the car and looked around. No one was outside. Two small mixed-breed dogs were lying in the dirt in the shade of an oak tree in Maria's front yard. They raised their heads as I walked by, but didn't seem to care one way or another that I was there. I walked up the dirt path and knocked on the door. The door quickly opened and there was Maria. She hadn't changed a bit.

"Hola, Harry!" Maria exclaimed. She appeared very glad to see me.

"Hola, Maria!" I said as we gave each other hugs and cheek kisses and walked into the house. I followed Maria straight to the back and sat at the table. The kids were playing on the dirt floor nearby.

Immediately Maria inquired about her old friend. "Where's Tex? Why are you not together, Harry?"

"I don't know," I honestly said. "He took my car one day and I haven't seen him since."

"Well, I haven't seen him either," she said. "Fernando got lost again."

"I know. That's what we figured."

"Harry," she said, "I have some bad news, my friend. We had to sell some of the pot to get by. It was Christmas... and the kids... you know." Her eyes filled with tears and she could hardly speak.

"I understand, Maria. It's okay. How much is left?" I asked.

Looking me straight in the eye she said, "We had to sell about half of it, Harry."

That meant that there was about 25 pounds left, which was certainly better than nothing. I was amazed that anything was left. Here these people were, sitting on fifty pounds of pot, not knowing if they would ever see us again. Plus, Fernando had risked his own freedom to help us without asking for anything. Six weeks had gone by. I really was thrilled that anything was left. It was also a huge relief that Tex hadn't come back down to take the rest of it for himself. The incident at the border must have really scared him. He was the type to lie low for a period of time before cranking up his smuggling again.

I asked Maria how she would suggest getting the pot across to the U.S. "So what do we do now, Maria? Is Fernando still available? Can we still get it across the border?"

"Yes," she said, "but we will do it differently this time. The river is very shallow right now, so we have more choices on where to cross. I will get Fernando and he will help you."

"Okay," I said. "What do you want me to do?"

Maria went on. "You need to drive back across the river tonight, then drive down towards Del Rio on the same highway. You know. But before you leave town there will be a turn to the left. The sign will read *Eagle Pass City Dump* and you just drive on in. There isn't a locked gate or anything that will get in your way. Drive slowly down to the spot where people have been dumping their garbage, turn off your lights and wait. It's not hard to see the spot. Fernando will be waiting and you will be on your way."

I thanked Maria for all her help and told her I hoped to see her again, although we both knew I probably wouldn't. Being a smuggler was way too stressful for me. Those days were over, but first there was business to finish before all was done. I drove off from Villa Fuentes, crossed the bridge without a search and drove to the city dump as instructed. I stopped the car, turned off my lights, and waited. After a minute or two Fernando came out from behind the piles of debris carrying a big suitcase. I stayed in the car. He opened my trunk, placed the suitcase in it and shook my hand through the window.

"Muchas gracias, amigo," I said to Fernando.

"De nada," he answered. "Good luck, amigo. Don't speed."

I turned the Skylark around, drove out of the entrance of the dump and looked both directions before turning on my headlights and pulling back on the road in the direction of San Antonio. It was a nerve-wracking drive back since the border patrol was always lurking about ready to stop any suspicious cars for a search. On that night, I saw none of them and I guess they never saw me. Driving straight on through to San Antonio with the pot, I arrived at my friend's house unscathed. I walked up to the door and knocked. Abby was anxiously waiting for me and swung open the door.

"You made it!" Abby exclaimed and gave me a huge hug. I squeezed her tight because none of this would have been possible without Abby's help.

"Yes," I told her. "Everything will be okay now."

I walked in, opened the suitcase and there was the prize. Abby, Gene, and I all just stood there looking at the wrapped bricks. It was twenty-five pounds of pot, just like Maria said it would be. Enough to get us back on our feet and pay our debts.

It took only a few days of selling lids before Abby and I had enough money to buy plane tickets back to LA. I called several of my old friends who smoked but were not dealers. They were very happy to see me and pick up some pot at the same time from Gene's house.

There was less security in those days and it wasn't that big of a risk to just check luggage with pot in it. It was my first time on an airplane. Sunny had borrowed a car to pick us up at the LA airport. We grabbed our baggage off the conveyer belt without a hitch and proceeded out the glass doors to find our ride. At first we didn't see Sunny, but soon heard his voice in the distance. "Hey, Harry!"

Abby was so short she couldn't see over the crowd, but I saw an arm waving out of a car window and then saw it was Sunny, who got out and had the trunk open when we reached the car.

"Man, it's good to see you two," Sunny said as we all exchanged hugs.

"Good to see you, too," said Abby.

"I'm so glad to be home with you guys again," I told them.

After throwing our bags into the trunk we drove out of LAX and home to Silverlake. Nothing had really changed while I had been gone, except the apartment was so much nicer without Tex in it. Sunny, Abby, and I sat together in the living room and talked for hours. At one point, we all stood up and just hugged. I told them all about the trip. Sunny didn't like trouble so it made him uneasy to hear about my Mexico ordeal. He put his hand up as if to say *stop* and just wanted to know what was going to happen next.

With tears in his eyes, Sunny explained that he was uncomfortable living in that apartment now. Tex drove off the girl Sunny had fallen in love with there and, after spending some time alone in the apartment while Abby and I were gone, he felt like we should all find another place to live. Sunny said the Silverlake apartment was starting to creep him out. To him, we were a threesome and he wanted us to stay together. Abby and I agreed with Sunny and decided to look for a new place. We all wanted a fresh start.

Abby made a few phone calls to our friends who had given me money for the trip. They didn't all come at once but by the second day home, we had given all of them the pot they had invested in. Ray drove over about three days later on his Indian. I told him what had happened on my trip and why I had to charge on his credit card so much. I was embarrassed.

"Tell you what," Ray said. "Those charges haven't started coming in yet. It sometimes takes a while for out-of-state charges. Just pay me as they come in each month. I'll bring 'em over. As long as I can pay the bill on time, I'm not going to worry about it."

That arrangement sounded great, so I agreed to pay the bill when Ray needed me to. With the money from the pot we had left, Abby, Sunny, and I could rent a new place, start selling lids again in Hollywood and pay Ray back completely what we owed him over time.

Now we needed a vehicle. Abby bought a newspaper from the corner store and found another Buick listed in the classifieds. Buicks were always the choice of my family because of my father was in the Buick business. I just needed some transportation and Buicks were pretty darn reliable. The seller brought the car right to our apartment that day and signed over the title. My new four-door sedan was big with faded blue paint and it was cheap enough at $500.

Once we bought the car, the three of us sat around the kitchen table with the classifieds again and Abby read the ads out loud. One rental sounded promising. It was in Hollywood and was part of a group of small one-bedroom bungalows arranged on either side of a courtyard. The three of us drove over to check it out. The address was 1518 N. Saint Andrews Place. The alley behind the complex was shared by a row of small shops on Hollywood Boulevard.

We parked and walked through the gate at the end of the courtyard. The first bungalow on the right had a small sign that said *Office*. Sunny and I started to look around while Abby knocked on the door of the office to ask if we could see the bungalow for rent. A narrow concrete sidewalk went down the middle of the courtyard and smaller sidewalks turned in to each bungalow entrance. A dry concrete fountain sat in the center of the courtyard and the bushes and plants within the complex made it so once you walked down the sidewalk of the courtyard, no one could see which door you went into or came out of. People who looked like us were walking around or sitting on their steps talking. Several of them said hello as we walked by.

"This place is perfect," I whispered to Sunny. "We can deal out of here all day long and not be noticed."

Sunny nodded his head up and down but didn't say anything. Soon Abby came walking up to us and had a key in her hand. She said the place cost $100 per month and the manager was pretty cool.

"Number 6," Abby said, while looking at the numbers on the bungalows, then pointed at one a few doors down on the right and said, "That one."

Abby, Sunny, and I looked over at the bungalow. It looked identical to the others. We walked up to it and Abby opened the door with the key. Sunny and I followed her in. It had a large front room and the entrance was centered on the front wall with tall windows on either side. A hallway was even with the entrance on the other side of the room and a kitchen door was at the far left corner of the room. The bedroom, bath, and closet were down the hall. The kitchen was in the back on the left. A nice little floor plan, except that we needed two bedrooms –– one for Abby and me, and one for Sunny.

The house was perfect for the three of us otherwise. Sunny said that he needed a bedroom because he was dating and girls wouldn't sleep with him unless he had a private space. Abby and I understood his problem but we didn't like it very much. Abby suggested that she and I put our mattress in the opposite corner from the kitchen at the back of the living room.

"Look, there isn't a window there and we can put up the Pier One tapestries we have and make a corner tent," Abby said.

"Okay, okay," I relented. "So you are cool with it, Sunny?"

"Sure. Let's do it!" he said.

So our little family walked back down to the office. Sunny and I stood outside in the courtyard while Abby rented the place. She came out and said, "We got it." After walking back to the car, I drove us back to Silverlake to pack. It didn't take long to make our move, especially with the large trunk of that Buick. We had accumulated a lot of big stuff that had to be hauled back down the Silverlake stairs and sidewalk steps to the street so it wasn't exactly an easy move. Some of the bigger furniture had to be strapped on the back of the car. Once our things were in, we began to decorate the place and put things in order.

Everything we owned was old. Some of our things were bought at Hollywood junk stores. Most of it came from the streets where people put things out for the garbage truck. Residents in Hollywood could put virtually anything out on the curb in front of their house and the garbage truck guys would pick it up. So furniture was easy to come by. It was an old-school recycling program before most people had even heard of such a thing.

We placed the sofa, large coffee table, and comfortable chairs on the left wall of the living area, just outside the kitchen door. The coffee table was made from our old wooden dining table. I took off the legs and sat it on several concrete blocks for support. The coffee table was used for eating and whatever else we needed it for. The table was surrounded by a sofa and several over-stuffed chairs, so plenty of friends could sit.

I built a wall of wooden shelves behind the sofa for all the stereo equipment, books and the small TV, although we didn't watch that much television back then. The choices of TV stations were very limited and the depressing Vietnam War was always on the news. Instead we enjoyed talking and listening to music together.

We created our tent-bed in the far corner of the living room as Abby had suggested and it worked out very well. Those tapestries imported from India made a great tent. I attached the corner with a cord going to the central light fixture and they hung down just outside the edges of the king-size mattress on the floor. I also stapled them to the inside wall to complete the effect of sleeping in a tent. We enjoyed the warm glow coming through the fabric when we were in the tent.

After finishing placing the furniture, Abby, Sunny, and I drove to the Safeway together and bought enough food to stock the refrigerator.

Since Abby and I had been gone from Silverlake for so long, we pretty much had to start all over with everything. We would take fifty dollars to the grocery store, buy most of what we needed and come home with ten full brown paper sacks of groceries. The three of us would laugh that no matter what we bought, it always averaged out to about five dollars per bag.

    We pulled the Buick down the alley to the back door of the house. This made unloading easy since we were able to carry groceries right in from the car to the kitchen. After unloading, I had to move the car back around to the front to find a parking spot on the street.

    Wednesdays were days the street sweeper would clean the even-numbered side of the street. Thursdays were for the odd-numbered side of the street. It was illegal to park on the side of the street between certain hours when the city workers needed to clean. The police wrote tickets constantly as people forgot about having to move their cars to the other side of the street. I was no exception and got numerous tickets for forgetting what day it was and leaving the car parked on the wrong side. My car was often parked a block away and, some weeks, we hardly drove the car at all because it was easier to just walk a block or two for quick groceries.

    Abby and I liked to walk a few blocks away to buy Saki from the little corner liquor store. We also just liked walking down the street and mingling with the constant flow of street people. It was fun watching all the action and observing the crazies that Hollywood was known for.

    One beautiful summer day, the three of us were packing up the car for a trip to the beach at Malibu. The Buick was parked in the back alley of the cottage and we carried stuff out through the back door and loaded it up. I hopped in the driver's seat and started up the car. Abby and Sunny got in and, all of a sudden, a police car roared down the alley and stopped right in front of us. We were all thinking that this was just another time when the cops harassed the hippies and sat there quietly as one approached the car.

    The deputy asked for my driver's license and I politely handed it to him. He took it back to his car and called it into his office. Those were the days before the police had laptops and could pull up your record in a few keystrokes. He came back to the car and asked me to get out. I did so and he handcuffed me, took me to his car and *Poof* –– off I went to jail. A warrant had been issued because of my unpaid parking tickets. I didn't know they were such a big deal!

Abby got help from one of the neighbors and bailed me out before nightfall. I was in a holding tank. It wasn't that bad. I went in front of a judge before they let me out and promised to pay the tickets. It was one of those big spoilers for what could have been a wonderful beach day.

---

The days flew by and people came and went, usually with a lid tucked into their pants or their purse. We did a lot of sunbathing around the courtyard fountain. Those were good days, relaxing and fun.

My trusty dog, Jack, loved the courtyard too and would walk freely from door to door seeing if anyone would give her a snack, which they usually did. Everyone loved Jack, as well as two of her sweet puppies that we kept, Dizzy and Dopey.

Dizzy had long wispy black hair like Jack. Dopey was a bit larger with short hair. He was the most beautiful dog in the courtyard with an equal amount of large black and white patches. Dogs were everywhere in the courtyard and had just about as much fun as we humans did. None of them ever thought of running off.

Jack left quite a legacy of dogs in LA in the three years she lived there and, yes, we should have had her fixed. I get that now. I think she had eight litters in all. I will have to say that after fifty years, there must be tens of thousands of little Jack's running around by now. Jack would live to be seventeen years old in Texas before dying of cancer. I've rescued and loved many dogs after Jack, but no dog would ever really replace her.

We made a lot of friends at that bungalow. A couple with a newborn baby lived just across the courtyard from us. Dee and Bill were their names. They were a little older than we were and both of them were a little strange. Dee was a large girl with a very light complexion and long red hair, which she usually had pinned up on her head. Dee often wore a big T-shirt that covered most of her body and never wore a bra.

Bill was skinny with short, black hair and a mustache. Bill was a filmmaker. He scratched out a living making pornographic "B" movies. Dee was one of his porn stars and sometimes they would have filming sessions in their house. We didn't really think much of it then. Hippies accepted everyone without trying to judge them. Dee loved to talk and laugh. Bill was less vocal and had a deep voice. He had a somewhat sinister looking smile and an odd sense of humor.

An older guy that called himself, *Crystal Jim* lived by himself to the left of Dee and Bill's cottage. He had short hair that was turning gray with a long mustache that hung down like a western gunslinger. Jim had grown up in Crystal City, Texas, and dressed like an old Texas rancher, complete with cowboy shirt, leather belt, and worn-out cowboy boots. He liked to call me *Homey* because I was also from Texas, although I had never been to his hometown that was near the Mexican border.

Crystal Jim was what we called a *speed freak*. Every day he gave himself injections of crystal meth, which we called *speed*, wherever he could find a decent vein -- arm, hand, leg, wherever.

It was a source of pride to say that neither Sunny, Abby, nor I had ever shot up anything. All we did was smoke pot and occasionally take a tab of acid. Crystal Jim was something else altogether and boasted of our friendship because of our Texas connection. He was really a pretty straight-up kind of guy and I enjoyed being neighbors because he was such an interesting character. I put up with his drug abuse just to talk about interesting topics with him. He made his living dealing speed. Some pretty shady and desperate looking characters came and went from his place. I never saw him eat. He was thin as a rail.

Crystal Jim's bungalow was filled with junk he had found on the streets. Some of it was fairly valuable. Every inch of wall space was covered and floor space was at a minimum with antique furniture in stacks. He had a large collection of sterling silver and pewter bowls, cups, and flatware hanging around like fish on a stringer. When Jim needed some money, it was off to a pawnshop. Every nook and cranny had something in it. When I walked over to visit, he would pull out his latest find and explain what it was. Crystal Jim was a master at refinishing furniture and showed me many of his techniques.

On the night before trash day in Hollywood, the curbs were crammed full of people's discards. Jim would start out on his collecting journey about midnight when the streets were quiet and had less traffic. He would shoot up with speed, grab his grocery cart, and take off on his search. Crystal Jim kept asking me to go with him, but to start something like that at midnight seemed a bit ridiculous to me. My marijuana high didn't exactly match his speed high. While I was mellowing out, he was buzzing full blast. I made a good listener and that was about it.

One night I gave in and went *trashing* with him. The speed Jim shot up gave him a huge energy boost. My legs literally couldn't keep up with his pace and, hell, I was young and still in fairly good shape.

The part of Hollywood where our bungalows sat was at the base of the Hollywood Hills. Jim would push his shopping cart up and down the hilly streets stopping at pile after pile of people's trash only momentarily to see the nature of their castoffs. Tenants who were evicted would have their belongings put out on the curb by the landlord.

Crystal Jim had a special knack for deciding whether to dig deeper into the piles and explained his theories to me as we walked.

"It's just bad karma to take anything from those people," Jim said. "They may come back for it." He could tell by the stuff that they had been evicted and would just walk on by.

I stopped following him that night after about two hours of hiking. He almost had his shopping cart full by then but wanted to go on.

"Hey, man," I called out, "I'm getting tired. Going to call it a night!"

Jim begged me to stay with him. "Homey, I have a feeling something is just over that next hill. Just a little more."

But I held my ground. "No dude, I'm heading back. I need a joint."

Jim waved his arm without looking back at me and yelled, "Well, okay, Homey. See you sometime tomorrow."

I headed back to the bungalow. I stopped, turned back around, and watched Crystal Jim's dark silhouette reach the top of the hill. Then he disappeared. I thought about how powerful speed was and knew that Crystal Jim wasn't going to live that long at the rate he abused his body. He was an addict and with all his wrinkles and dark rings around his eyes, he probably looked a lot older than his actual age.

I had run across addicts before and tried to keep my distance. But Jim was so likable. I hated to watch his health go south, but didn't really know how to help him. Several times when we were talking, he would pull out a needle, cook some speed in a spoon with a cigarette lighter, and shoot up without skipping a beat of the conversation. Then just seconds after the injection, he would experience the rush from the speed. Jim fell over several times as if fainting and I would lift him back up on the sofa and wait until he woke before I left to go home. That usually only took a few minutes. After I made sure he was okay, I would make an excuse to leave because the conversation often became unpleasant after he did the speed.

Crystal Jim had a powerful personality and he acted like he was the older and wiser person that was teaching me about life. It was impossible to argue with Crystal Jim because to him that type of relationship was plain boring.

Sunny and Abby stayed clear of Crystal Jim's house and wanted me to also. I didn't go over there often, but I still enjoyed visiting with him. Even though the old coot repeated himself a lot, I still liked listening to his stories and talking about all the things in his house that had been collected from the streets. Most of his furniture was restored since he knew furniture making from his younger days. Crystal Jim would shoot up speed and spend countless hours rubbing and scraping a piece of furniture until it looked perfect. Speed freaks rarely got enough sleep and sometimes would be awake for days until crashing into long hours of sleep to make up for it.

The people who came to Crystal Jim's house did so only to buy or sell speed. It was easy to tell if they were speed freaks. Their eyes were wild looking, their teeth rotting, and skin rashes covered their faces. Visitors to Crystal Jim's house usually wore long sleeves and long pants to hide the places they shot their drugs. I was sad for Jim and slowed down my visits just because it wasn't so interesting anymore. I felt sorry for him. But I didn't know how to save him from himself.

After a few of months living at St. Andrews Place, there were many people who would come and go from our house on a regular basis, primarily to score some pot, but they were different than Jim's people because they weren't addicts. Visitors to our house were good people who just liked to get high. We had a lot of fun with our unusual group of friends.

---

Sunny still had his job at Studio Instrument Rentals. Bands playing in clubs and auditoriums in LA would rent equipment from SIR instead of hauling their own around the town. Roadies were hired when the bands toured, but not when they just had a gig locally. Sunny was one of the guys who would deliver and set up equipment prior to the band's performances, often setting up big organs and rolling in grand pianos.

Once he asked me if I wanted to go with him to make a delivery of speakers that a musician had purchased for his home recording studio. Sunny came by the house in the white company van and I climbed in. Two large boxes sat in the back of the van.

"I've got a surprise for you," Sunny said. "We're on our way to Neil Young's house."

"No shit?" I said. "That's very cool."

We drove out Sunset towards Santa Monica, then up Highway 1 a little ways and turned on Topanga Canyon Road to reach the house. The address we were looking for was 611 Skyline Trail. Sunny turned on one of the roads and started the steep climb up to the top of the mountain. The van had a difficult time going up the steep driveway that led to Neil Young's house. At the top, Neil Young's driveway opened up to a gigantic gravel area that could hold about ten cars. We stopped in front of his two-story California-style redwood house.

Neil Young moved to this house in Topanga in 1968 after leaving the band *Buffalo Springfield*. He was quoted as saying, "I just needed to get out to the sticks for awhile and relax." Neil had used a $17,000 advance on his first solo album to buy the property. In his biography he wrote, "Morning on the deck began with coffee overlooking the canyon, watching everything start to move below as the day unfolded."

The famous musician enjoyed breakfasts at the Canyon Kitchen Café, served to him by a strawberry blonde waitress named Susan Acevedo. He said the atmosphere in the cafe was always stimulating. Neil and Susan would marry six months after meeting.

Neil Young heard us driving up, came out of the house, and walked up to the van. Two cars were parked over on the left side. We could hear music from outdoor speakers mounted on the structure. It was his private recording studio with a view to die for. I sat there for a moment just taking it in. I could see all the way to the Pacific Ocean from his driveway.

"Hey, guys," Neil said, walking towards the van, "How's it going?"

"Great," Sunny said. "Had a hard time getting up the hill, but we made it."

"So you have my…" Neil Young stopped in mid-sentence and yelled into the studio door, "A little more base, Steve!"

"Okay!" came the voice of his sound engineer from inside the studio. "How's this?"

Neil listened for a moment and then yelled, "That's better, Steve. Just give me a minute and I'll be in!"

By then Sunny and I had gotten out of the van to open up the back. Sunny pulled out one of the boxes, set it on the ground, and opened up the end with his pocketknife. I held the box while he pulled the speaker out. Neil looked at the speaker and said, "Nice looking. Now if it sounds better than the last set I put in this studio, I'll be very happy."

"I hope so," Sunny told Neil.

Young grabbed the large speaker Sunny had pulled from the box and carried it into the studio. Sunny and I unpacked the second box and I carried it up to the studio door and he took it out of my hands.

"Why don't you guys come in and check this out?" Neil said.

"Sure," Sunny said, and we followed him in.

The view was spectacular through the large windows of the control room. The other room was dark and padded for soundproofing. Sunny had been in a lot of recording studios due to his job and was extremely impressed by the beauty of what Young had built next to his home.

"I don't leave this place much anymore," Neil told us. "I can do a lot of my own music here and it's so peaceful. Canyon life, you know."

"I get it," I said, and we all laughed a little.

After a few minutes, Sunny said we needed to head back, and after shaking hands with Young and his engineer, we threw the empty boxes into the van and took off for Hollywood. I thought of how it must feel to have enough money to build such a cool place to create your music. Yet Neil Young seemed like one of us when we met him and that was comforting.

## Chapter Fifteen

Jonathan King, also known as *The King*, was Tall Tom's acid connection in LA. Tall Tom had bought the acid from him when he was arrested coming off the plane in San Antonio. Tall Tom had given me The King's phone number to put in the little black address book I carried and I decided to use it.

We needed a contact for good LSD because most of what was circulating around LA was junk. The King owned a huge drug paraphernalia store on the corner of Hollywood Boulevard and Las Palmas called the Psychedelic Supermarket. It was the largest head shop in the country.

The King made a lot of money and had a lot of toys. One of his hobbies was *funny car* racing. He had a long, silver rail dragster in the driveway outside his Coldwater Canyon home. When racing, he wore a shiny, silver fireproof suit that covered his entire body, including a hood for his head with glass in front to see through.

The King was known for going to Hollywood parties actually dressed like a king. He even had a suit of armor he would sometimes wear, but most of the time he paraded around the Strip dressed something like King Henry the Eighth.

I called Jonathan King and was surprised when he answered the phone. I explained who I was and got directions to his house. He told me to come over the next evening. I drove out to his house alone because there was no need to put Abby in any danger. I really didn't know what to expect.

I parked my car in his driveway and walked past the dragster. It had a custom cover over it to protect the body from the weather. I knocked on the door and Jonathan answered. The King was a thin man and stood about six-foot-four inches. He had a long, thin face that was exaggerated by his long, thin black hair, mustache and beard. His face looked dark and rough, maybe even scarred. I wondered if he had been burnt in a racing accident.

"Come on in," he said in a very deep voice, "I'm Jonathan."

"Hi, I'm Harry," I said, as we shook hands and he gestured to come in.

His house was on the side of the canyon road and had at least two stories and maybe another below because it hung off the side of a cliff. I followed him into the house. No one else was there that I could tell and it was quiet.

"Come on up here," he said walking down a narrow hall to our left. "That's where I do my business."

He pointed to a wooden ladder and started to climb it. I looked up and saw that the ladder went to some kind of loft above the living area. Following him up, I sat down on a pillow on the floor of the loft, across a small table from him. Large pillows and tapestries covered most of the loft, along with empty food containers and clothes that were strewn around. There was a syringe kit tucked over in the corner. It was sticking out from under a pillow just enough for me to tell what it was. I was getting tired of running into so many addicts who were dealers, but I didn't say anything about it.

Jonathan wanted to know about our mutual friend. "So, how is Tall Tom?"

"I haven't talked to him in a long time. I kinda lost track of him," I said.

"I hope he's okay," Jonathan said. "I like that guy."

"So do I."

"Tall Tom has the funniest laugh," Jonathan said laughing.

"Yeah, man. He really does. I miss that," I said with a smile.

"So, what can I do for you?" Jonathan asked. "Are you looking to buy something?

"Yeah, I'm looking for some good acid. I'm living out here now and Tall Tom said to look you up if I ever wanted to score some stuff at a decent price."

Just then, The King pulled a pistol out that he had tucked in his belt and put it on the carpet. I wasn't sure if that meant anything or if it was just uncomfortable and he decided to remove it. I didn't react and acted like I didn't notice.

"Well," he said, "I don't have a lot right now, but I can give you what I have and get more whenever you need it."

"Okay, Cool. What do you have?" I calmly asked.

Jonathan started rattling off names of drugs. "I've got about fifty hits of Sunshine, a hundred or so hits of Purple Barrels and I don't know, maybe two hundred Black Molly's… and … and some other stuff. I'm not exactly sure, but we can look."

He seemed super distracted by something, but I kept talking trying to get this over with. I had a funny feeling that I shouldn't be there any longer.

I quickly blurted out. "How much for the hits of Sunshine and the Purple Barrels?"

"Uh, I'll take a dollar per hit for both of them," he said.

That price sounded great to me. "I'll take all the Sunshine and Purple Barrels."

"Okay," The King said, "They're in the kitchen so let's go back down and I'll count them out for you."

"Terrific, 'cause I really need to get going," I said.

"Sure, you have the cash on you?" The King asked.

"Yep, no problem," I told him. "This should be easy."

We climbed down from the loft and I reached into my front pocket and pulled out my wallet. I counted the bills and handed them over to him. He took the stack of bills from my hand without looking at or counting it, and put the money in an old cigar box that was next to him on the kitchen counter. Jonathan reached up to the cabinet above the sink, pulled out a fishing tackle box, placed it on the counter and opened it.

Inside I could see a lot of little bags and prescription bottles. He reached in and pulled a couple of packs out. He held the first one open and pushed it at me to look inside. I looked at the yellow tabs and they appeared to be the real thing so I nodded. He did the same with the second bag and I saw the purple-colored cylinder-shaped tabs.

"Want me to count them?" The King asked.

"No, I trust you," I said.

I took both bags out of his hands and placed them in my jeans pocket.

"Cool, man," he said.

I turned toward the door ready to get the hell out of there. "Well, I gotta go."

"Okay," he said, "That's cool."

He followed me through his living area to the front door.

"Thanks, man," I said, as I started to walk out.

"Wait," The King said, and he quickly shoved his arm out in front of my chest as if to hold me back.

Then he stepped out of the door ahead of me, looked down both sides of the street and stepped aside for me to leave. I took the hint and walked on down the sidewalk to my car. Everything was wet. It must have rained while I was inside.

"Call me anytime," The King said.

"I will, man. Thanks," I said as I got in my car.

I drove home without any problems, put the acid under my mattress for safekeeping then told Abby that we could sell the acid easy for two dollars a hit and double our money, which is what we did for the next two weeks. Most of the acid, she sold herself. Abby was a good little businesswoman. You learn all about hustling for money growing up in Queens.

After getting the easy money from that sale, it was hard not to visit The King to score at wholesale prices. But having gone back two more times, I finally decided that going to his house again was too risky so I stopped going. I never saw or heard from The King again. We were not really friends and I'm sure he could have cared less that Tall Tom's friend didn't return.

———

One of the guys who used to come over to our cottage was Sean O'Malley. Sean was Irish and made sure we knew it right away. He was a little older than all of us and had been raised in the Hollywood Hills by his mother. Sean's complexion was pasty white and his head was shaved smooth. His original hair color must have been blonde because his eyebrows were blonde. Sean was in his seventh year studying martial arts, Tai Chi to be exact, and loved to show off his moves on every visit. Our Irish friend explained that, upon reaching the end of his seventh year, his teacher said he could begin to speed up the Tai Chi moves. So far, Sean had been doing all the moves in slow motion. He explained that the moves would become so natural and fast after doing them for so long that his body would become a lethal weapon.

Sean boasted that a Tai Chi master is so fast he could bust his fist through a person's chest, rip their heart out, and show it to them before they die. That didn't exactly make us want to become a Tai Chi master. Sean was also a vegetarian and didn't take any drugs at all. He stopped doing drugs after starting his Tai Chi training, but wasn't critical of those of us who still did.

I gave Sean a ride up to his house one day when his bicycle broke down and thought how cool it would be to have a house like that one in the Hollywood Hills. Sean's house sat on a hillside, as did many of the houses in the Hollywood Hills, with part of it sitting on the land next to the winding street and part of it hanging over the cliff supported by steel pipes and braces. The view of LA was spectacular from his windows.

The house had been his mother's. She had moved in with her boyfriend in Beverly Hills and left him to live in the house alone. Sean didn't have a steady girlfriend but, according to him, he dated lots of girls. We never saw him with one. His huge bed was round and elevated in the middle of the living area. It had a large round mirror with a wooden frame attached to the ceiling above it. He bragged about how great sex was on the bed looking up in the mirror. I was impressed and wondered if I would ever have anything that cool.

Martial arts weapons were hung all around the living area. Tai Chi was what Sean lived for and all he talked about. During his visits to our home, all conversation stopped. He had to have all the attention in the room. Sean never stayed very long so it didn't really matter to us. He was so interesting! People did enjoy listening to his stories and watching him demonstrate his moves and would return back to their conversations when Sean announced he was in a hurry and needed to go.

Sean didn't have many friends, but he did have one friend from Texas that he said we might want to meet, someone who also dealt the *good* drugs and was looking for more contacts to work with. Sean didn't want any part of it himself, but was just putting two people together that he trusted. Abby and I said we would like to meet this Texan.

Sunny didn't participate in any dealing, just Abby and I, but Sunny didn't care what we did as long as he felt safe. Lots of people were doing it in Hollywood to make a living, or just for some extra money, so it didn't seem like such a big deal to us at the time.

One day, Sean brought over his friend Texas Mike. Lots of people had a nickname in those days. No one cared what people's last names were, so Mike became Texas Mike because he was from Texas, where else? Of course, I was from Texas myself, as was Crystal Jim across the courtyard, but Texas Mike was from Dallas and had a very distinct Dallas accent.

Texas Mike was a tall, well-built, and handsome guy with long, dark brown hair and a full beard. We hit it off really well and he started coming over often, sometimes to do a deal with us, and sometimes just to hang out and smoke some dope.

Texas Mike dealt in both pot and cocaine. My friends and I had snorted a little coke, but it wasn't something we sold or did very often. Texas Mike had a contact that had a considerable amount of it so he always had some and would share a little with us when he came over. One afternoon, Texas Mike came by and wanted me to *front* him a pound of pot so he could deal some lids and make some quick money. He had been in a financial bind lately and needed some help. Abby and I agreed that we could do that. He paid us for a portion of it when leaving our house, but still owed us a few hundred dollars for the rest.

   Three weeks went by before Texas Mike dropped by again. Abby had gone into downtown LA with friends and Sunny was at work. I told him that we needed our cash really soon. Texas Mike said that he didn't have the cash, but did have an ounce of cocaine if I would take that instead. I thought that we could probably make a good profit on an ounce and took the deal. I also thought it would be nice to have a little cocaine around the house to enjoy ourselves. Sex was spectacular with a little cocaine and I thought Abby would like that too.

   In the following days and weeks, we all snorted a little cocaine and enjoyed it. I did more than Sunny and Abby. In fact, I was doing more and more every day. We stopped selling it because the freaks who came by to buy it were not your typical pot smokers. They were a different sort of people –– hyper, paranoid, and definitely not one of us. Dealing cocaine made us extremely nervous. We started to realize just how dangerous it was to be exposing ourselves to this dark side of Hollywood. When a buyer came by, one of us would just say it was all sold. That did the trick, although we still had about a quarter of an ounce. So the three of us just used it ourselves and I used it more than my fair share.

   It was hard to stop because the more cocaine I did, the more I needed to get high. Its effects didn't last very long so when the high started wearing off, I would just put out another line of white powder on a mirror. After arranging the powder carefully in a neat row with a razor blade, I used a rolled-up dollar bill to snort it into my nose. It was quick and easy and I could still function fine while feeling like I was on top of the world.

   I was sitting in my usual position on the sofa when Sunny and Abby walked up together and asked if they could have a serious talk with me. We had had talks before, trying to somehow recover from whatever trouble we had gotten ourselves into. But Sunny and Abby had never asked to talk to me together like that. I said I would be glad to talk and followed them out the front door of the cottage. We sat closely together on the concrete steps in front.

Abby and Sunny told me that the coke was becoming a problem and that my personality had changed from using it. Neither of them liked how I had been acting. Nothing had seemed different to me, but I listened to them. I trusted and loved them both. I knew in my heart that they were right and it took a lot for them to confront me with it. I apologized to both of them and explained I didn't know the coke was affecting me like that. I promised to stop, and did -- cold turkey. They were relieved and we three sat there on the steps and hugged for a long time.

I called Texas Mike the next day and asked him to help me sell the last of the coke. He was glad to exchange it for money now that he had some cash.

So that was the end of my cocaine run. I was lucky to have good enough friends to sit me down and have that talk. I was becoming one of those people who we had decided not to deal with anymore. It was hard to notice the change myself. I just thought maybe I was moving too fast, but it was the personality change that threw me. From then on, I went from thinking cocaine was cool, to feeling sorry for people with the addiction. Eventually they would all crash and burn from the cocaine.

---

Abby, Sunny, and I loved our trips to the beach. It was about a thirty-minute drive from Hollywood down Sunset to Santa Monica if you hit all the lights right. We usually kept driving north right to Malibu on the coast highway or to our favorite stop, Zuma Beach.

Once it was just Abby and me. She didn't have a bathing suit and, looking back, I'm not sure she ever learned how to swim. The water in California was too cold for us anyway.

Abby wasn't the bathing beauty type. She usually wore blue jean cutoffs and baggy T-shirts at the beach. Like most hippies, I didn't have a swimsuit either. Surfers had board shorts and hippies had cutoffs, but if given the choice hippies would have preferred skinny-dipping.

On this warm California day, we parked in one of the parking spaces along the highway at Zuma and walked down the dunes. Abby and I strolled about a hundred yards up the beach away from the traffic and past some large rocks to a place that looked more private. No one was in sight.

Jack was with us, of course. She always went where we went and never needed a leash. As usual, she ran up and down the beach chasing the gulls. They would fly up when she came by and then land back down at the same spot until Jack came running back towards them.

The Pacific Ocean was deep blue and beautiful. The sky was light blue with a few puffy clouds slowly moving from left to right. It was late morning by the time we arrived and the sun was beginning to warm the air and sand. We spread out our beach towels in a nice spot near the edge of the surf and close to the rocks.

I took off my T-shirt to get some sun on my chest and laid back. Abby took off her T-shirt and did the same. She didn't think anything of it and I figured no one was looking. Abby didn't even own a bra, much less a bikini for sunbathing. So we laid there, eyes closed, enjoying the sounds of the crashing waves and the chatter of the gulls and just soaking up the sunshine.

"Hey, you kids!" a woman's voice yelled from a distance. We definitely heard the woman but didn't pay any attention at first. We were hoping she wasn't yelling at us.

"Hey, you can't go topless here. Put your damn clothes on. I live here and this is my beach!" the woman yelled.

Abby and I both sat up and turned around behind us to see a woman screaming from the balcony of her house about fifty yards away. We didn't even realize this was a spot where people on the beach could be seen from a house.

"If you don't leave, I'm going to call the police!" she yelled.

This pissed off Abby to no end. Being a New Yorker, she was used to yelling. Her family yelled all the time. Just walking in New York was a symphony of yelling. Cab drivers honking, people hitting the hood of the cab that was in their way, both yelling obscenities at each other. So Abby's first response to people yelling at her was to yell obscenities back at them.

"What? You own the whole fuck'n beach?" Abby yelled. "Screw you, lady, we're not doing any harm to you. If you don't like it, don't look!"

Well, needless to say, that didn't go over too well.

"If you two don't leave right now I'm going to call the Sheriff!" she yelled.

Abby and I had enough. We got up and both put our T-shirts back on, picked up our towels and walked back down the beach to the car. This beach bitch had spoiled our day and we weren't going to get back to the wonder of the beach sitting in front of this lady, clothed or not. So we decided to drive on back to Hollywood from Santa Monica on Sunset. Sunset is a beautiful, curvy drive and passes by UCLA. We always enjoyed that ride.

---

Small-time dealers in Hollywood in the late 60's ended up meeting and knowing a lot of people. Heck, everyone looked like a drug dealer and most of them were dealing in one way or another. Lots of people helped their friends buy a lid just as a favor without getting any markup. If you added money to the cost for your favor, that made you a dealer. The closer the person was to someone who had a large quantity available, the more dangerous it became. So most people were very low in the chain of distribution and felt fairly safe buying and selling.

In our courtyard people came and went regularly. Some were friends and some were friends of friends. Others were strangers. The streets all around us were full of people walking around at all hours of the night. The chances of getting caught were slim, even though you sold pot to many different people. Everyone was a *head*. If you had the right look and talked the right language, you were trusted until proven otherwise.

Things were changing for our group of friends during that time, however. I guess eventually everything changes. I didn't see Rich or his friends anymore. He quit working at Lunde and moved up to Carmel. He loved the mountains and the Northern California coast and he hated all the traffic, smog and multitudes of people in LA. Rich just had to get out. I never heard from him again.

---

When I lived in the old Coronado house across from Lunde, there was an old man named James who bought and fixed old trucks that he would sell for a small profit. They were ugly, but mechanically sound. Abby and I were looking for something that could be turned into a camper -- a truck or van that ran. We had visions of taking off to the mountain states and maybe finding a commune to join. Abby thought we would be welcome if we drove into camp in an old converted truck. I agreed.

Old James worked on the vehicles in the dirt lot beside my old house. He was missing one of his arms, but didn't let that get in his way. This self-taught mechanic just figured out how to do everything with only one. James was a broad-shouldered, heavyset man about fifty years old and wore old, dark work clothes. His overalls and skin were always covered in grease. When I lived next door, I would sometimes walk up and talk with him while he worked. I was amazed how he would work with only one arm. Using a lot of leverage, James never had to ask for anyone's help.

Abby and I drove back over to that neighborhood one day. James was there working on an old delivery truck. We parked our car, then walked over and watched for a minute while he finished tightening something under the hood.

"Hi, James," I said.

"Oh…hello there," James said, as he pulled his head away from the front of the huge truck and looked at us. "Haven't seen you in a while."

"No, I moved and just haven't been back here much," I said.

"Nice ride!" Abby said to him.

"Well, it's for sale, ma'am. I'm just finishing it up," James said. "It don't look too good but it runs good."

"Pretty cool," I said, as I turned and started to look closer at the truck.

Abby and I slowly walked around the vehicle and James went back to work under the hood. It was a 1960 three-ton Metro Delivery Van, something very similar to the UPS trucks of today. It looked like it may have been a bread delivery truck or something like that at one time.

The big, ugly truck had a two-tone paint job, mainly a dark brown color and a dirty white part along the sides and top that had almost faded away. Some signage on the sides had been painted over with a white rectangle that didn't match the other color. It had faded, too.

Abby and I talked quietly about the delivery truck as we stepped up into the truck. We could even stand and walk around inside. Someone had already been converting it to a camper, but had stopped before finishing it. There was a wooden shelf and counter on one side of the back with a small sink with a faucet but no water. Across from that was a built-in wooden bed with a thin mattress on it that folded up and latched.

The driver's seat was the standard UPS-style but the passenger's seat was an upholstered living room chair attached to the floor. It was the perfect hippie truck. A little large but what fun we could have with it camping!

"How much do you want for it?" Abby asked.

"Five hundred and you guys can drive it off," James said. "I've just rebuilt the engine and it should run great."

Abby and I looked at each other. She shrugged her shoulders and said, "I don't know, Harry, that's more than we have."

I responded with, "Yeah, I know, Abby."

Then I turned to James and said, "That's too much for us, James. Will you take three-fifty in cash?"

James wiped his wrench off with a rag and said, "Okay, when can you pay?"

"I have enough with me now," Abby said, lifting up her purple velvet purse that she always carried.

"Then, it's a deal," James said. "I have the papers and the title. You can drive off with it today if you want."

We spent the next hour waiting for James to finish up the work he had been doing. The engine sits between the seats so I wasn't sure what he was working on in the front, but he had the grill off and I thought it might have something to do with the radiator.

"Don't you want to test drive it?" James asked.

Ha! I should have thought of that. "Uh, yes, we probably should."

"Why don't you drive it around the block while I go get the paperwork?" he said. "The keys are in the ignition. You know how to drive a standard?"

"Sure, haven't driven anything this big before, but I'm sure I can do it," I said, as I climbed up into the seat.

Abby hopped into the passenger's chair next to me. Abby never learned to drive a car and said she didn't want to. There was no need for a car in her old neighborhood. If it was too far to walk, Abby and her friends took the bus or the train. And if they had enough money, they would take a cab.

I felt clumsy up so high in such a large vehicle. I drove off the dirt lot and onto the street just trying to get used to the different feel of the clutch and gas pedal. We returned after a quick spin around the block, gave him the money, finished the paperwork, and told him we would be back the next day to pick up the truck. I had Bill follow me back over and I drove the van back to the house. We already had a car and now we had a camper truck. We were ready for some hippie-style travel!

---

A new couple from Abby's hometown of Flushing, New York, came onto the scene. Bob and his girlfriend, Chris, had just arrived by car. People called him by his last name, Schneider. He was a mechanic by trade and cars were the only things he liked to talk about. Abby had known him and Chris both in Flushing, but wasn't that thrilled that they had come to California.

Abby told me that Schneider was a recovering *junkie* –– the term most of us used for heroin addicts –– and that she didn't know Chris all that well. Chris was a young girl of Irish decent, maybe seventeen if that –– probably a runaway, but very street-smart. Chris had long black hair like Abby, but was slightly taller. She always wore a tight-fitting tank top with no bra and short cut-off jeans. She had a really nice figure and I found myself somewhat attracted to her.

Schneider was about Chris' height and reminded me a little of a young Eric Burdon of *The Animals*. The new arrivals both had New York accents and loved to make fun of my Texas slang. I immediately thought that Schneider was a jerk. He'd laugh at his own jokes when they weren't funny. Schneider rubbed me the wrong way from the beginning. He was looking for a job as a mechanic in town. No one was hiring him.

Chris and Schneider argued constantly. It was easy to tell that they were both unhappy. One day, Chris admitted to Abby and me that she was only with Schneider because she wanted to get out of New York and he was her ticket. California had quite a magnetic pull for New Yorkers who longed for warmer weather and the laidback hippie life. Chris found a cheap apartment and they moved in together.

Sunny continued to work at the recording studio and Abby and I dealt lids out of our house. Lots of people came and went. Ten dollars still bought an oversize ounce. We spent a lot of time sitting in our living room cleaning pounds of pot and making nice fat lids. People would come and go from our cottage, day and night. When we weren't bagging lids, we spent time sitting around our big wooden coffee table smoking dope, drinking beer or wine, and eating whatever we felt like cooking up. We had an open door policy and we had lots of friends. They would just give a little knock and open the door and we'd yell, "Come in!" Our doors were never locked.

At that time I was buying my pot wholesale from Fast Eddie, or at least that's what he wanted to be called. He lived on Coronado Street, the same street where I used to live when I worked at Lunde. Abby struck up a conversation with him one evening while we were sitting on the front steps of the house. He was always walking fast down our sidewalk on his way to the liquor store across the street. Abby and I talked with Eddie a lot because he walked in front of the house at the same time every day. Eddie had an Italian heritage. He had black hair, a black mustache, and a heavy New York accent. He came from the Bronx, but had lived in LA for five years. We never became very good friends. Our relationship was strictly business.

One frequent visitor to the bungalow was a young guy named Mitch. His father owned a big construction company and his family lived in Beverly Hills. Mitch always seemed to have plenty of money. He had recently graduated from high school and would spend hours at our house smoking dope and enjoying the circus of people who made their way in and out of our house each day. We all had great conversations about anything and everything.

Mitch had a great entrepreneur's spirit for a nineteen-year-old. He would talk about promoting my artwork and kept saying that I was going to be a famous artist. It wasn't clear what I was going to be, but I liked to paint and make things.

Just for fun, I made roach clips that had little wheels on them. They would stand up when you set them down and you could roll them around on the table. Roach clips are made from what they call *alligator clips* normally used in electrical work. The roach clip holds one end of the joint so a person could smoke the last bit of it without burning themselves or staining their fingers yellow from the smoke.

Mitch liked to talk about how many of the roach clips I could make because he was interested in financing their production -- going into the roach clip business. We never got much further than talking about that kind of thing and, no, I wasn't going to get anywhere in life making roach clips that rolled on a table, but it was so much fun to talk about it with Mitch over a smoke from my water pipe. His big ideas matched mine. I loved it! He was becoming a close friend and came around often to buy a lid and talk.

---

Abby and I had been steadily dealing and were able to put away a nice chunk of cash. Abby had dealt in Queens while living with her parents so she knew a lot of people who wanted to buy pot. Abby was convinced that if she could get some pot back to her hometown, it could be sold for a lot more money than we were getting in Hollywood.

"Harry, I've been thinking," Abby said one morning. "What about sending me back to New York with a few pounds? I could be visiting my parents in Flushing and sell from there like I used to do. Then I could come back with the dough and do it all again. We could make a ton of money Harry. I know it!"

"Man, flying with a lot of pot sounds risky to me," I said.

"Listen, babe," she said. "I look so young, no one would suspect me. All I have to do is put on one of those little girl dresses and they will think I am twelve."

"Well, that's true. Even though you are twenty, you do look like you are twelve. I'll think about it," I said, and we didn't talk about it for the rest of the day.

The next day, Chris and Schneider came over to the house. They would come over every other day or so. Chris liked to smoke dope, but Schneider didn't. We were all sitting around the table when Abby spoke up again about her idea.

"Hey, do you all think I could sell pot out of my parent's place back home like I used to do?" Abby said.

"Does a bear shit in the woods?" Schneider said.

"Sure, you could," Chris said. "It would be easy."

I was still not convinced. "I don't know," I said. "It worries me for Abby to be flying with that much pot into New York." I suspected that drug enforcement would be greater there.

"Well, I need to go back East for a while," said Schneider. "Why don't you ride with me, Abby? Chris can stay here with Harry and you can either fly back or wait until I come back. I have to pay for the gas anyway. It would save you some money."

"Sure," Abby quickly agreed. "We could help with the gas. What do you think, Harry?"

"Uh, I guess that sounds like a better plan. No flying." I said. "When are you planning on going, Schneider?"

Schneider spoke right up. "I don't have a day yet, but I can be flexible. You tell me."

"Okay, we will buy the pot and let you know. It should only take a few days before we have it," I said.

"Far out!" Abby exclaimed. "I can't wait to see my friends. My parents will be happy, too. I think I have a little dress that would work," and she left the room and opened the hall closet to look at her clothes.

Abby came back into the room and said, "While I'm in New York, Chris can move in our place and take care of Harry while I'm gone. It'll work out perfect." Chris and Schneider moved their things over to our bungalow the next day.

Schneider hadn't been able to find work in LA after weeks of looking, so he wanted to go back to New York and took most of his tools with him. He said he might have to get a job to make some money before he came back. Abby was so excited she could hardly wait to leave. Chris was glad she wasn't going back to New York because her life there had been less than desirable. Plus, she was glad to be rid of Schneider, at least for a while.

Two days later, I picked up ten pounds of pot from Eddie and brought it home. We were paying about $60 per pound in those days. Abby said the going price was $30 for a lid in Flushing, which would make us a good profit. I wrapped it all well in plastic and packed it in a suitcase. Abby packed a second suitcase for her things. Chris and Schneider slept on our sofa that night.

The next day everyone woke up early. We were all nervous and excited at the same time. Abby and I talked about how much money the pot would bring in New York and how much we would miss each other while she was gone.

"I'm gonna miss you, Harry," Abby said while we laid in bed.

"I'll miss you too, Abby," I replied. "I hope you are not gone too long." Then, we made love and cuddled up together for the last time.

Schneider said he just wanted to get out of town. Sunny didn't like our plan at all and kept quiet about it. Chris did the same.

We all hugged and said our goodbyes and off they drove in Schneider's car. I would miss Abby's laugh and warmth in bed, but at least Chris would be here to help around the house, do the cooking and cleaning, and keep Sunny and me company. She loved Jack and made sure Jack's water bowl was always full.

---

The hippie culture was known for peace, free love, and flower power. But Abby and I had an odd relationship. We had sex but the passion seemed to be missing. She just didn't seem very into it.

Abby and I made a fun couple and did everything together. I loved her as a friend, but in my heart, I knew I was not in love with her. I felt pretty sure she was bisexual, because of how she was with Wendy, but I was never quite sure. She probably loved me the same way I loved her. We never discussed it. Maybe over time, we could be more passionate, but I had been in love with a cute cheerleader back in high school and I knew the difference.

While Abby was in New York selling our pot, Chris took good care of me. In fact, she took care of me way more than Abby would have ever thought. Unlike Abby, Chris grew up in a family where the mother doted on the father, bringing him coffee in the morning, serving him seconds of the food he liked the best at dinner, and making sure he had everything he needed -- that kind of stuff. I had never been with a girl like that.

I don't know if Chris had a plan, but it didn't take more than a week of Abby being gone for me to start thinking about Chris in a different way. Chris moved from the sofa and into my bed and took care of me in that way, too. Looking back, I'm not too proud of that, but at the time, it felt right so I guess I just went with it. Sunny wasn't happy about Chris taking such good care of me, but wasn't openly critical. I knew him well enough to know how he felt. He was a gentle soul. He liked things just the way they were and hated any kind of change -- particularly change on an emotional level.

Another week went by. Chris and I were having a good time together -- in other words, lots of sex. Plus, she was a great cook. Sunny and Chris were getting along. Life was pretty good, at least for a while.

I had talked to Abby twice since she had left and things sounded like they were going well in Flushing. Abby was enjoying catching up with friends as they came and went at her parents' apartment. I tried to pretend everything was fine back in Hollywood when we talked. But it wasn't fine. I felt guilty as hell. Abby was going to return and find out Chris had taken her place. I felt bad, but also felt that I had a right to be happy. After two years with Abby, I knew she was not the one for me. Again, I didn't want to hurt her.

The next day the phone rang unusually early and woke me up. It was Abby and she was in a panic, talking fast and crying. I could feel my heart beating fast at her voice.

"What? Slow down, I can't understand you!" I said.

Abby blurted out why she was so distraught. "They came in last night and tied me up! All our money is gone! All our pot is gone!"

My mind was racing now, too, and Abby was still crying. It was a few seconds before I could speak. "Oh God! Who was it? Are you okay?"

"I'm okay, I guess. It was some guys that I had not met before. They knew Jerry. Remember Jerry?"

"Yes, I remember Jerry," I said, using a calmer voice than how I was feeling.

"Well," Abby went on. "I was in my bedroom and they came in to score. My parents were watching TV and didn't pay much attention to what was going on. I always had lots of friends coming and going."

"Okay, get to it. What happened? I asked.

Abby started explaining. I could hardly keep up because she was talking so fast. "There were three of them. The last one shut the door and one of them pulled a gun and pointed it at my face. I was like freaking out."

"Did they hit you or anything?"

"No, they didn't hurt me but they would have. One of the guys turned me around on the bed and tied my hands together with my sheet," Abby said.

"Then what?" I asked.

"Then, they searched my room and took all the money and the pot that was left."

"How much did they take?"

"Five grand!" Abby cried. "Five grand!"

"Oh babe, I'm so sorry," I said.

"That's all we had, Harry," she said. "I don't even have the money to come home."

"Don't worry about that," I said. "I will wire you some money and you can fly back whenever you are ready."

"I'm ready now," Abby said.

That same day I went to the Western Union office and wired Abby enough money to get to the airport and buy a ticket home. She told her family goodbye and left the next morning. Chris and I picked her up at LAX and drove home to St. Andrew's Place where we unloaded her luggage and fixed her dinner.

"I don't think Schneider is coming back, Chris," Abby said while eating the spaghetti Chris had made. "I talked to him the other day and asked when I could get a ride back to LA. Schneider said he got this good job and didn't know if he was ever coming back."

"Schneider's a schmuck!" Chris yelled out. "That junkie is better off back in New York. He never fit in here anyway." Chris was talking to Abby like everything was normal. It was not. I just couldn't let this go on much longer without telling Abby about Chris and me. I felt horrible. Abby was going to want to share the bed with me that evening and I wasn't looking forward to dealing with that. So I went to Chris when she was alone in the kitchen and told her she needed to leave for a while because I had to tell Abby about us. Chris didn't want to be around for that. She was a little scared of Abby so she left right away and Abby didn't notice.

I went up to Abby and sat down next to her. "Abby, I need to talk to you about something serious," I said, in a calm, low voice.

"What?" she said rather loudly. Sunny was sitting on the other side of the table.

"Why don't we three go out and sit on the steps and talk," Sunny said. "I've been part of this threesome for a long time and I have a right to be there."

"What are you talking about?" Abby said.

We all got up and went outside. I'm not sure why outside was better than inside but Sunny thought so. We sat close together on the narrow front steps of our house. Abby sat in the middle with Sunny and me on either side.

"You know how Chris stayed here to take care of me?" I said.

"Yeah," said Abby. I turned and looked right at her. Sunny looked off into the distance.

"Well... she took better care of me than she was supposed to and now I want to be with her, Abby. I'm really sorry."

Sunny started to tear up as he put his arm around Abby. He always had a hard time with emotional issues and this was a big one. "I don't want this to end," Sunny said. "I love you two so much."

"I can't believe this," Abby said.

"I know this sucks," I said. "But I don't know what to do. That's just how I feel, Abby," and I put my arm around her, too.

Abby had her head down trying to figure out what to say. Then she lifted her head up quickly and said, "It's okay... I'm okay. Really. I can take care of myself. Look what I just went through. I'll be out of your hair in no time."

"Please Abby, you are sounding mad. I want to be friends," I said, taking my arm away.

"Okay, sure. We're friends," she said, "but I'm not going to stick around and watch Chris and you be together."

Sunny continued to cry and hold onto Abby. By then I was crying, too. Abby's face was red and tears started coming down her cheeks. I put my arm back around her.

"I'm really sorry," I said through my tears. I could hardly talk. "I didn't plan this. I didn't mean for it to happen. It just did."

We stopped talking. There was just not much more to say. The three of us just sat there for a long time with our arms around each other. Our last hugs on that little porch. This was the end of an era -- the end of a partnership that couldn't be replicated. I didn't know what was to come next, but I knew that the three of us were no more. It was a very sad day in Hollywood. It still makes me sad to think about it. Jack sat on the sidewalk in front of us.

It didn't take Abby long to clear out her things from the bungalow. She moved in with her New York friends, Alan and Stephanie, and never looked back. Before long, she had moved to San Francisco to start another chapter in her life.

## Chapter Sixteen

Chris was younger than Abby and had graduated from high school. Abby had gone to a junior college before moving to California so at least she had some college education. Chris had none. Abby had wanted to be involved in our decision-making and always offered her own perspective. She was sharp. She was a leader. That's why Abby and I called each other partners. Chris pretty much went along with anything I wanted to do. She was a follower. That made me miss Abby. But Chris was so warm, sexy, and cuddly. She wanted to make me feel good all the time. It seemed I was just a sucker for her affection.

I went over to visit Crystal Jim across the courtyard one night and he told me that some guys were in town and had five kilos of pot to sell. He said they were Cuban dealers sent to him by his old buddy from Texas. But rumor had it that they were soon going back to jail. The Cuban dealers were looking for someone who could turn their pot fast and give them the cash.

Jim didn't sell pot and offered to introduce me to them. He said maybe that could help us get back in business again after what happened to Abby in New York. Eddie, my regular supplier wanted cash up front for his pot, so this deal sounded pretty good.

"Cubans, huh?" I said. "So do they speak any English?"

"I'm told they speak a little, Homey," Crystal Jim said. "When do you want to meet them?"

"Tomorrow would be fine," I said.

"Okay then, I'll set it up," he said. "How about right after dark here at my house?"

"Great," I said. "I appreciate it."

"No probleeemo, amigo," he jokingly said, as I walked out his front door.

Two Cubans showed up the next night at Crystal Jim's house carrying five kilos of pot in a brown paper grocery sack. I could see that they had arrived from my front door so I walked across the courtyard, knocked, and went in.

Crystal Jim introduced us and we shook hands. I had a hard time understanding their names but I was pretty sure the tall skinny one called himself Emilio. He was the one who seemed to be in charge and did most of the talking.

The other guy was named Jose. He was shorter than Emilio and heavyset. Both had short, black hair with mustaches and wore old jeans, cotton shirts, and work boots. I'd seen a lot of guys from Mexico with that look and wondered why Cubans were in LA in the first place. I thought they all went to Miami or Tampa. After about two weeks, I had sold most of the pot and needed to let the Cubans know we were ready to settle with them. Chris, however, had a different idea.

I often told Chris and Sunny about how nice Texas was and how much they would like it. All three of us were getting sick of Hollywood and especially dealing for a living. Sunny was getting nowhere at his job. He thought working in a Hollywood recording studio would get him discovered. It didn't. In my mind, the California adventure needed to be over. It was time to grow up and move on. I was thinking about going back to Texas.

Sunny, Chris, and I spent one whole evening talking about the possibility of the three of us moving to San Antonio and trying something new. I wanted to finish college, only this time my major would be in art instead of architecture. Sunny thought he could sing in clubs and make enough money to live. Chris wasn't thinking much at all. She talked about owning a farm and raising animals, although she actually had no clue how to do that. I just let her ramble on and wondered how she would really do in Texas. I wasn't sure I was going to take her with us.

I had accumulated some decent cash from selling the Cubans' pot and we kept our money well hidden at the bungalow. Chris proposed a dubious plan after dinner that night. The three of us were sitting around our big table.

"Listen, guys," Chris said. "I have an idea."

"What's that?" Sunny asked.

I was smoking pot from my glass water pipe. I took a long hit and passed it to Chris.

"As far as I can tell," Chris said, stopping in mid-sentence to draw a deep hit on the end of the pipe. She held it in as we looked at her then blew smoke out slowly across the coffee table towards Sunny. "About the only way we are going to escape this God-forsaken city is to use the Cubans' money to do it."

I was taken back, so I looked right at her and said, "Hey, I've never ripped anyone off before, Chris, and I'm not planning on doing it now!"

"These aren't the kind of guys who you want to rip off," Sunny said. "Shit, they'd kill us in the blink of an eye!"

"We have to find a better way than that," I said. "We've made a profit from their pot. We need to give them their cut."

"It's just an idea," said Chris. "Just an idea."

"Well," I said, "Crystal Jim thought they were heading back to jail soon, but I'm still not interested. Anyway, I'm not sure why the Cuban guys are out of jail now when they are supposed to go back to jail. What kind of system allows that?"

"Yeah, that doesn't make much sense," Sunny said.

"I don't know," said Chris, changing the subject, "but Dee and Bill have some Sunshine! They said we could all get together at their house and do it tonight if we want."

"Okay, I'm in. I could use a nice trip," I said. "How much are the tabs?"

"Five bucks a hit," Chris said. "But it's the real deal, so it's worth it."

"Okay, let me know when they want us to come over," I said.

---

It had been a month since I had taken acid. I had slowed down because I was having problems recovering from the last few times I had dropped. Doing acid was just fun for me. I always had a great time tripping along with exaggerated colors all around me -- objects moving and undulating as I stared at them. I would be lost for hours. I absolutely loved it.

No one I knew ever had stomach pain when coming down from an acid trip, but I was. The pain would last for about an hour. Bill and Dee's party really sounded like fun though. The pain wasn't all that bad, plus Chris and I had not dropped acid together. She told me that she really wanted to make love while tripping. Well, she talked me into it.

We all got together in the early afternoon. Dee said she and Bill had already dropped their tabs. I thought she and Bill were acting strange when we got there so that made sense.

I gave Dee ten bucks and she handed Chris and me each a yellow tab of Sunshine LSD. After about half an hour, we were all having a great time. Everyone got along. No one had a bad trip. It was just fun and I enjoyed lying on the floor on pillows just talking and listening to music with everyone.

By midnight, things had slowed down and the acid had started to wear off. And like before, my stomach was starting to ache a little. The pain usually went away on its own without me having to take any medicine. Besides, I didn't know what medicine to take for it anyway because I didn't know why it was happening. What was I supposed to do? Go to a hospital and say, *Can you help me, doctor? These pains start every time I am coming down from taking acid.*

Chris and I told Bill and Dee goodbye and walked across the courtyard to our own cottage. Jack led the way home. Sunny was sitting in his chair watching TV and eating a bowl of cereal.

"About time you two came home," Sunny said, trying to be funny.

"The party is over anyway," Chris said. "Dee and Bill were going to bed so everyone else left. Harry doesn't feel good."

"Again?" Sunny moaned.

"Yeah, it's those same pains coming down from acid," I explained as I headed for our corner bed. "They'll go away like they always do. Don't worry about it. I'm just going to lie down. I'm sure I'll be back up in a little while."

"It's after midnight anyway, man. Just try to go to sleep," Sunny said. "I don't know. Maybe you should just stop taking acid, man."

"Okay, okay," I said, "I'll think about it."

Then I went over to my corner tent, pulled back the tapestries, and crawled into bed. As I laid there I could hear people talking. Sunny was playing his acoustic guitar and singing a new song he had written. But instead of feeling better, I slowly started feeling worse. The pains coming down from acid usually went away. This time the pain was getting stronger -- really stronger. Jack crawled up on the mattress and curled up at my feet like she usually did.

*This can't be constipation,* I thought to myself. *So what is wrong with me?*

The pain was getting unbearable. I called out softly for help but with Sunny playing and people talking, no one could hear me. It became obvious to me that I was in trouble. I could hardly move.

Thoughts ran through my brain. *This is getting serious. I'm not sure I can get out of bed. Am I dying?* Jack was sitting at the foot of my mattress looking at me. I think she sensed something was wrong.

About thirty minutes more went by and I didn't think the pain could get any worse. That's when our friend, Mitch, walked into the bungalow and sat down with the group. Sunny stopped playing to greet him and Mitch said, "Where's Harry?"

It was about 2:00 a.m. and he had been out all evening. Mitch often came over late at night to smoke a bowl with us and chat for a while before heading home.

"Harry's not feeling good and went to bed," Chris said.

"Oh," Mitch said. "Maybe I should check on him."

Mitch walked across the room to my tent and pulled the tapestry back. The flickering light from the table lamps on the other side of the room gave a warm glow to the inside of the tent. I was on my back looking straight up and holding my stomach with both hands. He looked down at me and I looked up at him with a grimace on my face. I made a moaning sound but couldn't speak.

"Are you okay?" Mitch asked.

I couldn't get a sound out. I shook my head and got out a faint, "No."

Mitch called out to the others in the room, "Harry's really sick. I'm taking him to a hospital!"

"He always feels like that after taking acid," Sunny said. "He'll get over it."

"No, not this time," Mitch said.

Sunny said, "Whatever, man, I doubt it's that bad, but you do what you want."

Chris didn't say anything and kept talking to friends. I'm not even sure who was there that night but evidently, Mitch was the only one concerned about me.

Mitch looked back at me and said, "Hang tight, I'll be right back."

Sunny started playing again. Mitch drove his convertible around to the alley and stopped right in front of our kitchen door. Then he came back into the house, bent down, and lifted me up from my bed. He carried me out to his car. Mitch put me in the back seat where I doubled up in pain. Mitch quickly got into the driver's seat and sped off down the alley. I remember the lights of the street going by above me as he drove. He turned on Sunset Boulevard and drove fast about twenty miles down to Santa Monica and UCLA Medical Center.

When we got to UCLA, the parking lot was almost empty and everything was quiet. Mitch got as close as he could to the emergency entrance, then ran into the door, and came out rolling an EMS-type stretcher. He helped me out of the car and up onto the stretcher. My pain was intense as Mitch rolled me into the hospital entrance and up to a desk. The lights were bright and I felt like I was fainting. All I saw was white.

I will always remember Mitch's words, "This guy's really sick. You gotta do something!" The hospital clerk behind the desk sprang into action, taking the cart from Mitch, and rolling it through a set of double doors. I don't remember much after that but evidently a surgeon did an emergency operation to repair my ruptured appendix. *Acute Appendicitis* they called it. Not sure if Mitch hung around that night, but I survived the operation and was put into a room to recover.

A heavy dose of Demerol through an IV helped me cope with this new kind of pain, but this new pain didn't even touch the excruciating pain from the night before. There was now a four-inch opening on my right side about at my waist and two rubber tubes coming out of it onto the bandage pads.

As I laid there in a stupor, I did a lot of thinking. In a nutshell Mitch had saved my life. What more could a friend ask for? How lucky I was that he was who he was and that he happened to drop by our house exactly when he did. My thoughts wandered. *Mitch, old buddy -- my guardian angel! I bet Abby would have done something if she were still there. Man, I made a big mistake leaving her for Chris. How stupid I have been. What did I do?*

I was dozing off every few seconds. The Demerol was a constant drip, drip, drip. It was not a high I was used to. Demerol in drug talk would be a *downer* and I didn't do *downers*. They just slowed you down and made you dumb. Demerol reminded me of being drunk and that was not a feeling I liked.

So there I was, in and out of a dreamy state. I dreamt about flying over LA at night like Superman, waving my arms to turn on the lights in the different parts of the city. Big swoops and swishes of lights as far as the eye could see. I enjoyed the fact that I could keep the same dream going as I went in and out of consciousness, returning to it each time. *Now that's hard to do without heavy drugs,* I thought to myself as I drifted back off to sleep and into my dream of dreams.

UCLA Medical Center was a teaching hospital, so each morning I was surrounded by as many as eight interns watching as the dressing on my wound was changed. With a ruptured appendix, poisons are released into the cavity of the abdomen and that wasn't good. Once a day each of the two tubes coming out of my side would be removed about half an inch one at a time. It felt like my insides were being pulled out with the tubes. After a few days of dreaming, the doctors must have lowered the amount of Demerol I was getting through the IV because I became more aware of my surroundings. I discovered I was not alone in the room.

Mr. Blankenship was in the hospital bed next to me and we slowly began talking to each other. I don't remember a lot of the conversation but I know my new roommate told me that he was the National President of Boy Scouts of America. He had been in LA on a speaking engagement when his appendix became inflamed so his was taken out as well. But since his appendix had not burst, Mr. Blankenship was not in as bad shape as I was. He was eighty-nine years old, however, so maybe they kept him in the hospital longer than usual as a precaution. His daughter had flown in from Chicago to watch his recovery. She came to visit once in the morning when the doctors made their rounds and once late in the afternoon. She didn't want much to do with me.

I remember talking with Mr. Blankenship about Scouting and how much he loved it. We watched TV part of the time, mainly the news about the Vietnam War and the anti-war protests going on around the country and the intense anger focused on President Johnson. Mr. Blankenship and I disagreed on most of the issues on the war, but I was careful not to argue with him. I preferred to respect his age and opinions. He was very patriotic to the degree that he didn't think the country could do any wrong. I was very patriotic, too, but felt the country and its leaders could definitely make mistakes and the Vietnam War was one of those mistakes.

Sunny and Chris came up to the hospital on a Saturday. They said I had been there for a week and they had come before, but I was out of it when they tried to talk to me. I didn't remember their previous visit but was glad to see them. They were glad to see me, too, because the Cubans had moved into our house and wanted the money we owed them.

Chris leaned over my bed and whispered to me so my roommate couldn't hear, "This can be our chance to escape Hollywood, Harry."

Sunny stood there listening and let Chris do the talking. He looked freaked out just being in a hospital. His light colored face always developed red patches when he was stressed out.

"Sunny and I are scared of them," Chris said, still keeping her voice low. "They both have guns and have been threatening us. They won't leave!"

"I'm freaked out!" Sunny said, also in a low voice as he leaned over my bed.

"Do you still have their money?" I asked.

"Yes, we still have it hidden," Chris said.

I tried to explain the seriousness of the matter to Chris. "You've got to give it to them, Chris."

"No," Chris said. "I want out of here. I want to go to Texas like you said."

"Look, "I implored. "You guys are gonna get hurt and I can't help you laid up in here."

"You let us worry about that," Chris said.

I asked for Sunny's opinion next. "Sunny, what do you think about all this?"

"Look, man, I don't know," Sunny whispered. "I'm pretty freaked out. But I like the idea of going to Texas. It would be a fresh start for us, Harry."

"Well, this is an extremely dangerous idea," I said, "but this isn't my decision anymore. I just almost died. I can't deal with this now."

"The Cubans are demanding to know where you are," Chris said, "but we haven't told them. It's like they are holding Sunny and me hostage. I lied that Sunny and I were going grocery shopping and would be right back, so we snuck up here."

"Have they done anything to hurt you?" I asked, still feeling a little out of it.

"No, these guys are smoking our pot almost 24/7 and that calms them down, but they aren't going anywhere without their money. They're sleeping on the sofas," Chris said.

"And eating our food!" Sunny added.

"Shouldn't they have gone back to prison by now?" I asked.

"I talked to Crystal Jim and he said they are supposed to," Chris said, "but we don't know when or anything. Jim just thinks you will pay them off when you get out of the hospital. He said to tell *Homey* to get well soon."

"I don't know why they need money if they are going back to prison," Sunny said.

"I don't know either, maybe for their families or maybe they owe money, too," I said. "What are ya'll going to do now?"

"We've got to do something fast," Chris said. "I think they are figuring out that we are lying to them. What if we just leave for Texas right away? They will never find us there. We can start a new life, get jobs, and get out of this place for good."

"Mitch came over the other night while the Cubans were there," Sunny said.

"He was freaked out by them, too," Chris said, "Mitch could tell something was wrong. He and I were in the kitchen and I told him what was happening."

Sunny chimed in, "Help seems to be on the way, Harry."

"I like your attitude, Sunny," I responded.

Chris continued, "Mitch said that he's going to visit you again... soon. He's already been here but you weren't awake."

"That's cool," I said. "Listen to Mitch. He's a smart guy."

Sunny and Chris both nodded and I continued. "I don't know how long I have to stay here but the last doctor to come in said he thought it would be another few days before they would release me. So you two need to figure this thing out before you both get murdered. It would be safest to pay these guys off. After all, it is their money. So come on, we can always find a way to go to Texas." I could tell my voice was getting hard to understand and my eyelids were closing -- end of conversation.

I must have dozed off again because I didn't remember Chris or Sunny leaving my room. I was super tired from the stressful visit and just wanted to drift back to my Demerol-induced dreams. The good dreams, however, had turned into bad dreams about the Cubans.

At that point I felt trapped. Somehow the Cubans found out where I was. Maybe someone who came over didn't know they were unfriendly and slipped, I'm not sure. But about two days after Sunny and Chris' visit, these two guys showed up in my hospital room. They looked the same as I remembered and had the same heavy accents.

"Heeey! There you are, amigo," Emilio, the tall one, said as they walked in. "We've been waiting for you."

"Obviously, I've been seriously ill," I whispered.

"We want our money," the other one said. "Give us the money you owe us and we will leave you and your friends alone."

That moment with the Cubans was a tipping point for me. I made the final decision that Sunny, Chris, and I were getting out of LA one way or another. For some reason, there seemed to be no other choice. I didn't want to tell them that Chris had their money and get her hurt, so lying to the Cubans seemed the best route to go. It was a life decision that I don't regret. Almost dying woke me up and made me rethink what I was doing out in California. At any rate, I just went for it.

"I don't have the money right now," I said. "We've spent some of it and this guy owes me the rest of it and I can't get it until I get out of here."

"I think you are lying to us, gringo," Emilio said.

They were standing on each side of my bed and the grins they had when they first came in had turned to frowns. Jose started pulling on my IV and it hurt. Emilio gave me a little slap across my face and said, "You better do something quickly to get us our money or somebody is going to get hurt."

"We're not kidding you, amigo," Jose said, pointing his finger in my face.

"You'll get your money," I said, "It'll only be a few days, I'm sure. Chris and Sunny don't know where the money is. I'll go and get it from the guy when I get out of here."

I didn't say anything more and just looked at them. They didn't say anything else either. They smiled at one another and left the room.

I was shocked that the Cubans had found me, but knew that Sunny and Chris wouldn't have told them where I was. That worried me so I called the house and Chris answered.

"Hello?" Chris said.

"Chris," I blurted out, "the Cubans were just here."

"Oh, shit!" Chris said, and yelled to Sunny who was sitting in the living room. "Sunny, the Cubans were at the hospital!"

"Did they do anything to you?" Chris asked me.

"No, have they hurt either of you?" I replied.

"No, but they've started acting more aggressive," Chris said. "Sunny and I were wondering where they were."

Then Chris gave me a bit of good news for a change. "Mitch called us and is coming over to see you today."

"Good, good. It will be good to see him, but I'm not sure what Mitch can do to help."

"Don't worry," Chris said. "We'll figure this out. They haven't hurt us yet."

I said okay and we both hung up the phone. By then, I was allowed to take a walk down the halls rolling my IV rack and bag along with me. Walking farther and farther each day was part of my recovery and would soon come in handy. My gut had been cut open so there was tremendous pain when I got out of the bed to walk. But the good news was that the drain tubes had been taken out and there was just a bandage over the stitches.

I was about thirty feet down the hall from my room when nurses started coming down the hall shutting doors and asking all patients to go back to their rooms. I rolled my IV back to my room and a nurse shut the door behind me.

Later that day, a black woman in a blue business suit came into my room with a clipboard in her hand.

"Mr. Stevens?" she nicely asked.

"Yes," I answered.

She started talking in a more serious tone. "I'm from the business office and need to talk to you about your ability to pay for your surgery."

"Okay," I said, "but I don't have any insurance."

"That's what I understand," she said. "Are you working?"

"No, not right now," I told her, "but I'm looking for a job."

Her next question came quickly. "Do you think you would be able to make payments on the bill?"

"Yes, I believe so," I said.

"Well, Mr. Stevens, according to this you are scheduled to be released on Tuesday, so please stop by the Business Office on the first floor on your way out so we can make your payment arrangements."

"Okay, thank you. I will," I told her.

She nodded her head and started to walk out.

I said, "Excuse me."

"Yes?" she said, stopping to reply.

I hesitantly asked, "Can you tell me what happened a while ago when we all had to leave the hall and shut the doors?"

"Well, we had a patient pass away today and the nurses don't like to roll someone down the hallway with a sheet over them in front of the other patients," she explained.

I looked at her and said, "Oh, thanks." and she walked on out.

The next day, Mitch came strolling into my room.

"Hey, man. How are you doing?" Mitch said as he came closer to my bed. I remember the concerned look on his face.

"I'm okay, man. Or at least I am feeling better, I guess," I said. "They've removed those stupid tubes and have sewn me back up. But, Mitch, dude, I gotta get out of this place. I'm worried about Chris and Sunny."

"I know, Harry," Mitch agreed with me and added. "I'm going to help you guys."

"Thanks, Mitch. Any and all help will be greatly appreciated," I said.

"Look," he said, "I've talked to Sunny and Chris and we have a plan. It will get you back to Texas. We've all decided that you need to go home."

"That's fine with me," I said. "What is the plan?"

"Can you walk?" Mitch asked.

"Yes, slowly. They've had me walking down the halls."

"Well, just hold tight and we'll take care of the details," Mitch said. "I'll see you early tomorrow morning," and he left the room.

"Okay," I said and waved at him.

I was afraid to call the house after Mitch left in fear of making the Cubans suspicious that something was going to happen. I waited for a call from Chris, but never got one. Then I fell into a deep sleep from mental and physical exhaustion. The next day, the Cubans had been at our house all morning. Chris and Sunny woke up early. They each were doing some small packing but nothing obvious. They mainly walked around and looked for the things in the house to take to Texas. Sadly, most of the stuff belonged to me. They only had a short time to throw what they could into the truck and take off. Chris later told me how all this came down.

---

"We go to super mercado," Emilio said. "No leave." He got up out of the chair and walked towards the door. Jose got up and followed him out. Chris peeked through the slits in the wooden blinds at the end of the living room and watched as the two Cubans walked down the sidewalk and out to their car.

"They're gone," she said. "Let's go, Sunny!"

Sunny jumped out of his chair. He walked out and down the sidewalk, being careful that the Cubans had actually driven off. He jumped into our big truck and drove it around the back alley to the kitchen door. Chris started handing stuff out the back door to Sunny, who loaded it into the truck.

He yelled back at her, "Don't forget Jack, and get all Harry's stuff you can!"

"I think I know what he will want the most," Chris said.

Sunny and Chris continued to place things into the truck but were running out of time. Sunny went back in and started carrying out some of the smaller furniture. He grabbed the stereo and speakers and just pulled out the wires.

"No time for kitchen stuff," Sunny yelled.

"Just some pots and pans," Chris said.

"What about Harry's tools? This tool box is heavy," Chris said.

"Bring 'em, we may need them," Sunny shouted back.

After about fifteen minutes of frantic loading, Sunny and Chris stopped and looked at each other.

"That's it," Sunny said. "Let's get the hell out of here!"

Jack was smart. She knew that when things were being loaded, we were moving and wasn't about to be left behind. Jack was already in the truck sitting up on the living room chair. You didn't go anywhere without Jack going with you.

Neither Sunny nor Chris had very much stuff of their own. Sunny had his clothes and his guitar. Chris had the clothes on her back and just a little more. They could have put what they owned in a backpack and hiked down the street. So even though they were scared to death, they still took the time to get what they could of mine for me. At the last minute, Chris pulled out the cash she had hidden under the kitchen sink. There were clothes, photos, artwork, and record albums that were important, but taking care of Jack was most important to me. Jack had been with me since I worked at Hemisfair.

Sunny drove off in the big ugly delivery truck that the one-armed man had sold to Abby and me, and Chris followed behind him in my big Buick. She had asked me to teach her how to drive, but she never got her driver's license. So, off to Texas they went –– to escape the Cubans and start a new life.

A nurse came into my room early to check on me and walked back out. Mr. Blankenship had already checked out a few days before so I was alone in the room. I looked up at the clock on the wall. It was 5:00 a.m. All was quiet up and down the hall. I was only awake for a short time before Mitch came into my room.

"Here," he said, "I brought you these if you need them."

Mitch handed me a brown grocery bag with some clothes in it.

"No, look in my closet," I said, as I pulled my legs over the edge of the bed and felt the pain on my side.

"Oh, here's your clothes," Mitch said as he took them out of the closet.

"Check for my wallet, will you?" I remembered to ask.

"It's there, Harry." Mitch spoke quietly. "Here," and he handed it to me.

"Thanks," I said. Both of us were whispering.

"Quick, get your pants on. We don't have all day," Mitch said looking down the hall from the doorway.

"Well, I can't move too fast," I said. "These stitches are still healing and I can hardly walk."

Once my clothes were on I felt like a human again. Mitch helped me up from the chair I had sat down in and steadied me as we walked out the door of my room. We went slow but steady. Mitch and I just walked out of the hospital without saying a word to anyone. No one noticed.

It was still dark outside when we reached the parking lot. Mitch helped me into the front seat of his car and shut the door. He looked back and didn't see anyone coming.

"Looks like we are home free," Mitch said as he drove us out of the parking lot and down the street.

"You're going to stay at my house until the plane leaves, Harry," Mitch explained.

"A plane? Okay, when does the plane leave?"

"About six this afternoon," Mitch said.

"Man, that's a long time." I sighed.

We drove up into the driveway of Mitch's house in West Beverly Hills. It was a nice little street with tall palm trees on both sides and well-manicured lawns and sidewalks.

The house was very similar to others on the street, white stucco with terracotta tile roofs -- Spanish California style.

"You can stay here all day until I take you to the airport. No one should come home until this evening."

"Okay, thanks," I said.

"There's some big planning meeting going on at the company and all my family members will be there," Mitch explained. "I'll come back and get you when it's time to go."

"What time will that be?" I asked.

"About four-thirty," he said. "Okay?"

"That's fine," I said. "I just appreciate your helping us like this, Mitch."

"Don't mention it, Harry." Mitch answered. "You would do it for me. Just sit here quietly all day and don't disturb anything."

Mitch shut the door. The sun was up now and I could see him through the lace curtains that covered the front picture window as he got into his car and drove off. I couldn't believe his family all got up to go to work that early in the morning, but they did.

I stayed there all day and fell asleep for a couple of hours in the middle of the day. There was time for a lot of thinking, but mostly I read magazines his family had on the coffee table. I could tell it was getting late in the afternoon because the sun was coming in from the windows on the other side of the house now. I looked at the clock in the kitchen. It was four-thirty.

*Mitch should be here any minute,* I thought.

Just then, he came driving up into the driveway. Mitch was in a hurry when he came into the house.

"Ready?" he asked.

"Sure," I said.

"I don't have much time to take you and get back before my father realizes that I'm not there helping him," Mitch said.

"Well, let's go!" I said, and he again helped me down the steps and into the car. My side felt like a large hand was squeezing it hard all the time, causing me to stop every step or two and regain my composure.

Off we went to the LA airport. There was a lot of traffic at that time of day. When we finally got there and stopped at the curb, Mitch handed me a small packet.

"Ah, my ticket," I said.

"Yes, it's on me," Mitch said.

I was visibly touched. "You didn't have to do that, man."

"It's fine. I've got the money. You need it now. Just don't worry about it," Mitch said.

"Well, thanks again," I said, as I got out of his car. "I'm not sure if I can ever repay you."

"Don't mention it," Mitch said. "Good luck in Texas!"

Then he drove off and gave me a wave behind his head -- as if this was an everyday occurrence for him.

Mitch, the friend who saved my life, was in traffic again heading back to Beverly Hills. I was heading out of LAX. He had every reason to stay. I had every reason to go. Only by the grace of God had I somehow survived that wild ride in Hollywood, and now I was definitely ready to go home to San Antonio and try to do something with my life. I was done with this lifestyle. Done with dealing. Just done.

I felt bad about the Cubans and felt even worse that Crystal Jim had introduced us. I hoped they wouldn't hold him accountable for what we did. But I just went with it and wasn't going to regret my decision this time.

There was no assigned seating, so I just found a seat next to a window, rested my head against it and looked out as the plane taxied down the runway. I couldn't see very far because of the smog, with its bluish somewhat brownish, haze -- dirty, ugly and about to be history for me. I thought about how clean the air would be when I landed in San Antonio.

The engines of the jet suddenly roared to a high pitch and the plane began to move. We slowly taxied our way out to the end of the runway and waited our turn behind several other planes. When it was our turn, the pilot didn't even stop. He just made his turn and off we went, rumbling fast down the tarmac for takeoff.

I had never experienced anything quite so exhilarating. It seemed like it was taking a long time before we finally took flight.

The plane shook like it was trying to hold onto the ground and not lift -- holding me down, not letting me go -- somehow trying to thwart my escape. I pulled my seatbelt strap a little tighter and closed my eyes.

My heart was racing. The front of the plane tilted up high and the thrust pushed me back against the seat as my whole body vibrated with the engines and runway.

I felt the tires of the plane finally jerk loose from their grip on the tarmac. I thought about that grip. That grip that dealing drugs had on me. It's been lifted, too. No more. I'm done. I made it out, and someday I will write my story.

---

There was no telling what was to come next in my life, but it had to be better than what I had just been through. My parents sent me to Hollywood to get me away from the drug scene in San Antonio. Well, I guess it worked, but not like they thought it would. Of course, they never knew.

It would be years before I would see cousins Hugh and Christine again but I never really had the chance to say goodbye and thank them for all they did for me back then. Hugh would move to the desert near Palm Springs and become somewhat of a recluse. Morten closed his business and died of dementia several years later.

A few years after losing Morten, Christine attended her Beverly Hills High Class of 1956 Reunion and reunited with her high school sweetheart, the boy her mother didn't want her to marry. They finally did marry and retired in Florida.

Sunny, Chris, and I did make it to Texas together, but it wasn't what they expected. It would only take three months for them to want to leave and I would never see or hear from them again. Sunny went home to Torrance, California, where he grew up surfing with the Beach Boys. He died sometime after 2007. Chris flew home to Flushing -- good riddance. In 2015, Abby died of cancer in New Jersey. She had spent 35 years with her partner, Betty.

Soon after Sunny and Chris left San Antonio, I reunited with the girl I should have stayed with in the first place, the beauty I met at Hemisfair '68 –– Brenda Miller. It was 1971 and we moved into a small apartment with Jack, married seven months later, and we shared a wonderful life together for over fifty years.

But before Brenda agreed to marry me, she made me promise to never deal drugs again and to this day I have kept that promise. Brenda got a job as a service representative at Southwestern Bell Telephone Company and I went back to college. I eventually earned a BFA from the University of Texas at Austin and enjoyed an award-winning career as an advertising/publishing art director and creative director until I retired in 2002. Brenda has been a wonderful wife to me and a wonderful mother to our three children. How lucky can a man get? I think this story tells how lucky I am.

Oh, and guess who showed up at our wedding in 1971? Mitch. He had done very well for himself and flew in for it like the good friend he was. I owe you my life, Mitch, and so do my kids and grandchildren. You stood up and did the right thing when others didn't. You are the real hero of this story. Thank you, my friend.

Made in the USA
Middletown, DE
05 January 2019